Two Laps Around the World

Two Laps Around the World

Tales and Insights from a Life Sabbatical

Bob Riel

Jane and Steve —
Best wishes and happy travels!
Bob Riel

iUniverse, Inc.
New York Lincoln Shanghai

Two Laps Around the World
Tales and Insights from a Life Sabbatical

Copyright © 2007 by Bob Riel

All rights reserved. No part of this book may be used or reproduced by any means, graphic, electronic, or mechanical, including photocopying, recording, taping or by any information storage retrieval system without the written permission of the publisher except in the case of brief quotations embodied in critical articles and reviews.

iUniverse books may be ordered through booksellers or by contacting:

iUniverse
2021 Pine Lake Road, Suite 100
Lincoln, NE 68512
www.iuniverse.com
1-800-Authors (1-800-288-4677)

Because of the dynamic nature of the Internet, any Web addresses or links contained in this book may have changed since publication and may no longer be valid.

ISBN: 978-0-595-44391-8 (pbk)
ISBN: 978-0-595-69078-7 (cloth)
ISBN: 978-0-595-88720-0 (ebk)

Printed in the United States of America

The views expressed in this work are solely those of the author and do not necessarily reflect the views of the publisher, and the publisher hereby disclaims any responsibility for them.

Credits:
- Cover design by Phil Worcester
- Cover photos by Bob Riel

For Lisa,
my partner in travel and life

Contents

Acknowledgments xi

PART I: TRAVELING EAST AROUND THE WORLD

Introduction 3
Turkey 13
Kenya 47
Southeast Asia: Bali and Thailand 71
Northeast Asia: Beijing and Tokyo 105

PART II: TRAVELING WEST AROUND THE WORLD

Interlude 137
Southeast Asia: Vietnam and Cambodia 141
India 173
Singapore 203
Middle East: Egypt and Jordan 215
Central Europe 247
Home 261

Life Lessons and Global Rules 265

Acknowledgments

A book is an interesting creation. Although it requires one person to be willing to sit alone at a desk for hundreds of hours, most books couldn't be written without the help and support of dozens of other people. So I want to express appreciation here to those individuals who, in big and small ways, played a role in the birth of this book.

First, of course, is everyone we met on the road, whose stories are scattered throughout these pages. Some of the names or details have been changed because people who met us didn't know they were going to end up in a travel memoir. But I owe many thanks to the friends who hosted me and Lisa, to those who showed us their cities, to the people who eagerly talked to us about their cultures and to the many new friends we made along the way. Without all of you, there would not have been a travel experience to write about and so I am most grateful for your hospitality and friendship.

When I decided to write this book, several people graciously agreed to read early versions of the manuscript and give me comments. John Stacy and Liz Callahan, in particular, went beyond the call of duty in the time they spent and the feedback they provided. Many others also read sections of the book and made helpful suggestions, including Marc and Amy Vachon, Dave Eaton, John Mason, Cate Reavis, Kelly Chang, Louise Patane, Kim Hill, Jeff and Kristen Lehouillier, Kristina Irwin, Craig Herreman, Tamara Montano and Mara Gerst.

Then, of course, there is my very large and diverse family, some of whom also belong in the above list for giving editorial feedback and all of whom have provided emotional support. This includes my parents (Bob Riel and Ellen Bourget), step-parents (Charlie Bourget and Maggie Losardo), siblings (Theresa Riel, Patty Reynolds, Ken Riel, Debbie Cooper, Wendy Spradley, Robin Galipeau, Jen Cunanan, Kelly Johnson and Jim Richardson), and Lisa's parents and siblings

(Judy and Darrell Obert, and Kelly, Kacey and Katy Obert), who have welcomed me into their family. Whew. It's unfortunate that we're all scattered across six states, but fantastic that we're all still such good friends and I am truly grateful for that.

I would be remiss if I didn't mention the organization that was responsible for my earliest international experiences. My first trip abroad was with the Up with People student leadership program. There are so many individuals who helped sparked my interest in travel and culture that I couldn't begin to name them all, but Blanton Belk founded the organization and has devoted much of his life to building understanding between cultures.

I also want to acknowledge two friends who played a role in bringing this book to life, particularly because of their considerable enthusiasm. Early in the process, Rick Von Feldt encouraged me to take a chance on a bigger, more personal project in my life, while Tommy Spaulding later talked through the concept with me and helped convince me to publish the book. Thanks to both of you. I appreciate the conversations we've shared over the years.

Finally, and most important, there is my wife, Lisa, who has been so much more than a travel partner. She has always believed in me and provided more support and encouragement than I can probably ever repay. Thank you for sharing this life journey with me.

Part I

▼

Traveling East Around the World

"Strange travel suggestions are dancing lessons from God."
—Kurt Vonnegut, *Cat's Cradle*

Introduction

It was 6:30 a.m. when three guards approached us on the Cairo train platform, guns slung over their shoulders.

"What nationality are you? English?" one of them asked.

I hesitated. "... No, American."

"American?! Aye!" he shouted.

Walkie-talkies crackled to life. All we heard was a string of Arabic, laced several times with the word "American."

"Come," the officer said and motioned for us to follow him.

On most days, our early arrival in Cairo after an overnight journey from Luxor would have been a mundane event. This is, after all, a well-worn path on the Egyptian tourist trail. But this wasn't the most common of days. Just over 24 hours earlier, terrorist bombs had shattered the country's composure.

My wife, Lisa, and I had heard about the bombings the previous morning when we went to meet a guide who was scheduled to take us to Luxor's Karnak Temple. When we saw Mohammed, though, he had a stricken look on his face and said to us: "Did you see the news? Three bombs exploded during the night in Sharm el Sheikh. More than 80 people killed."

It's always shocking to hear news of any such attack. Even when we are not in London or Madrid or Bali or New York, it's impossible not to be moved by the tragedy and appalled by the senselessness of the violence. But not only were Lisa and I in Egypt when this occurred, we also happened to be on our way to the Sinai Peninsula the very next day. In fact, we'd recently been debating whether to go to Sharm el Sheikh or Dahab, two contrasting towns on the Red Sea coast.

There we were, standing alongside the Nile River, about to visit the ancient temple complex at Karnak, and our guide was telling us there had been a terrorist attack a few hours earlier in a region of the country that we would soon be visiting. We looked around at the street and the river. Everything seemed normal. If we hadn't been told this news, it would have appeared like any other day.

"It is very tragic," said Mohammed, "but you should go on with your plans today. There is more security here now. It will be very safe. You should focus on the moment."

We decided to listen to him, so for the next few hours we toured Karnak Temple. As the morning wore on, though, and the desert sun grew more intense, Mohammed began to share some of his thoughts.

"This is not a war against the West," he said to us, "this is a war against humankind. These are the worst kind of Muslims who do these acts. They are using their religion for bad aims. In Egypt, we believe in a tolerant Islam. I don't know what kind of people can do this, to kill people like this!"

At another moment, he swept his arm around. "Look at all of these boats on the river. They may all be empty soon if tourists don't come to Egypt; and these merchants, and taxi drivers, and restaurants. So many people rely on tourism to make a living."

"Do you think there may be another attack?" asked Lisa. "Are you afraid? Is it dangerous?"

"Ah, what is dangerous?" whispered Mohammed. "You can have danger in your home or crossing the street. You must live your life, I think."

What is dangerous? We couldn't get that question out of our minds for the rest of the day. What, we wondered, is the proper reaction to a terrorist attack in a foreign country, when you happen to be traveling in that country on the day the bombs explode? Should you leave immediately? Or, if you decide to stay, is it possible to go on with your trip as if nothing happened?

News reports later indicated that at least half the tourists in Egypt did leave in the day or two after the bombings. But a sizeable number also chose to remain. Some of them just assumed there wouldn't be a second attack; others refused to give in to the terror (like the woman we met on the train later that evening who said, "I don't like to be bullied by terrorists"); and some were just hardened to terrorism in general after a string of attacks in all parts of the world. In the days ahead, a common refrain that we heard among tourists was, "where can you consider yourself safe now, anyway?"

In the end, Lisa and I also decided to stay in Egypt. I'd like to say that it was a heroic decision, that we wanted to live our lives and not be bullied, and, yes, we certainly carried some of that sentiment inside. But we still would have put our safety first had we felt seriously threatened. There was no single reason for our decision, but rather a web of interconnected ones. Most importantly, we didn't feel unsafe among the Egyptians, who had been gracious and welcoming to us.

So it was that the following morning we found ourselves standing on a train platform in Cairo. We'd arranged for a van to meet us at the station and drive us to St. Catherine and then onto Dahab. But as we watched almost all of the other travelers disappear into the early morning haze, there was still no sign of our driver. Now, three armed guards were asking us to follow them.

At the front of the train station, one of the guards asked if we were waiting for a ride.

"Yes."

"Give me the name of your driver."

I fished around in my backpack and pulled out the name and number of the Egyptian company through which we had arranged our transportation. He took the piece of paper and disappeared. The other two guards remained close by.

"Is everything all right?" I asked.

"He go to phone your driver," a second guard said.

Phone my driver? I exhaled. Jeez, why didn't he say so? These guys were just trying to help us locate our ride, I realized with a sigh. This was nothing more than Egyptian hospitality. Well, with guns as props. Once we understood what was happening, it didn't seem like such a bad thing to have our own security detail. A few minutes later, the lead guard returned and all three of them stood and waited with us until we were safely in the van and on our way.

Shortly thereafter, we left Cairo, leaving behind a sea of brown buildings and murky skies. Then we drove for six hours, past Suez and into the Sinai, through a dry, empty desert landscape that became progressively more rugged and lunar-like. Though it offers very little in terms of vegetation, the Sinai is an important piece of land. It serves as a bridge between Asia and Africa, and between the Red Sea and the Mediterranean, and has a significance that dates to the Old Testament.

In early afternoon, we arrived at St. Catherine, a small village that is located at the base of Mt. Sinai, the biblical mountain where Moses is said to have received the Ten Commandments from God. St. Catherine's Monastery, from which the town's name is derived, is the keeper of a bush that is believed to be descended from *the* original burning bush. The monastery is the starting point for tourists who hike Mt. Sinai in the predawn hours to watch the sunrise from atop its summit.

I gazed at the harsh, sunswept terrain and reflected on the fact that Moses may have walked on this very ground. What would he think of the world today, I wondered? The words and beliefs that descended with him from Mt. Sinai live on, yet several thousand years later we are still engaged in battles between religions and cultures.

After settling into our hotel room, Lisa and I went for a walk in town and, strangely, failed to run into a single other traveler. We stopped in a one-room store on the deserted main street to buy supplies for our hike. A flickering television in the corner broadcast news reports about the carnage in Sharm el Sheikh. We asked the proprietor, a local Bedouin dressed in a *galabayya*, a traditional white robe, about the news.

"Foolish people, those terrorists!" he said to us. "Why kill? Why? It is crazy!"

This was just one of a string of encounters with Egyptians who, like Mohammed the previous day, were suddenly very willing to open up to us. Many of these conversations were with people who relied on the tourist trade for their livelihood. They were despairing over the terrorist attack, and I sensed that in their anguish some of them spoke to us with a candor they might not have otherwise.

"You are Christian, I am Muslim," said one person. "But we both have blood, we are both human beings. This is not Islam, to kill like this."

To be honest, it was easy for Lisa and me to feel self-conscious when we first heard the news about the bombings. After all, we are citizens of a country that had enraged many Muslims with its policies, particularly the decision to go to war in Iraq. It would be easy, we thought, for the Egyptians to be furious with America and Americans, even if the recent attack was not directed specifically at the U.S. That is not, however, what we discovered.

"Look," said another individual, "it is true that we don't like Bush. And we don't like decision to go to war in Iraq. But American people we like. People are not government. We know there is a difference."

It was a validation, in a way, of our decision to remain in Egypt. We had some terrific experiences and conversations with local people in the days ahead. The Egyptians had always been friendly, but now it was as if they felt compelled to inform us that their culture and religion did not condone such acts of random violence.

That night in St. Catherine, Lisa and I struggled out of bed at 2 a.m. to head over to Mt. Sinai. It was hard to believe that just 20 hours earlier we had been standing on the train platform in Cairo. Improbably, we had still not seen another tourist since then, so we wondered if we were destined to be lone travelers hiking the trail in the dark, chasing the spirit of Moses. When we arrived at the trailhead, though, we saw a few dozen other people in the vicinity, including a group of French visitors who had come on a tour bus in the night.

From 2:45 to 5:15 a.m., we navigated our way by flashlight up a gravelly track that climaxed in a steep set of several hundred steps cut into the stone of the mountainside. Along the way, we were kept company by Bedouin tribespeople who hawked hot tea, cold coke and camel rides in the moonlight.

Finally, atop the rocky summit of Mt. Sinai, we sat down to rest our tired legs and await the dawn. The sky inched its way out of blackness, with a swatch of crimson light peeking over the edge of the earth and glowing steadily brighter. It provided a glimpse into the jagged, ethereal landscape that surrounded us and, as the sun prepared to rise in the eastern sky, it truly seemed as if the mountain were being blanketed in celestial light. It was not very difficult to imagine Moses having a divine encounter there.

Abruptly, then, the sun made a dramatic appearance—a globe of fiery brilliance climbing above the mountainous peaks of the Sinai to a round of applause and gasps. There we were, amongst a group of travelers from the Americas, Europe, Australia and Asia, standing atop Mt. Sinai at sunrise. For a moment, at least, the specter of terrorism seemed far away.

A few minutes later, I leaned back against a boulder that was still cool from the nighttime chill. I lifted my face to the warming rays of the sun, which was rising in a clear blue sky next to a still visible sliver of the Moon. An orange dawn illuminated some of the rock-strewn path that we had hiked during the night and we watched as Bedouin men began to lead their camels back down the trail to St. Catherine.

This, I thought, is a reason to travel. Not just for this moment, but for everything that led to this moment. The overnight train ride, the armed guards at the station, the anxiety over terrorism, the conversations with Egyptians about religion and politics, the overnight hike up a rocky mountain path alongside Bedouins, camels and fellow travelers. All of these episodes coalesce, finally, into the memory of a single sunrise, and when we return home at the end of our journey with this memory, we return also with the perspective of a traveler who has had all of the accompanying experiences. The perspective of someone who has discovered that the people of the Middle East are some of the most hospitable individuals anywhere, who has been surprised by the lingering beauty of the Islamic call to prayer, and who has learned that the world is both more complex and more magnificent than it ever seemed to be from the comfort of a living room at home.

Thankfully, Lisa and I weren't returning home just yet. We still had more than a month left on the road, but our trip was nevertheless beginning to wind down. As I sat there in the growing daylight I couldn't help but reflect on the path that had led us here, to the top of a biblical mountain in the middle of an Egyptian desert.

This journey, in a sense, had begun more than three years earlier. For some time, we'd been dreaming about taking time away from our daily lives in order to travel. Although we had seen a great deal of North America and Europe, a large part of the planet was terra incognita to us and we yearned to know more about this wide-ranging world that we inhabit. We also wanted to have an adventure together before starting a family and were drawn to the prospect of carving time away from our careers for an enriching life experience now, rather than waiting several decades in hopes that we'd have a similar opportunity during retirement.

But how? Quit our jobs? Stop everything in order to travel and then hit the re-start button on our lives after we returned? Our dream was laden with obstacles, particularly for two people who were in the middle of their careers. One day, though, we hit upon the idea of traveling during a leave of absence from work. If we could arrange a job sabbatical, we reasoned, we'd be able to travel for several months without causing a drastic break from the rest of our lives.

The idea proved surprisingly easy to orchestrate. Lisa had worked six years for the same company and she managed to convince her director that losing her for a few months was preferable to losing her permanently and that this experience would make her even more productive in the long run. In my case, I had been self-employed as a writer and consultant and so was able to make the necessary arrangements to not be available for a period of time.

As we watched our plan grow into reality, Lisa and I decided to plot a round-the-world itinerary with a focus on non-Western countries. It would be an ideal means of interacting with multiple cultures and we also appreciated the symbolism involved. We would travel in a circle around the globe, returning to the place we left but with an abundance of memories and new experiences.

I also became increasingly intrigued by the concept of framing the trip as a sabbatical. Merely thinking of it in those terms, as opposed to calling it a leave of absence, seemed to exalt it with the promise of a longer-lasting, more memorable experience, because a sabbatical has traditionally been a time of contemplation or a means of reinvigorating oneself.

This is an ancient idea, since the term sabbatical derives from the word sabbath. In religious and spiritual practice, every seventh day was meant to be devoted to rest, family time and spiritual reflection. Likewise, it was applied to the practice of resting agricultural fields every seventh year, giving the land a chance to restore itself and return to greater productivity. The custom of a work or academic sabbatical derives from this same notion, the belief that time off from the everyday rigors of a job can provide individuals with a chance to rest and reflect, or to conduct research, thereby returning to work with renewed energy and ideas.

In our society, this concept is often relegated to the confines of academia, with most people either never contemplating the option or at least pushing off the possibility to their later years. But many individuals could benefit from a sabbatical—whether to travel, do volunteer work, learn a skill or take up a new hobby—even if it simply means returning to the same routine with increased enthusiasm or more varied knowledge and interests. The journey that Lisa and I were embarking on, I realized, could best be termed a "life sabbatical." We wanted an adventure, sure, but we also wanted to learn about the world and return home recharged for the next stage of our lives.

This notion spurred me to view our travels as an opportunity to gain insights into myself, my aspirations and my beliefs. By getting away from my normal daily routine, I hoped to better understand myself; and by getting away from my home, I hoped to gain a better perspective on what it meant to be an American in today's world. My goal, I decided, would be to travel, listen, reflect and see what I could learn from the encounters we had and the people we met. I wanted the trip to surprise me.

And surprise me it did. I not only kept a journal, but as the trip wore on I also began recording insights that arose from our experiences on the road. When I began, I didn't know whether I'd collect three insights, or seven or 20. I didn't know if they'd be life-changing or mundane. I didn't know if I'd share them with people or bury them in my journal. Eventually, though, I put them together on one page and realized that some of them were personal and applied to the way I wanted to live my life, while others were more universal in nature. So I formed two collections, called "Life Lessons" and "Global Rules," which you will find throughout this book. They are not earth-shaking insights, but they provide clues as to how my own perspectives ripened and unfurled during our sabbatical.

Thirteen months after we were married, then, and four months after we'd begun making actual plans for our trip, Lisa and I left Boston and began journeying east around the world.

During that trip, we sipped apple tea amidst the historic wonders of Istanbul. Watched Masai tribespeople kick up crimson dust as they danced atop the red soil of Kenya. Discussed Buddhism and American foreign policy with a young monk in Thailand. Met a middle-aged rickshaw driver in Beijing who invited us into his tiny apartment for tea. Spent a memorable 12 hours in Tokyo with a Japanese family who adopted us for a day and insisted on showing us their culture. And more. So much more.

The trip was everything we'd hoped it would be and we returned to Boston planning to buy a house and start a family. But something unexpected happened. Or didn't happen. We had difficulty finding an affordable home in Boston's then overheated real estate market and found ourselves continuing to put off having children until we were "more settled." Before we knew it, two years had gone by, the children hadn't arrived and the travel bug hadn't left. Not only that, but we found ourselves now staring at the possibility of a cross-country move to Arizona. Lisa was a native of the state, she had an intriguing job prospect there and the real estate prices in the Southwest seemed a whole lot easier on the budget.

So we made a surprising decision. Surprising, at least, in comparison with what our plans had been two years earlier. We would move to Arizona, but first we'd take time off for another trip, which in a sense would be a continuation of our earlier sabbatical. There was more of the world to explore, we decided, there were more adventures awaiting us, there was more to learn and there were more insights to collect.

This time, we made a more definitive break from our lives. We packed up our belongings and put them into storage in Arizona. We drove cross-country and left our car with Lisa's family. Then we set off on a second trip, to Vietnam and Cambodia, India and Singapore, Egypt and Jordan, and finally some of central Europe. Since we had trekked east during our first adventure, we decided now to travel west around the planet and to complete a round-the-world journey in both directions.

Perhaps if we'd had one longer excursion in the first place, rather than two different trips that added up to nearly seven months, we may not have felt the need for a second journey. But that is just the way it worked out for us and today the two voyages seem to blend together in our minds as a single experience. One life sabbatical that spanned two laps of the world.

Turkey

EDGING AWAY FROM THE WEST

As the ferry slipped through the water, Lisa and I sat on deck and quietly watched the morning sun rise in the East while the Greek shoreline faded from view behind us. If I had to choose a single moment when our journey seemed to begin, this was it.

We had decided to start our trip with ten days in Greece, mostly as a way to get our travel muscles limber and as a transition from our jobs and lives at home to our sabbatical experience. During that time, we visited the Acropolis, lounged on the island beaches of Santorini and Samos, drank wine in Greek tavernas and soaked in the magnificent light that drenches the Aegean Sea. Now, though, Greece was melting into the horizon, the Turkish coast was growing large in front of us and our travels were about to kick into a new gear.

Only three kilometers of water separates the Greek island of Samos from Turkey. It is a negligible distance that could be covered by a good long distance swimmer. But while Turkey is on the edge of Europe and its history is intertwined with Greece's, it is also a Muslim nation that has as much in common with the Middle East as with the West. In this short boat trip, we were leaping a cultural border as much as a national one. Before long, Lisa and I would begin to see such a border crossing as a mundane event, but on this day, as we began edging away from the Western world for the first time in our lives, we were consumed with a restless wonder over what we'd find on the other side.

The ferry pulled into the dock at Kusadasi and we stepped off onto Turkish soil. Once through immigration, we walked onto the street and were immediately besieged by touts for various hotels and pensions.

"Merhaba! Hello!"

"Looking for a room? Please, sir, come with me."

"No, this way. I have the best deal."

We walked forward through the maze of persistent salesmen who crowded the ferry exit. One young man walked with us down the sidewalk.

"Sorry, we already have a room," I said.

"Where?"

I told him. We'd booked a room via the internet and the guesthouse had promised to send a van to meet us here at the boat dock.

"Oh, that place is full, my friend. I just saw the manager."

"Yes, but I already have a reservation."

"But my rooms are better," he said, "because they are very close to here."

We eventually tracked down our ride, climbed into a van and set out for Selcuk, a nearby town that we had chosen for its easy access to the ruins at Ephesus. Soon, we were bumping along the road out of Kusadasi, climbing above the sea and into the hills. Twenty minutes later, we found ourselves amidst the crowded lanes of a small town. The van pulled into a narrow street and stopped in front of the guesthouse. The staff then showed us to our $12 room, with its lumpy mattress and single sputtering fan to provide relief from the summer heat.

This was another sign, I thought, that our sabbatical experience was truly getting underway, because from this point on we'd be watching our expenses more than we had in Greece—partly because of our budget and partly because we didn't want to insulate ourselves from the real experience of travel. Our quest would be to seek out the middle way, to stay safe and maintain a modicum of comfort while not getting trapped in a tourist bubble.

As we settled into our room, we opened the window to let in some air and soon heard the Islamic call to prayer for the first time. In every Muslim country, people are called to prayer five times each day, from dawn to early evening, when a muezzin chants prayer verses that are broadcast around town via a loudspeaker on the mosque's minaret. By the time Lisa and I realized what was happening, though, the chant was about over.

We then decided to go for an early afternoon walk through Selcuk, where we observed women picking out vegetables from a street market and men chatting with other men in teahouses. But we also began sweating through our clothes in the afternoon sun and, after a while, Lisa said she didn't feel well. So we went back to the guesthouse and relaxed in a downstairs sitting room, where there were drinks, snacks and a computer. We struck up a conversation with Andrea, a middle-aged British woman who had lived in Selcuk since moving there two years earlier to be with a Turkish man. We also met Kelly, a woman from San Francisco who blew into the room as a ball of energy, introducing herself to everyone and shooting off questions in every direction.

A short while later, Kelly and Andrea left and Lisa decided to write some emails. I tried to read, then wrote in my journal, then went for a walk. When I returned, Lisa was still on the computer. Somehow, this wasn't quite the way I envisioned our first day in Turkey unfolding. "We did our relaxing in Greece," I said to myself. "Isn't it time to begin having real travel experiences?"

I fidgeted around for a while and slowly grew more impatient. Ironically, there were many other times in the weeks ahead when I wanted nothing more than some down time to relax. But at this moment, for some reason, all I could think was that time was slipping away on our first day in Turkey and I wasn't doing anything noteworthy.

"What's going on?" I finally asked Lisa. "How long are you going to be on the internet? If you're not really sick, we could have found something to do this afternoon."

"I'm really not feeling well."

"So go lay down then. It's not going to do us any good if you stay sick for a few days."

"I just thought it would be a good time to write some emails to my family," she said. "I'm not stopping you from doing anything."

Arggh. I planted myself back in the sitting room and flipped through a two-week old magazine. I was joined there by Will, a fiftysomething Canadian man who was in the middle of a three-week visit to Turkey with his adult son. He joked about how he had to adjust his expectations in order to travel with his son, who subsisted on a few dollars a day in austere lodgings.

"I did the whole backpack thing in my university days," he said, "but I've gotten accustomed to a little more luxury since then. Still, it hasn't been bad. This is the way my son travels, and it's been a nice experience to spend this time with him. When we first discussed the possibility of a trip together, we considered going to China. I'm glad we came here, though. Most of us in the West don't know much about Turkey, but I've found it to be a fascinating country."

Eventually, Lisa finished her emails and joined us. Will left to meet his son and we went back to our room to rest. She slept and I read. By dinnertime, Lisa was feeling better and we went down to an open air restaurant in the back courtyard of the guesthouse. Now that she was more relaxed, Lisa admitted that a lot of things were hitting her all at once earlier in the day.

"From the time we got off the ferry, everything just seemed so different," she said. "It hit me suddenly that we were going to spend the next few months in unfamiliar cultures and I thought, 'What have I gotten myself into?'"

"So that's why you didn't want to do anything this afternoon?"

"No, the sun was also incredibly hot and I didn't sleep much last night. I really didn't feel well. I think I just needed some time to myself and being able to write those emails helped me relax."

"Well, I just didn't know what you were thinking," I said. "All you had to was tell me. I only knew that you said you were sick and yet you didn't seem to want to get off the computer."

"I know. But I'm better now."

Within minutes of our conversation—as if on cue, it seemed—we again became aware of the Islamic call to prayer. When we heard it earlier in the afternoon, we were too distracted with other thoughts for it to really register. Now, however, the sonorous chant rang clear through the evening air.

Allahu Akbar ... Ash hadu an la ilaha ill Allah ...

The sound was hauntingly beautiful. A deep and melodious hymn that seemed to cascade from the heavens. It brought home to me that this call to prayer was a common, everyday occurrence and actually a very beautiful way to be reminded of one's religion. It was nothing more, nothing less, than the sound of faith.

About this time, Kelly appeared and asked if she could join us at our table. During the course of the next hour or so, we traded stories and discovered that we enjoyed each other's company. We learned that Kelly, a late twentysomething Asian-American from California, was a lawyer who had quit her job on a whim. She decided to go on the road for a month and was traveling alone, mostly in Turkey and Greece before meeting some friends in France.

Since the three of us had similar plans to see the ruins at Ephesus the following day, we made plans to meet for breakfast and spend the day together.

John, Paul and Mary

When discussing ruins from the classical era in the West, the first sites that come to mind are those in Athens and Rome. These cities were the centers of ancient empires and are still important capitals, which perhaps explains the primacy of the Parthenon, Coliseum and Roman Forum. But, by themselves, these are not more impressive than the ruins at Ephesus.

Two millennia ago, Ephesus was one of the largest cities in the Western world, with a population that reached 250,000 at its height. The seaside city was a trading hub and a center of worship for Artemis, the goddess of fertility. The Temple of Artemis, in fact, was larger than the Parthenon of Athens and was considered one of the seven wonders of the ancient world. Although this temple has long since disappeared, many other Ephesian ruins still exist.

Lisa, Kelly and I took advantage of a free morning ride to Ephesus from our guesthouse. Upon arriving, we stood face-to-face with the remnants of a city that had vanished beneath the waves of history. Ephesus wasn't buried by volcanic lava or burned to the ground by an invading army; rather, its influence waned as a result of natural and historical forces. Through the centuries, the harbor that brought prosperity to the area silted up and disappeared. Additionally, Christianity and then Islam became predominant in the region and future rulers were not concerned with maintaining a city that had been a center of worship for a pagan goddess. Ephesus became a ghost town and was forgotten.

Until the advent of modern tourism, that is. New armies of foreigners now descend on Ephesus, but we come to gaze at relics of a lost age. So, armed with our guidebooks, the three of us set out down Curetes Street, a boulevard that was once paved with marble and lined on both sides with statues. We wandered freely among the solitary arches, the broken pillars and the marble-strewn fields of a once magnificent city. Further down the road, we saw the crumbling remains of Ephesian homes and were impressed and amused by the well-preserved public latrine, a row of marble benches in a communal room with a channel of water below that connected to a municipal sewage system.

"I don't think I've ever seen a 2,000-year-old public bathroom," I said. "This must be where Ephesians would come to relieve themselves after a night of wine-drinking in the local tavernas, or after going out to the theater."

Other tourists from around the world were evidently as amused as we were. By the dozens, they lined up to take pictures of themselves sitting on these ancient toilets.

"Hey, take a picture of me sitting here with a newspaper."

The humor eventually ran its course, so we continued to the much-photographed Library of Celsus. Built early in the 2nd century, this was once home to 12,000 books, or rolled papyri, making it one of the largest libraries of the classical world. Next to this was the Sacred Way, the city's main street. Here was the Great Theatre of Ephesus, an amphitheater that could seat 25,000 people and is still considered a marvel because of its perfect acoustics. It is beautifully situated at the base of Pion Mountain so that, from the seats, an audience could have looked out over the marketplace to the nearby harbor.

This theater is featured in the Bible, in Acts 19, which conveys the tale of St. Paul's visit to Ephesus. At the time, local artisans used to sell small images of the goddess Artemis, but Paul's Christian preachings cut into this trade. A silversmith named Demetrius managed to incite a near riot by suggesting that Paul was not only being disrespectful of Artemis but was also threatening the prosperity of the city. One day, thousands of people gathered in the Great Theatre, angrily shouting "Artemis of Ephesus is great!" The crowd was eventually calmed, but Paul left Ephesus shortly thereafter.

To me, what was most fascinating about the area was that it contained the ruins of an entire community. A theater, library, temples, fountains, market stalls, private homes and public toilets. Two thousand years ago, these grounds were filled with people—shopping, working, going to the theater, raising families, worshiping, arguing about government, spending time with friends. But all that is left are the skeletal remains of a major city and the accumulated dust of the centuries. It certainly underscores the transitory nature of our existence.

I pondered this also when I sat in the Great Theatre and read the story of the uprising directed at St. Paul. Here was a pagan community that resisted Christianity because it threatened not only a way of life, but also generations of deeply held beliefs about the nature of existence. Who could have known that, several centuries later, Ephesus would become a Christian community when that religion became the official faith of the Roman Empire? Or that another few centuries down the road, Islam would be brought to Ephesus by Turkish tribes from Central Asia as they established a new empire on the Aegean? It makes one wonder what our own cities and civilizations will look like to people two millennia from now.

Ali, the manager of our guesthouse, said to call him when we were finished at Ephesus so that he could meet us for lunch. We were touched by his kindness, although as the days passed we learned that hospitality toward guests is part of the essence of Turkish culture. He took us to a nearby restaurant, where we removed our shoes and sat on cushions at a low outdoor table in the shade.

The eatery specialized in *gosleme*, or Turkish pancakes, and we ordered several varieties, filled with potatoes, cheese and eggplant. Ali took us to the kitchen, where elderly Turkish women sat on the floor and rolled out dough on knee-high wooden tables and then cooked the meals in a fireplace oven.

Back at our seats, as we ate our lunch, I asked Ali to tell us something about Turkish culture.

"In our culture, we share a lot," he said. "For instance, in the West, when you eat, it is common for people to eat individually, or with one other person. Here, we like to eat together. And instead of ordering individual meals, we order many dishes, put them on the table and all share."

Mehmet, the owner of a local carpet shop, told us much the same thing on another day. Speaking about nomadic Turkish people who traditionally sit around a *sofra* (a carpet on which they place food for meals), he said, "The tribes consider it bad luck if you eat alone. Families always eat together. It is believed that God blesses the house where food is shared."

Lisa then asked Ali how much of a role Islam played in daily life in Turkey.

"Faith is important here, of course," he said, "but it is not a 'hot' Islam as in the Arab countries. Turkey is a secular country, and Islam is not as strict here."

"Do most people pray five times a day, whenever there is a call to prayer?"

"Most people do not," he said. "Myself, I maybe pray once or twice in a day, maybe none on some days. At prayer times, the mosques are filled with older men, not so many young people."

"So when you are old you will start going to mosque?" I joked.

"Yes, yes, probably," he laughed.

Later, Ali asked us what the American people thought of Turkey.

"Well, the people we talked with who had traveled here really enjoyed it," I said. "They told us how beautiful the country was and how nice the Turkish people were. But others are more afraid, I think, because of the Islamic culture and the closeness to the Middle East."

He nodded in understanding. But sitting here in this peaceful setting, enjoying Ali's kindness, I couldn't help but think of the fear that so easily grips us when we don't have personal experience with other people and cultures. I smiled when I remembered the anxiety that even Lisa and I had felt just one day earlier over the cultural border we were about to cross.

"So, Ali," I said, "now tell me what Turkish people think of the United States."

"We very much like Americans," he said. "When we meet Americans, they are always very open and friendly. But we don't always like your government. George Bush is kind of a cowboy, I think, and not so interested in the rest of the world. Bill Clinton was good, though. He was tolerant and was interested in other cultures. He came here to Ephesus when he was in Turkey."

After lunch, Ali and a co-worker were gracious enough to drive us the seven kilometers to Maryemana, or Mary's House. This small, serene spot, located up a twisting road on a hill above Selcuk, is an interesting place of pilgrimage, as it is widely thought to have been the home of the Virgin Mary during the final years of her life.

Some people believe that St. John took Mary into his care sometime after Jesus' death and brought her to Ephesus. It is generally acknowledged that John moved to Ephesus in the mid-first century and perhaps wrote some of his gospels there. He was also exiled for a time to the nearby island of Patmos, now a part of Greece, where he received inspiration for the Book of Revelation. Near downtown Selcuk is the Basilica of St. John on Ayasuluk Hill, built long ago on the spot where John was thought to be buried.

If we accept that Mary came to Ephesus with John, the evidence is then that she lived in a house by the harbor (near what later became the Church of the Virgin Mary), before eventually moving to a home on Bülbül Mountain. In reality, most of the actual details surrounding Mary's later life were lost to history, but local villagers kept alive a story about Mary's death in the area. Then in the 19th century a bedridden German nun named Catherine Emmerich had visions of Mary spending her final days in the hills near Ephesus.

Her description of the site proved surprisingly accurate and, in 1891, an expedition discovered the ruins of a building that matched the nun's description and had a foundation that was dated to the first century. The building was later restored and declared a pilgrimage site. With visits by three Popes now since 1967, the Catholic Church has lent credence to the belief that this was the last home of the Virgin Mary.

It is a very peaceful spot. The front room of the restored home is a small chapel and when we walked in an elderly nun was sitting there in solitude, as flickering candles cast dancing shadows on the stone walls. Just to the west of the building are fountains that flow from a natural spring. Here, an entire wall is wrapped in tiny bits of white cloth. Each piece of cloth was tied there by a Muslim and represents a prayer, similar to the practice of Christians who light candles inside a church.

It's fascinating to come here and see this is a pilgrimage site for both Christians and Muslims and to reflect on the fact that Islam and Christianity sprang from the same roots. Muslims respect Jesus as a teacher and prophet and they also venerate Mary. If only we could get back to these roots of a shared spirituality, I thought, what a different world we would inhabit.

Threads of Understanding

On our last night in Selcuk, we had dinner at the guesthouse. Despite the stark nature of the rooms, the pension served good food in an outdoor courtyard filled with plants and flowers. Kelly, Lisa and I shared a table and two bottles of Turkish wine. Ali joined us for a while. He was sipping clear liquid from a small glass.

"Ahh, you're drinking ouzo," said Lisa.

"No. You are in Turkey," he admonished gently. "We do not call this ouzo, we call it raki."

Ali sat down and reminded Kelly that she had promised to go watch the sunset with him. "But every day you are busy. You are a tease, I think? You say you will join me, but then at sunset you have other plans."

"I'm sorry, Ali," said Kelly, not knowing whether he was truly saddened or merely having some fun with her. "You joke a lot. I didn't know you were serious about watching the sunset."

Indeed, we didn't always know when Ali was being serious or comical. He had a running joke with us about a helicopter that he allegedly owned. He offered to take us to our next destination in Turkey via this helicopter, so long as we paid for the gasoline. It was preposterous, of course, to think the manager of a guesthouse in a small Turkish town actually owned and piloted a helicopter. But his humor was so dry, his demeanor so serious and sincere when he broached the subject, that the line between fact and fiction blurred when we were with him.

We had quite a different experience with Mehmet, who owned a nearby carpet shop and spent a lot of time at the guesthouse. He was friendly enough, but everything else about him indicated a silky smooth salesman. One afternoon, when we looked over some of his carpets, he tossed us his sales pitch.

"Selling carpets is not about money for me," he said. "It's about art, it's about loving carpets. I don't want you to buy from me unless you really love a piece."

Not surprisingly, though, when we declined to profess our love for any particular carpet and made a move to leave his shop, he insisted that we examine more of his inventory.

"You really must love a carpet," he continued, ordering an assistant to unroll more samples. "What is love? How do you explain it? You can't explain it, can you? Well, it's the same with your feeling for a carpet. You see one and you know immediately that you love it."

After hearing this song and dance about carpets, we were suitably surprised when Mehmet showed up in the restaurant that evening, joined us at our table for a drink and began talking, not about carpets, but about people and politics. He began innocently enough, telling us about his experiences with Americans.

"The Americans are good people," he said "Very pure-hearted, trusting, optimistic. I like Americans. But I must tell you that most Turks know more about the U.S. than Americans do."

This was a laughable statement, but since Turks know more about the U.S. than the average American knows about Turkey, we cut him some slack.

"Although I like Americans," he went on, "your government has a lot of problems. The U.S. sells weapons to countries all over the world, and then complains when some countries get too strong. They want to control the entire Middle East for its oil. If there was no oil, they wouldn't care about the Middle East. And Bush is a bad president. He knows nothing about the world."

This wasn't the conversation we wanted to be having on this otherwise relaxing evening, but none of these statements were terribly shocking. We let him go on for a while, figuring he'd have his say and be done with it. But he wasn't finished.

"Did you know that Bush knew about the September 11 attacks ahead of time, but did nothing to stop them?" he asked us.

"Look, everything else you said was debatable, but why would you think this?" I asked him.

"Because it's true. Bush knew that he was elected illegitimately in 2000. So this would boost his popularity."

"So you're trying to tell us the American government would let its own people die?" asked Lisa.

"Every cause has its victims," said Mehmet. "These people were sacrificed for a larger reason. Bush knew this would be good for nationalism. The United States always needs to have an enemy. This is all common knowledge to us. It's just not being reported as widely in the United States."

Interestingly, although this conversation took place during our first stop in Turkey, no one we met in the rest of the country ever expressed such an opinion. That said, it's obviously not uncommon abroad to hear questions about various U.S. government policies.

Such as, "Why does the U.S. support an authoritarian government in Saudi Arabia but insist that the Iraqis and Palestinians must be democratic?"

Or, "Why does your country have trade relations with Communist China but isolate Communist Cuba?"

Or even, "Why do Americans profess concern for the environment yet drive such big automobiles?"

There are never any simple answers, but while any conversation among people from diverse backgrounds has the potential to be difficult and exasperating, it can be equally enlightening. It's natural that we're perplexed when other people so easily see our nation's faults but seem blind to our strengths. On the other hand, I wonder, must it also be true that we see our own virtues but are blind to our weaknesses? Is the truth actually in that maddening gray area in the middle?

On this evening, we debated back and forth with Mehmet before calling a truce and finally agreeing to disagree. Eventually, Mehmet left and we stayed, draining our wine bottles and letting the candles in the middle of the table burn down to nothingness. Ali came back and sat with us. Will, the Canadian man, had dinner at the next table with his son. Two students from Sweden were there, as was a Japanese couple.

I looked around the courtyard, as we sat under a canopy of stars on this velvety Turkish night, sharing wine and stories and beliefs with other travelers. The flicker of the candles reflected in our wine glasses and for a moment it seemed to me that we were conversing around a campfire. But instead of watching hot embers or tiny bits of flame shoot off into a darkened sky, we were sending out little sparks of ourselves, and as these tales and opinions swirled together in the moonlight I understood more than ever how travel enables us to spin threads of understanding across the planet.

That night, I wrote a few thoughts in my journal, which eventually became Global Rule #1. *It is only by interacting with others, and even debating them, that we can ever begin to know each other.* We are stuck in a world in which too many people believe they are absolutely right. Which, of course, means that anyone who holds a different opinion has to be wrong. But absolutism leads nowhere, except to conflict. It's not that everyone should always agree, but rather that we should be able to reach some sort of common understanding of our differences. We should at least be able to appreciate what it is that we disagree about. Most travelers, I believe, understand this. Many politicians, unfortunately, do not.

"Goreme?"

Leaving Selcuk, we set out for a long journey to the region of Cappadocia in central Turkey. Since Kelly was on her way to the same place, the three of us decided to travel together. We boarded a bus and rode for half a day through a fertile, olive-colored valley framed by chestnut mountains. It was the type of stark beauty that one finds in unpopulated regions of the American West, complete with isolated villages that look as if they'd been dropped from the sky into the middle of an empty countryside.

Our schedule called for us to reach the town of Denizli in mid-afternoon, where we would have 30 minutes to transfer to an overnight bus going to the town of Goreme in Cappadocia. It seemed easy enough, but when we stepped off the bus in Denizli we were startled to find ourselves standing amidst the madness of a Turkish *otogar* (bus station). There were dozens of rows of buses distributed throughout a massive parking lot and a chaotic tangle of people, vehicles, buildings and open air restaurants. As we took in the tumultuous scene, it was apparent that we'd need help to locate our ride. So I walked up to what appeared to be a ticket window.

"Goreme?" I asked, hoping the man at the counter would smile and point me in the right direction.

Instead he gave me a blank stare.

"Goreme?" I repeated, this time with a different pronunciation.

Still nothing.

"Goreme?" I said, with an emphasis now on different syllables.

Hmmm, how many ways could there be to pronounce Goreme, I wondered? I finally showed him my ticket receipt. In return, he gave me a lengthy explanation in Turkish of what I was supposed to do.

Now it was my turn to look dumbfounded.

He explained it to me again in Turkish, but this time in a louder voice. Which helped a lot. Nice to know, at least, that it's a universal trait to raise one's voice when someone doesn't understand your language. Finally, he raised his finger in the direction of a nearby building. Off we went, only to find ourselves standing amidst a cluster of food stalls and news stands, but no ticket windows.

"We just need to know what bus we're supposed to be on," I said to no one in particular.

Eventually, the spirits of Turkish hospitality came to our rescue when a teenage boy, maybe 14 or 15, approached us.

"Need help?" he asked.

We thought he wanted to sell us something, but instead he just took me by the arm and led us through rooms and around corners to another part of the otogar and to a ticket agent. The man cheerfully accepted our receipt and printed three tickets, seats 43, 44 and 45 on a 46-seat bus. He told us the teenage boy was going to be our bus driver. They both laughed.

"Tessekkür ederim," we said. "Thank you."

They smiled, told us where the bus was located and watched us hurry off. We arrived with three minutes to spare.

The overnight bus trip turned out to be much more bearable than we'd expected. The seats reclined nicely and the bus had more leg room than most planes. There was even an attendant who occasionally made his way down the aisle, passing out water, tea, snack cakes, and lemon cleanser for our hands. We had a nice little international group at the back of our bus. Kelly, Lisa and me from the United States, three Italian women, two French men, and a father, mother and daughter trio from Hong Kong. This kept us entertained for a while, chatting about each other and our respective travels. Kelly had been born in Taiwan and spoke some Chinese with the Hong Kong family. In the front, an old Sylvester Stallone movie played, *Daylight*, in which commuters are trapped in a tunnel after a terrorist bombing.

It was a fun sort of absurdity. We watched Rocky battle terrorism on the video screen, listened to our new American friend speak Chinese to a Hong Kong family, and accepted tea and snack cakes from a bus attendant, all while watching the miles accumulate on the lonely roads that carried us ever deeper into Turkey.

After a few hours, people drifted off to sleep. The bus made a rest stop around midnight and I got off to use the facilities and buy a drink. In the bathroom, there was an equal mix of Western-style toilets and Asian-style squat toilets (a hole in the floor, with grooves on each side to support your feet as you, literally, squat and do what it is you need to do). Unlike me, the locals were naturally all accustomed to using the squat toilets, which were also notable for the presence of a bucket of water in place of toilet paper. The Turks, or the rural Turks I should say, are still traditional enough to see toilet paper as an urban innovation. Consequently, many people still use their hand for bathroom tasks. It is always the left hand, however, which helps to explain why the right hand is customarily used for eating.

For some reason, I recalled the sit-down toilets in the latrine ruins at Ephesus. I realized that those facilities, even 2,000 years ago, were representative of the West. The squat toilets, on the other hand, were a small reminder of the Asian roots of Turkish culture. So even at a highway rest stop in the middle of the night we couldn't escape signs of the intermingling of East and West here in Turkey.

After this, I stayed awake for a couple of hours. As other passengers drifted off to sleep around me, I began to ponder the journey that Lisa and I had embarked on. That in turn caused me to reflect back to my first travel experience, which had put me on the road to this moment.

I became infatuated with travel right around the time I found myself in the charming medieval town of Bruges, Belgium, and a young woman named Veronique made me a cup of hot tea with spices. It was my first trip abroad and I had only been in Europe for a few days. But already I was hooked. I was hooked on the narrow streets and the jagged orange rooftops, the coffee and the croissants, the art and the architecture. All of it enchanted me. Although, truthfully, it had petrified me just a couple of days earlier.

Like many people, I had long harbored dreams of traveling the world. My interest was especially sparked in my late teens and early 20s when I began spending time with a slightly older and worldlier friend, Scott. He was a painter and a fellow searching soul who had already traveled extensively abroad. We used to sit around our homes in Woonsocket, Rhode Island, discussing life and travel over bottles of beer. My favorite story was of the time he met the painter Salvador Dali in Spain and spent several hours with him, drinking wine and discussing art. And, yes, Scott had the picture to prove it.

Eventually, through a cross-cultural program for college-aged students, I was able to embark on my own two-month visit to Europe, beginning in Belgium. While most of my friends were housed with a roommate in Antwerp or Brussels, where most of our activities were scheduled, I found myself alone and in Bruges, a 40-minute train ride away from anyone I knew. Abruptly, my sense of excitement popped like a balloon and I realized I was terrified of what I'd gotten myself into. I don't speak Flemish, I thought. I've never been to Europe. How am I going to take a train back into Brussels on my own?

Fortunately, I was able to remind myself that, hey, I was in Europe! My friends at home were not going to take pity on me. Just go with the experience and live it, I told myself. Just a few days later, I had fallen in love with Europe and with traveling.

It wasn't just the atmosphere or architecture. I was equally absorbed by the fact that people were, well, different. Sure, they had jobs and families, hopes and frustrations, favorite recipes and sports teams, just like everyone else I knew. But there was something else. The very fact that it was a way of life to socialize over coffee (this was in America's pre-Starbucks age), that people walked to the market to shop for ingredients for that evening's dinner, that many individuals seemed more aware of U.S. politics than some Americans were. These were all small degrees of difference, but they were differences just the same. I found myself wanting to know more.

Then my host brother Peter took me around Bruges with his friends Greet and Veronique. They showed me the nooks and crannies of a town that seemed lost in time. I followed twisting canals along cobblestone streets, watched local women weave their magic on handmade lace and climbed the narrow steps of the Belfry tower looming over a centuries-old market square. One day, we went to Veronique's house for dinner. That's when she whipped up a family recipe of hot tea and spices. As I sipped the tea, I thought, "I'm traveling, I'm learning, I'm making new friends. I could get used to this."

My fascination continued to build and I eventually spent several years working with international students and traversing the western half of Europe, from Finland to France and Switzerland to Sweden. I later went to work for a cross-cultural consulting firm and spent the better part of a decade learning and writing about culture's influence on business. One thought long nagged at me, though, which is that there was a larger world out there that I hadn't been exposed to. Reading books and interviewing people from other regions of the globe was one thing, but I always wanted to build on that experience by traveling more extensively. I could never shake an urge to strap on a backpack and hit the road for a while longer.

And now, here I was. As our bus made its way down a dark highway into central Turkey, I began to believe more than ever that this trip of ours was taking place for a reason. Before leaving home, Lisa and I naturally had doubts and second thoughts about this life sabbatical. Now that we were on the road, though, I was more satisfied that our decision had been the right one.

The bus arrived in Goreme at 5 a.m. and we stumbled groggily into a dusty parking lot that adjoined some shops. It was an odd feeling to get off a long distance bus in the predawn darkness and realize that we didn't know where we were or where our hotel was or even if that hotel would let us in should we find our way there.

I fumbled for the town map that I had acquired earlier and stashed in my bag. Lisa gazed at me warily.

"If you don't know what part of town we're in now, how are you going to figure out where we're supposed to go?" she asked.

"It's a small town, it shouldn't be hard to decipher."

"Maybe we should ask someone."

"It's five in the morning. The place is deserted."

"Well, I don't want to wander around a strange town in the dark with my luggage, looking for a hotel."

"Do you have a better idea?"

I sighed. This has always been an amusingly common occurrence in our travels. Amusing because Lisa persists in asking these questions despite freely admitting that she has difficulty reading maps. She is otherwise extremely organized and makes me look like a complete slacker. When planning this trip, she helped book flights, arranged for our inoculations, prepared a health care package for the road, made backup copies of travel documents, arranged for bills to be paid and made sure our families had duplicates of important information. I thought I was organized before I met her, but now I don't even try to keep up.

Unfortunately, when it comes to driving or walking somewhere, unless you give her exact instructions she's liable to wander aimlessly around streets and city blocks. When we first met, I was confused by how an obviously intelligent person with a successful career could struggle with directions. It took me years to accept that this was merely the way her brain worked. So, although I'd be wary too if I were following someone else's lead in a strange town at 5 a.m., I'm still never sure how to react when my wife who has difficulty reading a map asks if I know where I'm going. It's one of the endearing yet maddening perplexities of traveling with a spouse.

Before our conversation could go any further, though, a man appeared like an apparition out of the early morning darkness and suggested that we all go to his office around the corner, where he would help us. We looked at him suspiciously.

"I'm not selling anything," he said. "I just have an office nearby and I will help you get to your hotels."

Well, why not? The man turned out to be a travel agent who only asked that we take some of his brochures. In exchange, he served us hot apple tea and pointed us to our hotel. And, in a stroke of good fortune, the inn gave us a room at 5:30 a.m. without any additional charge, allowing us to sleep in a bed for a few hours and have a hot shower before beginning our day.

AN ISLAMIC VILLAGE ON THE MOON

Cappadocia was the center of the ancient Hittite Empire, but its fame today derives from a fantastic landscape. Since we arrived in Goreme before sunrise we saw only faint glimpses of the terrain that surrounded us. When we awoke a few hours later, though, and went to the hotel terrace for breakfast we found ourselves in the midst of an otherworldly setting, surrounded by miles of strange, bizarrely beautiful rock formations and pillars of honey-colored stone.

This panorama was born ten million years ago when three volcanoes erupted and left a thick coating of ash. This hardened into stone, called tuff. Natural forces then sculpted a wonderland that today resembles a lunar landscape. Wind and water cut artistic grooves into rock walls, while large boulders lodged in the tuff and protected it from further erosion. This formed distinctive pillars of light stone that have darker boulders balanced on top. Entire valleys are lined with these odd creations that are shockingly phallic in appearance and which the Turks call "fairy chimneys," supposedly because they're so eccentric they have to be the work of fairies.

The other fascinating aspect of Cappadocia is that this stone is relatively soft and thus easy to carve. As a result, ancient peoples built homes in these rocks. Not only that, but a series of underground villages was constructed and early Christians fashioned cave churches out of the landscape. There are said to be more than 1,000 stone churches and chapels scattered through the ethereal Cappadocian countryside.

While gazing at the scenery that morning, we heard the call to prayer from a nearby mosque and listened as the soothing chant floated through the village and echoed across the valley. It seemed at that moment as if we were in an Islamic village on the surface of the moon.

The attractions of Cappadocia stretch across many towns, from Avanos and Uchisar to Kaymakli and Gülsehir, so we booked a day tour of the area. We actually reserved the outing with the same travel agent who appeared out of the darkness at 5 a.m. the morning of our arrival, so perhaps he knew what he was doing, after all, being in his office at that time of day.

We set out in the morning with a guide named Kemal, who was very short in stature and pleasantly cheerful. I quickly became entranced by the landscape, which seemed to stretch vacantly for miles in all directions. At one point, I watched a shepherd guide a flock of sheep across a field. It was a fleeting moment, but the image remained imprinted in my memory. The unbroken vastness of central Turkey in muted shades of brown and green and a solitary shepherd with his walking stick, navigating the emptiness amidst a flock of sheep.

One of the first and most interesting stops we made was at Derinkuyu, an underground city that burrowed eight levels below the surface of the earth. The living structure was first dug out four thousand years ago as a way to hide from invading armies. There were school rooms, food storage areas, water wells, animal stables, ventilation shafts and even a place for making wine. It could hold several thousand residents for up to four months. And all of it underground.

In mid-day, we headed to Ihlara Gorge, a ten-mile long canyon that was once a sanctuary for Byzantine monks. We walked down a long staircase to the canyon floor, where a church was carved into the rock wall. Kemal then led us on a two-mile hike along the meandering Melendiz Suyu stream, as copper-colored canyon walls towered over us. Along the way, we came across an older woman and a young boy who were pulling a load on a donkey. The woman was wearing a long dress and the traditional head scarf and was carrying a sack of small plums. She opened the sack and smilingly began passing out pieces of fruit. It was like a scene from another century.

By this time in the day, we had connected with a pair of humorous Brits, Matt and George. They worked a miners and bouncers at home and used their vacations to travel. When we met, we all went through the standard traveler greeting of name and country.

"You're from the United States?!" bellowed Matt in a thick British accent. "That's brilliant! We thought you guys had all stopped traveling. Nice to see some Americans on the road."

Indeed, Americans seemed to be few and far between in Turkey. Other than Kelly, we'd met only two other Americans. Most of the travelers were Australians and Europeans, with a few scattered Asians. Americans seemed to have given up on Turkey because of its Islamic culture and proximity to the Middle East. This at least provided a nice opening for us to converse with Matt and George. After this, we hit it off and had a fun few hours together. They were a riot to be around and were constantly cracking jokes.

At the end of the day, we made our way to the town of Avanos, where we saw a pottery making demonstration. After watching a master potter turn wet clay into a sugar bowl in a matter of minutes, the guide took a volunteer from the audience to try the same thing. He chose a young woman from Australia. You have to realize, when the potter's wheel is first spun, the clay is molded into a large pillar—I compared it to a fairy chimney, and honestly it looks like the growth of something very phallic—and the person at the wheel must move his or her hands up and down this clay pillar in order to shape it.

As this scene played out in front of us, with a young Australian woman massaging a growing pillar of phallic-looking clay, Matt drew a few chuckles by shouting at this young woman, "Oh yeah, baby. Keep it up!"

The Turkish guide then asked the woman working with the clay if she had ever tried anything like this before.

"Well, um, not with clay," she grinned, bringing down the house in a roar of laughter.

On another day, Lisa and I spent an afternoon wandering through Goreme's market area. By this point in Turkey, we had discovered there was a ritual to the shopping experience, which usually began when we made eye contact with a salesperson, or sometimes even when we didn't.

"Hello my friend. Where are you from? Please, come in."

Once inside a store, of course, it was difficult to free ourselves, as we would be shown one example after another of the carpets, clothing or souvenirs that were for sale. In many cases, this wasn't such a bad thing, as the sales pitch was often accompanied by an offer of hot tea. Usually apple tea, which is a Turkish staple, and always served in a small glass cup on a saucer with sugar cubes on the side.

We could always count on amusing back and forth bargaining, not to mention the tortured comedy of trying to determine a product's cost in U.S. dollars after fumbling with the exchange rate. Although Turkey introduced a new currency in 2005, when we were there the exchange rate was one dollar to 1.7 *million* Turkish lira. Needless to say, a calculator came in handy.

On this afternoon, though, while walking between carpet shops, souvenir stores and internet cafés, we were buttonholed by a shopkeeper who seemed to have something on his mind. He engaged us in some small talk and then asked where we were from.

"The United States," we told him.

"Ahh, you are rich?"

"Rich? No," we chuckled, "not hardly."

"Oh, my friends, you are young, you are from America, you have money to visit Turkey. I cannot afford to travel to United States."

We have just normal jobs in America, we told him. Our families are not rich. We like to travel, so we save our money to do this.

"I see," he said, unconvincingly. "Well, in any case, you must help us in Turkey. You know that your President Bush is thinking to attack Iraq? Please, please, when you return home, tell him not to do so."

I wanted to tell him that I didn't exactly have a direct line to the president, but he went on.

"Last time, when United States go to war in Iraq, many tourists decide to stay away from Turkey. We lose much money. Still today, many Americans afraid to visit Turkey. If there is another war, it is much worse for us. Many shopkeepers will lose their business, I think. Please tell your President Bush not to do this to us."

I didn't know what to say. It was true, in fact, that Turkey suffered billions of dollars in tourism and trade losses in the years following the 1991 Gulf War. Although I hadn't bonded in any way with this individual, I couldn't help but feel heartbroken for the people whose livelihoods relied on the tourist industry. It helped impress upon me the interconnectedness of events in our world, that an American war with Iraq could help drive a Turkish shopkeeper out of business.

TURKISH BATHS AND BACKFLIPPING PIGEONS

Public baths, or *hamams*, have long been a traditional feature of Turkish culture. In the days before indoor plumbing, people would venture regularly to these community centers, where they would enjoy a steam room, a massage and the company of friends. Although the need for hamams has disappeared, many Turks still see the bath as a pleasant social activity.

Since some of these hamams also cater to tourists who are eager to experience a slice of Turkish life, we booked an appointment at one while we were in Goreme. It was in Avanos, about a 20-minute drive away, and we made an appointment for late afternoon. Our hotel promised to arrange a ride, so Kelly, Lisa and I went off in our own directions for several hours and planned to meet again later in the day. When we returned, we discovered that Kelly had become acquainted with a local carpet dealer who offered to take us to the bath.

"Why would he just agree to drive us?" Lisa asked. "Doesn't he have a business to run?"

"Well, I did buy two carpets from him," Kelly remarked. "But he's a great guy. He just wanted to help us out."

We were dubious, but Mustafa arrived as promised. Lisa thanked him for his generosity.

"It's very nice of you to offer to drive us. But we could get a ride from the hotel. We don't want you to go out of your way."

"Oh, please," Mustafa smiled. "It is my pleasure. You are in my hometown, you know. This is Turkish hospitality."

We were beginning to understand. Most all Turks we had met were exceedingly polite. Some of them, of course, saw something in it for them, as they hoped we might buy something at their shop. But with most people, the hospitality seemed truly genuine. It was a deeply felt and very natural part of their culture.

Shortly thereafter, we were deposited in the front lobby of a nondescript concrete building that housed the bath. Mustafa told the attendant to call him when we were finished so he could pick us up. We were then shepherded into some dressing cubicles to change into our swimsuits. From there, we were taken to the steam room. The attendant stood at the door and gave us instructions.

"Sauna, water, sauna," he said, pointing alternately to a plunge pool of cold water in the center of an adjoining room and back to the sauna. "Sauna ten minute. Then water. Then sauna. Yes?"

"Yes."

The door closed behind us and we sat down to relax in the steam heat of the sauna. By the end of ten minutes, we were parched and looking forward to the coolness of the pool. Or so we thought. In fact, the water was barely warmer than ice. This is the idea, of course, which is why the Finns have a winter tradition of running from a sauna into the snow, but there is still no way to prepare for the shock to your body. We jumped in and out a few times, then retreated back to the steam.

From there, we were directed to a second room and told to lie on a large, heated stone table. Again, it sounds nice in theory. But this was hot! None of us could lie down for more than 15 seconds without the sense that our bare backs and legs were in a frying pan. An attendant gave us a hose of cold water to spray over the stones, which at least made it bearable for 30 seconds at a time. Then we lay on another table, where a different man came by, covered our bodies with soap suds and scrubbed us with a rough glove that was just a level or two softer than a brillo pad.

Right about this time, I began thinking, "A Turkish man whom we just met drove us 20 minutes to a tiny village and left us here. I jumped in a pool of ice water. I laid down on a stone table that was so hot it nearly cooked me. And now I'm lying on another table, having my skin scrubbed off by a guy who is dressed a blue loin cloth. Oh, the things we do for travel experiences."

Finally, one more attendant gave us a deep tissue massage and we were shown to a place where we could shower before changing back into our street clothes. By the time I made my way back out to the front lobby, I was surprised to realize that I felt thoroughly cleansed and relaxed. As we sat and waited for Mustafa to return, one of the men came by and served us some tea. I sat on a cushion and closed my eyes, perfectly content. Well, maybe it hadn't been so bad, after all.

True to his word, Mustafa didn't desert us at the bath. In fact, on the way back he even drove us to Zelve to see some particularly spectacular rock formations in what is called the Valley of the Fairy Chimneys. We walked around and marveled at the monstrous columns of soft stone reaching toward the heavens, glowing amber in the late afternoon light.

Back in Goreme, we went to Mustafa's carpet shop, where he served us Turkish coffee and we chatted for awhile. Then he asked if we wanted to see his trained pigeons.

Trained pigeons? Uhhh, yeah, sure.

He took us outside and coaxed a pigeon out of a cage in his yard. He rubbed the pigeon for a minute and released it into the air. Then, swear to God, the pigeon did a back flip. Mustafa took another pigeon out of the cage and repeated the trick. We continued watching while this carpet dealer-chauffeur-bird trainer began making strange sounds, calling for the birds to return from wherever they had flown.

I thought for a minute that maybe he had spiked my coffee and I was hallucinating. But, no, we had just seen pigeons doing back flips.

Hey, it's all in a day's travel when you give in to the whims of Turkey.

A Wine Bar in Cappadocia

On our final night in Goreme we went to a wine bar. There, travelers gathered in a cozy, crowded Turkish-style pub where they sipped drinks and puffed on hookah water pipes. A local man performed a selection of Turkish music and a woman joined in for a few songs and did a belly dance.

This was the last night we'd be with Kelly, as she was leaving the next day for Athens and we were trekking on to Istanbul. We had become close to Kelly in a very short time. Long-distance travelers always have something in common because of a common desire to see and understand the world, but in some cases the intensity of the shared experience enables friendships to develop more rapidly than they otherwise would.

That evening, as guitar notes stroked the air and mingled with the scents of apple tobacco and red wine, we talked for several hours. She told us how she'd become interested in a law career and about a recent relationship that hadn't ended well. After getting tired of the work and relationship merry go-round, she quit her job, bought a plane ticket and left the country to clear her head.

"Maybe it was just that I hadn't stopped, you know? From college to law school to being a lawyer. I was leading a life that I wasn't sure I wanted to keep leading, and I needed a mental break. I'm sure I'll go back and work again as a lawyer, but I needed to take a breather for a while to get off the treadmill I was on."

"So you're on your own little sabbatical then?" said Lisa.

"Yeah, I never thought of it in those words, but that's pretty much what it is."

Kelly asked Lisa and me about our relationship. What brought us together, she wanted to know? So we told her our story. How we met, when we were married. We even told her the prologue to our relationship, the story of timing and geography, which I had previously recounted in a speech to guests at our wedding.

One day, the story goes, I found myself in Freiburg, Germany with my friend Dave from New Hampshire. It was a warm evening in late spring. We put some bottles of wine and a Swiss army knife with a corkscrew in our backpacks, got on our rented bicycles and rode over to a grassy area next to a garden with a view of the city and the surrounding hills. There, nestled in the Black Forest of Germany, we drank wine and talked about life into the early hours of the morning. We gazed at the stars and watched the moon disappear behind the mountains.

Eventually, the talk turned to relationships, as it often seems to when you philosophize over a bottle of wine.

"It's all about timing and geography," Dave professed. "You might meet a great person, but if the timing isn't right for both of you, or if there are geography issues, then it won't work. Eventually, you'll meet a great person and the timing and geography will be right."

Sometime later, I moved to Tucson, Arizona for a job. I stayed for four years and grew to appreciate the unique beauties of the region. The multihued sunsets, the quiet blooming of springtime cactus flowers and the smell of the desert after a summer rainstorm. But I eventually felt a need to move back to my native New England. I wanted to be closer to family and had been accepted to graduate school in Boston. Also, I wanted to reacquaint myself with that part of the country. To sit by the ocean in summer, taste clam chowder by the beach, see the red and yellow leaves of October, and walk in the bright blue skies and crisp afternoons of autumn.

A few years after settling near Boston, I met and fell in love with Lisa. But, ironically, Lisa was from Tucson. After we met, we discovered that we'd lived for two years on the same block in Tucson, in adjoining apartment complexes. We probably crossed each other's path on the sidewalk or in the aisles of the local grocery store. But despite having lived a few feet from each other, we somehow didn't meet until we each moved almost 3,000 miles away.

And the coincidences didn't stop there. One night after we began dating, Lisa was at my apartment when I received a phone call from a friend, Kent, who lived in Colorado. He was calling about a fantasy football league that we were in together. Astonishingly, it turned out that Lisa and Kent knew each other. They had grown up together in Tucson from the time they were two-years-old. They lost touch after college and Kent didn't know that Lisa had recently moved to Boston.

Understandably then, I said, I often think back to that conversation in the middle of the night in the Black Forest of Germany, and I contemplate the mysteries of timing and geography.

"Wow, what a great story," said Kelly. "All those coincidences. Your relationship was meant to be. I want a story like that."

Well, it wasn't quite as easy as it sounds, we told her. As it turned out, Lisa had moved to Boston for a job and always expected her stay on the East Coast to be temporary, but I hadn't expected to leave New England and return to the

Southwest. So we soon found ourselves spending hours in debate over the relative merits of New England (summers by the ocean) and the Southwest (winters in the desert).

"The thing is," I said, "there is a lot to like about both places and Lisa and I are still strongly attached to certain aspects of each region. For me, although I don't love winter, I really enjoy the changing of the seasons. I like being near the ocean and having access to great seafood. I enjoy living someplace that is walkable. But I understand Lisa, too, when she reminds me about the warm winters, the beauty of the mountains, the good Mexican food. And another reason this has been a difficult question is that no one in her family lives in New England, and no one in my family lives in Arizona."

"So what are you going to do? How do you decide?" asked Kelly.

"Well, we decided not to decide, for now at least," said Lisa.

Geography seemed like a silly reason to not be together, we explained, so we chose to believe that love would overcome location. Life would give us the answers in time.

"We Don't Eat People, We're Vegetarians!"

Many hotels in the Sultanahmet district of Istanbul, even the inexpensive hostels, have roof terraces that provide jaw-dropping views of one of the world's most beautiful skylines. On our first morning in the city we ate breakfast on one of these terraces, under an explosion of sunshine. We looked out over the Blue Mosque and the Aya Sofia, which shone against the backdrop of an azure sky, giving the appearance that we were looking at a canvas and the buildings had been painted there. In the distance, the Sea of Marmara glittered diamonds in the morning light and blew a faint salt-water breeze in our direction.

After fortifying ourselves with bread, yogurt and coffee, Lisa and I set off to explore Istanbul. We walked down Divan Yolu, a busy boulevard that slices through the historic heart of the city, passed the ancient Hippodrome where chariot races were once held and found our way to the 1500-year-old Aya Sofia. We were dismayed to discover a long line to get inside the building, but soon struck up an amiable conversation with a local man, Selim.

"Where you from?" he inquired.

"America."

"Ahhh, beautiful country. What state?"

"Massachusetts. Near Boston."

"Boston. Boston Celtics!" he exclaimed.

"Yes, uh, you know the Celtics?"

"I love NBA basketball. I like Celtics when Larry Bird play there. They not so good now, but I still follow them."

"Wow. Well, nice to meet you, Selim."

"You know," he said, "there long line here at Aya Sofia. Line not so long at Blue Mosque. And mosque close early for prayers. It better to go to mosque first, then come to Aya Sofia later. It very nearby. If you like, I can show you entrance."

We were slightly suspicious, but we had seen so many other examples of Turks being helpful merely out of kindness that we accepted his offer. Soon, though, we began to have doubts over our haste when we realized Selim wasn't going to let us out of his sight. Even when we were obviously within sight of the mosque entrance, he was firm about staying with us the entire way.

"Don't worry, I don't go inside with you," he replied, walking alongside us. "I just take you there."

Then we arrived at the mosque entrance and he insisted on making sure we got inside. It seemed as if there had to be a catch, but we couldn't figure out what it might be. We were in the middle of crowds of tourists, he wasn't carrying anything to sell and he had walked us straight to the mosque. But, still, he wouldn't let go of us.

"It's very nice of you," I said, "but, really, we can figure it out."

"Mosque very big. I just make sure you find right entrance," he said. "You go inside on your own. Don't worry."

He showed us to the entrance, where there was indeed a much shorter line than at the Aya Sofia. So far, so good. He pointed out a box of scarves for women to put over their heads before entering and to the place where we were to remove our shoes.

"Thank you very much for your help, Selim," I repeated. "It's been nice to meet you."

"You go inside now," he said. "Take as long as you want. I will wait for you. When you come out, you come to my store, just one block away. Very nice souvenirs."

Aha. There was a catch, but Selim was very smooth about making sure the ploy wouldn't become apparent until the very last moment. Not only did the mosque not close early, we now realized, but the tourist entrance was at one end of the building and the exit was at the other end. He knew that he was leaving us at the only place we could enter the mosque and would be waiting for us at the only place we could exit.

That is how we were introduced to one of the spectacles of international travel and to the business of touts, who are ubiquitous not just in Istanbul but on the streets of most major cities in the non-Western world. They usually want nothing more than to make a bit of money, but they can still be pesky antagonists. Like most travelers, we were never completely successful in avoiding them, but we quickly became more aware of their tactics. Although it was frustrating to be taken in by this ruse on our first day in Istanbul, we at least had to give Selim credit for creativity.

It's easy enough, after all, to steer clear of people who are pushing their wares on the street and whom we could walk away from, but it's much harder to avoid those individuals who disguise their goal by being helpful in some way. It is also especially difficult to shun anyone who exhibits humor or personality. In fact, it was just a few days later in Istanbul that we heard one of the funniest lines ever from a man who was trying to entice us into his store. We initially walked past him, pretending not to hear his plea. But then we couldn't help but laugh.

"Don't run away," he shouted. "We don't eat people, we're vegetarians!"

Domed Mosques and Soaring Minarets

Turkey straddles the political, religious and cultural fault lines between West and East and no city is more emblematic of this border personality than Istanbul. It sits on both sides of the Bosphorus Strait, the geographic dividing line between Europe and Asia, it was the historic center of both the Christian Byzantine and Muslim Ottoman empires, and the streets are filled with a unique cultural stew of people, as women in modest Islamic dress and headscarves walk alongside secular Turks in mini-skirts.

There are any number of attractions in Istanbul, from shopping bazaars to ancient ruins, but for anyone with even a mild interest in exploring a world where the East seeps into the West, three buildings stand out above all others: the Aya Sofia, the Blue Mosque and the Topkapi Palace.

The first two of these, which stand facing each other across a park like twin beacons of spirituality, represent the two major streams of Istanbul's history. The Aya Sofia was built as a Christian church in the 6th century by the Emperor Justinian and is an artifact of the Byzantine Empire. The Blue Mosque dates to the Ottoman Empire and the 17th century reign of Sultan Ahmet I.

Following our morning encounter with Selim, Lisa and I began our explorations at the Blue Mosque, which is quite visually striking. The prayer hall under the vast dome is simply decorated with the beautiful geometric designs of Islam, but the blue color of the tiles and the artwork present an overwhelming effect, especially when combined with the hundreds of windows that allow light to stream in from every direction. I stood there silently for a long time, taking it all in.

It was my first time inside a mosque and, as I beheld the scene, I reflected that all places of worship are very much alike in one way, which is that they evoke the same silent sense of awe and wonderment over the mystery of life. Whether one is inside a mosque, a church or a temple, it's apparent that people of every faith are searching for a sense of meaning and are all similarly grasping for an awareness of our spiritual nature.

We eventually made our way back to the Aya Sofia (the name means "divine wisdom"), which was once known as the greatest church in Christendom. With a 183-foot high dome, it still ranks as one of the largest cathedrals ever constructed. When the Byzantines fell to the Ottoman Turks, however, the church was converted into a mosque. Then, in the 20th century, it was declared a museum.

Its beauty is now faded, but it is clear why the Aya Sofia once awed all who saw it. What I found especially interesting was the juxtaposition of Christian and

Muslim artwork inside. In the center of the sanctuary are various Christian-themed mosaics, including a large portrait of the Virgin Mary. Along the side walls are eight large wooden discs with the names of early Muslim leaders engraved in Arabic calligraphy.

On another day, we took in the third member of this troika of historic buildings. Though not as visually striking as the other two, the Topkapi Palace has a lot of history swirling about it.

The Ottoman Turks conquered Istanbul (then Constantinople) in 1453, bringing the Byzantine Empire to an end. The Ottomans then came to govern not only present day Turkey, but also much of the Middle East, North Africa and the Balkan region of southeastern Europe. The Topkapi Palace was the center of this far flung empire, serving as the home of the ruling Sultan for almost four centuries.

The palace was built in a series of four successive courtyards, with the innermost space being the exclusive domain of the Sultan. It was here that the Harem was located. This was the living quarters for the Sultan's family and accounted for nearly 400 rooms, including a Turkish bath, swimming pools and a hospital. We strolled through the Sultan's bedroom, his mother's chambers (the Sultan's mother ruled the Harem), an entertainment hall, the kitchens where the concubines worked, and the living quarters for 20 select women who were favorites of the sultan. The Harem was continually replenished by young girls who were bought or captured from distant regions of the empire. They worked as servants, but were paid well and allowed to retire at age 30.

The most beautiful or talented concubines who caught the Sultan's eye were given nicer quarters and were expected to be available to meet the ruler's "other" needs. Those who bore him a child, particularly a son, became one of the official wives. There was great competition among the wives to be the mother of the next Sultan, as this woman would gain great power through her control of the Harem.

Also intriguing to visit were the Sacred Safe-keeping Rooms, which contained a number of holy objects. When we went inside, there was an imam in the corner chanting verses from the Koran, which only added to the unreal effect of what we saw. The room contained a sword and sandals that were said to have belonged to the Prophet Mohammed, as well as hairs from his beard, a tattered copy of a letter he had sent to a Coptic Christian leader and even a mold of his footprint. We also purportedly saw the staff of Moses, as well as items that belonged to Abraham and Joseph.

Some of these objects were no doubt genuine, but others certainly stretched the imagination. Where exactly did one acquire the staff of Moses? And why was the mold of Mohammed's footprint larger than his sandals? But what was more intriguing to me, actually, was that sacred relics of Mohammed, Moses and Abraham were even on display together. Time and again in Turkey, we were faced with evidence of the common roots and overlapping strands of Islam, Judaism and Christianity. Although we were previously aware of the shared history of these religions, the obvious and public nature of these displays was still the least expected and most thought-provoking discovery of our time in Turkey.

One of our other enduring memories of Istanbul is actually of eating dinner several evenings at our hotel, on the roof terrace that overlooked the Blue Mosque and Aya Sofia. We enjoyed this restaurant not so much for the view but because we struck up an acquaintance with two of the waiters.

We first met Ur, who was good-natured and helpful. "My name means 'luck' in Turkish," he related to us. "So you can just call me lucky." Ur confessed that he had first seen me on the roofdeck in mid-afternoon one day, having a beer and writing in my journal.

"I would have talked to you, but you look like you are French. Sometimes I don't have good experiences with French tourists, so I leave you alone," he laughed.

During the next several days, we spent more time with Ur and a fellow waiter, Adem. Ur was married and glowed when talking about his young daughter. Adem was single and lovesick. He admitted to us that he was in love with a woman who didn't know his feelings for her, but that he was afraid to confess his desires for fear of rejection.

"Oh, you have to tell her," said Lisa. "How will she know how you feel if you never say anything?"

"Yes," sighed Adem, with a tinge of longing in his voice. "It is difficult, though."

One evening, when the restaurant was about empty and we shared a table with our two new friends, Adem dared to ask how we could afford to take such a long trip. Traveling on the U.S. dollar helps, of course, but were we rich, he wondered?

"We've gotten that question several times already," remarked Lisa. "Many people we meet seem to think all Americans are rich, but it's not true. We're certainly not, at least."

"You are rich in your heart," he said to her.

"That's so sweet," said Lisa. "Thank you."

As I watched my wife interact with Adem, I realized that when Lisa chooses to be outgoing, it doesn't take much time or effort for people to really enjoy being around her. Not that I don't also make friends easily, but she has more of an ability to be almost instantly sociable. Although this wasn't an entirely new insight, at that moment in Istanbul when a Turkish waiter complimented my wife I saw it more clearly than I had before.

That night, Adem recommended that we take a boat trip on the Bosphorus, so on our final afternoon in Istanbul we took his advice. The Bosphorus is the strait that connects the Sea of Marmara with the Black Sea and geographically divides Europe and Asia. The ferry we took cruised 45 minutes north up the European side of the Bosphorus, then crossed the river and returned along the Asian side.

At the end, we had a beautiful view of the city skyline from the water. Istanbul has a magnificent and distinct shape, with domed mosques and soaring minarets rising above a navy blue sea. Not far from the boat dock were the Aya Sofia, Blue Mosque and Topkapi Palace, while high on a hill to the right was the towering Mosque of Sultan Süleyman the Magnificent, right next to Istanbul University.

Once off the boat, we walked a short distance to the Galata Bridge. There, a few fishing boats sold sandwiches for $1 each. They grilled fresh fish, then slapped it into a large roll of bread with some slices of tomato and onion. There were few tourists here, so we shared some steps with a group of locals who were eating the same fish sandwiches. We watched as boats glided up and down the river, traditionally-dressed Turkish mothers looked after their children on the shore, and men and boys fished off the nearby bridge. It was a pleasant and agreeable way for our stay to draw to a close.

Kenya

"Hakuna Matata"

At the Istanbul airport, the secularism of Turkey quickly melted away. On our way to Kenya, Lisa and I had a flight to Nairobi via Dubai, so we traveled with passengers who were going to the United Arab Emirates, Saudi Arabia and other Gulf countries. As we waited to board the plane, we sat surrounded by Arab men in long white robes and women in black abayas. Some of the ladies peered out through eye slits and were covered from head to ankle in black. A glance at the crowd spurred Lisa to quickly zip on the bottom of her convertible pants so as to avoid being the only female with bare legs.

Once we were onboard, I ruminated on the effortlessness of culture-hopping in today's world. It's remarkable, I thought, how easy it is to close one travel chapter and begin another. Two plane flights of a few hours each and we would traverse the Arabian Peninsula and northeastern Africa in a mere hop, skip and a jump. This is the allure of air travel, of course, the ability to drastically reduce the time spent in getting from one place to the next. There is also a certain wonder associated with traveling by plane and I still marvel at the experience of soaring above the clouds and being almost magically transported to a new landscape.

That said, however, I do sometimes wonder what we miss by relying so heavily on air transportation. We aren't really able to engage in the full experience of a journey, as our ancestors did. By crossing an ocean in hours rather than weeks, we don't quite comprehend the vast distances that form our world. In hopping over mountains, seas and rivers, we can't identify with the geographic borders that shaped nations and cultures.

When Mark Twain undertook his own round-the-world journey in 1895, for example, which he wrote about in his book *Following the Equator*, he and his family spent three weeks on a ship crossing the Pacific. They and other passengers were even prevented from making a scheduled stopover in Hawaii due to a cholera outbreak there. During the trip they read books, wrote letters, played shuffleboard and stared at the waves. They may have been bored to tears, but they certainly appreciated how truly far Australia is from North America.

Now, if Lisa and I had forsaken planes during this sabbatical, an overland version of just this journey to Kenya could have taken us through Turkey, Syria, Lebanon, Israel, Egypt, Sudan and Ethiopia. Alternatively, we may have traveled by boat through the Eastern Mediterranean and the Suez Canal, across the Red Sea, into the Indian Ocean and around the corner of the African continent. Needless to say, we had neither the time nor the inclination for such an expedition. But while I'm not ready to give up the convenience of air travel, that doesn't stop me from wondering if we'd appreciate the vast diversity of our world even more were we to see it all from ground level.

Sometime after midnight, we landed in Dubai for our scheduled layover. Although most airports are closed and quiet at this hour, Dubai is a hub for flights between Europe, Africa and Asia, many of which pass through in the middle of the night. We got off the plane and discovered a veritable international shopping mall. There were hundreds of people passing time in pubs (The Irish Village) and coffee shops (Starbucks *and* Dunkin Donuts). Other travelers roamed the airport and shopped for jewelry, watches, perfumes, electronics, music and books.

When we checked in for our next flight, we were told the plane was full and we could not have two seats together. Well then, asked Lisa, can we reserve seats for our next flight, when we'll be flying through Dubai again on our way to Southeast Asia?

"No, I'm sorry," said the woman behind the counter. "We cannot reserve seats in advance."

"You can't?" asked Lisa, somewhat surprised. "But if you won't reserve seats in advance, then we end up like this, where I can't sit with my husband."

"I'm sorry, it is not possible. You must get your seats when you come to the airport."

"What if I call the reservations office in a few days?"

"I'm sorry, it is not possible."

Well, how exactly did families manage to sit together, then? No answers were forthcoming, at least from this woman, so we walked away in defeat.

Our Kenya Airways flight lifted off at 2:30 a.m. for the four-hour trip to Nairobi. Whereas our last plane had been filled mostly with Arabs, dressed in white robes and black abayas, we were now surrounded by a sea of Africans attired in vibrant reds and greens. Once more, we were skipping over a geographical transition area, lifting off the runway in one world and touching down in another.

Despite being fatigued from not getting much rest during the night, we were suitably excited as our plane landed a few hours later, in the yawning hours of early morning, at Jomo Kenyatta International Airport in Nairobi. Our sense of wonder diminished quickly, however, when we learned that our luggage had not made the trip with us, having disappeared somewhere in the night on a trip that involved two airlines and three countries. So for the next hour-and-a-half we waited in an interminably slow line to report our lost bags. The desk clerks would talk to one person in line, answer the phone, walk away, chat with a co-worker, then return and talk to another arriving passenger. Everything seemed to happen in slow motion.

Through all of this, to make matters even more vexing, Lisa was experiencing her first case of traveler's sickness. Her stomach went into convulsions and she ran several times to the bathroom. When we finally made it to the front of the line, groggy and worn out, the airline employees were extremely pleasant but nonchalant.

"Yes, this happens often," they told us. "We hope your luggage will arrive later today. Maybe we can deliver it to your hotel. But then again, maybe the customs workers will want you to come back to the airport to identify your bags."

"We're scheduled to depart for a safari tomorrow morning," we said. "What are our options if the luggage doesn't arrive today?"

"We don't know. You'll have to ask us later. Why don't you call us later today?"

That was it. One-and-a-half hours in line for a "maybe" and a smile. I sighed. I knew that these aggravations were simply part of the travel experience, but we were tired and all we really wanted was our luggage and a bed to curl up in for a few hours. Since our luggage was not there, we'd have to settle for a bed.

Lisa and I walked out of the international arrivals area and into the Nairobi airport terminal, where someone from the safari company was scheduled to meet us. Unfortunately, no one was standing there with our name on a sign. We couldn't be terribly surprised by this, since we'd been delayed in the arrivals area for nearly two hours. Still, we clung to a thread of hope and walked the length of the terminal.

Nothing.

We stood and contemplated the situation. We were exhausted, Lisa was still battling her stomach demons, and there was a chance our luggage wouldn't arrive before our safari departure. And now the ride we were expecting wasn't anywhere to be found. All we could do, really, was to laugh about the joys of traveling.

Happily, our situation improved considerably after that. We met a local taxi driver-tour guide in the airport terminal who was especially helpful and friendly. Ngugi helped us find a phone so we could call the safari company and check on our ride.

"Hakuna matata," he said, smiling. "No worries! Welcome to Kenya."

There was no answer at the safari company's office. That wasn't comforting but, after all, it was early on a Saturday morning. So we climbed into a taxi and set off for our hotel, in the Westlands district of Nairobi. Ngugi pointed out interesting locations along the way and taught us a few Swahili words.

"*Karibu* means *welcome* in Swahili," he said. "So, I say to you, karibu to Kenya!"

Later, he taught us about the words *mzee* and *mama*.

"These are terms of respect for elders. When you are older and you have a family, and you get grey hair like me," he grinned, "then people may start calling you mzee. It means you have reached a certain stage in your life, so that your community respects you. And in Kenya, we often call our older ladies mama. It is similar to the word mzee for a man."

At the hotel, we enjoyed a hot shower and a nap, although we did have to climb back into the same gritty clothes we'd had on since the previous morning in Istanbul. A few hours later, we finally talked to our contact at the safari company, Wanja. She came to our hotel to finalize the trip details and even offered to follow up with her contacts at Kenya Airways to check on our luggage.

With nothing to do now but hang out for the afternoon and evening, we walked over to the nearby Sarit Centre, a mall. We had dinner and bought some bottled water and other supplies for the coming week. On the way there and back, we walked past a long block of curio shops and had to surmount an entertaining procession of street merchants vying for our business.

"Jambo! Karibu! Come to see my shop," they shouted at us.

One of the more persistent hawkers walked with us down the street.

"Great souvenir from Kenya!" he said, showing us a small carving of a giraffe. "Only 600 shillings (about $8)."

"No, thank you."

"Oh, yes. Please. Great souvenir," he persisted, in a genial manner. "What about Mama?" he said, shifting his attention to Lisa. "400 shillings for Mama. No? OK, 200 shillings then."

Obviously, we were in another bargaining culture. Not to mention a culture where at least one person felt comfortable in calling Lisa "Mama." I joked that I was going to begin calling her that, but she didn't find the same humor in the term when it came from me.

Back at the hotel that evening, Wanja called to say that our luggage had arrived and that she would arrange for it to be delivered to us.

"That's great news! Thank you so much for your help, Wanja. We really appreciate it."

"Hakuna matata," she said. "Zachary will be your guide this week. He will pick you up at 7 a.m. tomorrow. Enjoy your safari!"

The Mosaic that is Kenya

The next morning, we climbed into the middle seat of Zachary's safari van, which had a pop-up roof and seating for seven passengers. Surprisingly, we were the only ones who had booked the safari for this departure date, so we had the van to ourselves. We had a six-hour drive ahead of us and would be in this vehicle every day for the next week, crossing the equator twice and bouncing along more than 1,000 miles of Kenyan roads.

"So, Zachary, we will be together for a week?" I said. "That means we will become friends."

"We are already friends," he said, smiling, in a comment typical of the culture. "Please, call me Zach."

Before long, we were out of Nairobi and off into rural Kenya. Only occasionally during the next week did we run into a small city, at places like Nakuru or Narok. On this day, we drove north past wheat-colored fields, banana and acacia trees and coffee plantations. The road took us through rolling foothills of green trees and deep red soil. These colors, and especially the red hue of the earth, became my lasting images of Kenya.

One of the biggest things I noticed as we drove were the number of people on the streets. Everywhere, even in what seemed to be the middle of nowhere between towns, we passed dozens of locals going about their daily lives. Many of them, especially the children, would wave as our van drove past. We saw women walking with huge loads of wood tied to their backs, young boys tending herds of cows, a person steering a donkey-driven cart. Near the tribal areas, people tended cattle or did laundry in a stream. Sometimes we'd see a solitary red dot or two on the horizon that, as we drew closer, would invariably prove to be tribesmen in their traditional red robes (*shukas*) who were out walking with herding sticks in hand.

We also drove past numerous small concentrations of shops, all with rickety, tilting wood frames and tin roofs. They were stacked side-by-side and marked by hand-lettered signs. At one point, we passed an open-air market, with food and clothing laid outside on carpets, surrounded by hundreds of people shopping for goods.

Wherever we stopped in Kenya, even just for gasoline, people descended on the van. Knocked on the windows, flashed souvenirs and postcards, told us how poor they were, begged us to buy something from them. It underscored for us the relative poverty of many Kenyans. Although several hundred thousand visitors spend millions of dollars annually in the country, profits from tourism actually benefit only a small portion of the population.

Another thing that was quite noticeable during our drive was the matatus, which are Kenya's version of public transportation. They are big vans, with enough room to squeeze in 12 or so people shoulder to shoulder. The matatus are also notable for being quite colorful and are all individually decorated and named. They were ever-present along the roadways and there were always touts hanging out of the front doors, scanning the street for new passengers.

Matatus are a cherished part of Kenyan culture, even though a few of the drivers are known to be somewhat less than safe. In fact, Kenyans suffer traffic accidents with disturbing regularity. On any day, one can pick up a newspaper and see obituaries for individuals who were "killed in a tragic automobile accident." Later in the week, we learned that Zach had even experienced this sort of heartbreak in his own family.

It was actually good to have so much to occupy our eyes on the trip, because the road was so rough it became impossible even to read or write.

"It's not even reasonable to call these roads pothole-filled," I said to Lisa. "They're really just a series of potholes that are sometimes surrounded by pavement."

Zach and other Kenyan drivers constantly veered from the left to the right side of the roads, and even drove on the dirt shoulder for miles at a time, since it was less shocking to the vehicle than the potholes were. Nor was it just bad roads that plagued us. Dust also proved to be a nuisance. When we drove on the dirt shoulder, or on one of the many dirt stretches of road that we encountered, we were inundated by dust, blowing in through the bottom of the van or through small openings in the window. It covered our bags and our clothes, coated our skin, dried our mouths, and irritated our eyes.

This was all part of the incredible string of contrasts that we experienced during our time in Kenya. We were frustrated by the crumbling infrastructure, the potholes and the dust. But we were enthralled by the landscape, the culture and the richness of the land. We were fatigued by the constant begging and selling of souvenirs whenever we stopped. But when we weren't besieged by individuals who wanted our money, we were delighted by amiability of the people, their smiles and their easygoing nature. We couldn't separate one from the other, so we just took it all in. It was all part of the mosaic that is Kenya.

An Untamed Earth

On that first day, we drove from Nairobi to the Shaba National Reserve. Shaba is just north of the distinctive snow-covered peak of Mount Kenya, Africa's second highest mountain, and is located along the Ewaso Ngiro River. It is one of three adjoining game reserves, along with Samburu and Buffalo Springs.

After one stop along the way for a flat tire, we arrived at Shaba in early afternoon and Zach gave us a few hours to shower and rest before taking us on our first game drive. He emphasized that it was just a warm-up and that we'd see more animals in the morning. Still, we saw a few zebra, elephants and buffalo. When there weren't animals to observe, we soaked in the sunlight that streamed in through the windows and enjoyed the fact that we were actually on a game drive in Africa.

"Be ready at 6:30 a.m. tomorrow," he said when the drive was over. "That is when more of the animals are out feeding. We'll have breakfast afterwards."

The next day, when we were roused from sleep before sunrise, everything seemed new and fresh and exciting. We drove through central Kenya that morning, as the earth broke open on the horizon and the first blue light of morning painted the sky. The acacia trees were still silhouetted as they stood sentry over the landscape and we gradually became aware of the unique smell of an untamed earth.

"It's a smell that is difficult to describe," Lisa said later, "but I hope I can remember it for the rest of my life."

As dawn seeped over the mountains, we saw our first giraffe, nibbling from the top of an acacia tree. We were so close, we could hear the animal chewing the leaves. In fact, we have a picture that Lisa snapped of me standing in the safari van, my head poking through the top, with a giraffe standing just a few feet behind me and dining on some foliage for breakfast.

Soon after that we saw groups of impala and oryx ramble by, gazed at zebras that were standing calmly in the middle of a field and watched a pair of gazelles lock horns. Later that morning, with the striking burgundy granite mountain Ol Olokwe looming on the horizon, we sat quietly as a family of adult and baby elephants lumbered across our path. Then, as the sun slowly rose in the sky, we came upon four lionesses as they meandered into some bushes.

Any distress that we might have felt in the past two days was quickly melting away. The overnight flight, the lost luggage, the potholes and the dust on the roadways. It's easy, in the end, for travelers to forget about such discomforts and challenges because they are ultimately replaced in our memories by moments such as these—watching lionesses, giraffes, elephants and gazelles frolic in the early morning sunlight in East Africa.

After a few days at Shaba, we moved on to Lake Nakuru National Park. This entailed another bone-rattling six-hour drive, although the first part of the journey was through the Buffalo Springs game reserve. It was interesting to casually drive by groups of zebra, giraffe and gazelles on our way from one destination to another. Quite a contrast to the normal morning commute in Boston.

By mid-afternoon, we'd arrived at our destination in the Rift Valley, a geographical crevice that runs through the middle of Kenya and stretches more than 3,500 miles across the continent. Nakuru is one of several soda lakes in this region, all of which have warm alkaline water as a result of ancient volcanic deposits and thus an abundance of blue-green algae. Fortuitously, for tourists at least, this algae is a staple of the daily diet for Kenya's pink flamingoes and hundreds of thousands of birds make their home in the area.

It began raining during our afternoon game drive at Nakuru, but we still saw an abundance of zebras, along with buffaloes and hippos by the water and a tribe of baboons along one of the roadways. We also saw two rhinos from close range and had a medium distance sighting of three leopards. This gave us the satisfaction of knowing that we'd completed our sightings of the so-called Big Five, as we saw lions, elephants and buffalo in Shaba.

We asked Zach why these particular animals made up the Big Five. After all, they weren't necessarily the five most popular safari animals.

"It has nothing to do with safari popularity," he explained, "but with toughness. These are the five 'toughest' game animals."

Lisa and I later decided there should be a Big Ten for safari purposes. The Big Five can retain their importance, of course—who are we to argue with them? But then we decided that giraffes and zebras should be included on our Big Ten list, being that they are unique, fun to gaze at and popular with tourists. Also, gazelles were worthy, since they are extraordinarily graceful and beautiful to watch.

For the ninth and tenth members of our club, we added animals that were top attractions in Kenya. These included the wildebeest, a popular sight during part of the year at Masai Mara, and pink flamingos, which are predominantly found at the soda lakes of the Rift Valley.

It was our experience at Lake Nakuru that prompted us to include flamingos on our Big Ten list. We'd heard they were an interesting sight, but we weren't prepared for the full impact of seeing tens of thousands of pink flamingos strutting around the perimeter of a single lake. This was one of the most visually interesting spectacles we saw on the safari. From a distance, it appeared the water was ringed with stretches of pink sand. But as we approached, it became apparent this was an illusion, caused by the presence of more pink flamingoes than we ever knew existed, all living together on the edge of a lake.

This was the only time all week that we were allowed out of the safari vehicle to approach animals. We walked along the beachfront and gaped in amazement at the thousands of pink flamingoes squeezed together in front of us—feeding, walking, flying, landing. And the noise. It's remarkable, the volume of sound that can be produced by all of those squawking animals.

Interestingly, as we walked towards the birds, who formed a ring perhaps 15 or 20 feet deep along the perimeter of the lake, they edged away from us in unison. They moved calmly, and not in panic, but a giant pink wave would invariably form opposite whichever direction we moved. If we walked straight towards the water, the birds in front of us would disperse into a semicircle. If we walked left or right, the wave would move in that direction. We felt like flamingo conductors.

It was raining fairly steadily at this point, but we were entranced and didn't want to leave the flamingos. So we stood there for long minutes on the edge of the lake, hoods pulled over our heads, no sound but for the clamor of birds and the drumming of raindrops, thousands of pink flamingos forming a dreamlike picture in front of us, and we breathed in the sweet smell of rain on a warm African afternoon.

Our final safari destination was the Masai Mara National Reserve, Kenya's most famous wildlife park. The Mara is located in the southwestern corner of the country, near the border with Tanzania, and it has the greatest abundance of animals of any of the nation's game reserves.

Covering more than 900 square miles of grassland, Masai Mara is the Kenyan side of the famed Serengeti Plain. The region is renowned for being the site of the annual wildebeest migration. Every year in July and August more than one million wildebeest move north from the Serengeti to Masai Mara in search of grass to feed on before returning south in the fall. In addition to the wildebeest sightings, a visitor to the park is likely to encounter large numbers of elephants, zebras, giraffes, gazelles, impala, lions, leopards, cheetahs, buffaloes, hippos, black rhinos, white rhinos and spotted hyenas.

Another distinguishing feature of the Mara is that it's more than 6,000 feet above sea level, nearly 4,000 feet higher than Shaba, and the elevation made for some surprisingly chilly mornings when we arose before dawn for a game drive.

"I never thought of it being this frigid in Kenya," I said to Lisa one day at 6:30 a.m., as a biting wind swirled in through the open top of the safari van and I tried to comfort myself by layering several t-shirts and a sweater beneath my windbreaker. Since the equator runs through Kenya, we had naively assumed it was warm year-round and forgot to consider the altitude of the parks. The weather did heat up considerably during the day, but the mornings were always pretty frosty.

Despite the cold, however, I came to the realization one day that, while I didn't like *getting* up before dawn, I sort of enjoyed *being* up at that time. At least in Africa. On that particular morning, I stood outside at daybreak and sipped a cup of hot Kenyan coffee while waiting with Lisa and other tourists for our safari vans. All around us, Africa was awakening from its nighttime slumber. There was no sound but for the murmur of the wind and the faint fluttering of birds. The morning air was brisk and fresh and it smelled of luxuriant earth and wild animals.

As I watched the steam rise from a half dozen other mugs and then slowly melt away into a misty violet-colored dawn, I had to admit there was an exhilaration about the early morning that didn't exist in the afternoon. Remember this moment, I told myself. Ignore the cold, warm your fingers on your coffee mug, remember the violet tint to the sky and the landscape.

The spell was broken, though, when Zach arrived.

"Ready to see some lions?" he smiled. "That will heat you up."

We began our drive that day just as the sun was becoming visible over the eastern hills. The morning clouds seemed to be lit from behind, as if they were on fire. Early on, we saw a large group of more than 100 wildebeest and zebra, milling about and munching on grass, as though they were at some mixed animal social.

"So, I guess the wildebeest and the zebra get along?" I said.

"Yeah," answered Zach. "Actually the zebra kind of take advantage of the wildebeest. If a lion attacks, the zebras have a much better chance of escaping. The lion can more easily catch the wildebeest. So we often see these animals together."

Sure enough, about 30 minutes later, in a different location, we came upon a group of vultures picking at the bones and leftover meat of a wildebeest carcass.

"Did you plan this?" we joked with Zach. "It looks like the zebras did escape, after all."

I took plenty of photographs, as I did on other days. But I wondered if the pictures would ever really be able to express what it was like to be out at dawn, with the morning sun rising over the mountain, and to see two dozen elephants walk past our safari van, almost close enough to touch. Or to feel we could reach up and grab the same tree that a giraffe was feeding from. Or to make eye contact with a zebra or a wildebeest, or with a gazelle just before it bounded gracefully away.

I began to notice, too, that it wasn't just the animals that transfixed me. It was the whole setting. There was something primal about being out on the African plain at sunrise, as if we'd been there before. Africa is in all of us, in our blood, in our soul. Is it our genetic inheritance? Remembrances of past lives? For whatever reason, it was all hauntingly familiar.

We all come from there on some level, I suppose. It's the birthplace of humanity and, deep down, we seemed to be aware of this. Being outside on a clear morning, feeling a strange kinship with the African landscape, watching a giraffe nibble from an acacia tree, observing lions and gazelles and elephants—it was primal, there is no other way to describe it. When we were there, Africa rose up from the depths of our being and burst forth so that the entire environment seemed to connect with us, seemed to become one with us.

Our final game drive of the safari fittingly turned out to be one of our more memorable experiences. It began quietly enough, with a sighting of three cheetahs lounging in the late afternoon sun. Then we came upon a massive herd of wildebeest. These animals are part of the antelope family, but they have an amusingly awkward appearance and are distinguished by a long beard and mane. The wildebeest are known to congregate in large packs and on that day we saw thousands of them, stretched for miles in both directions as they trudged single file toward the horizon. They moved slowly and methodically, lined up one behind the other for as far as we could see.

"How do they get in line?" I wanted to know. "Who begins? Who brings up the rear? How do they know when to start, whom to follow, where to go?"

All we know is that they annually migrate from the Serengeti Plain in Tanzania to the Masai Mara in Kenya and back again. They are nomadic animals who move in search of water and fresh grass. So when we saw them all heading off over a distant hill, Lisa declared matter-of-factly, "I guess that's the way to Tanzania," which Zach laughingly acknowledged was the case.

Near the end of the drive, we got a great close-up of some lions. Eight of them in all. They were resting, after having just killed their dinner. There were two unfortunate wildebeest lying dead a few yards away. We didn't see the actual kill, but the scene was so fresh we could almost visualize the lions circling the meandering wildebeest, sowing confusion and panic as the animals tried to flee, and then pouncing. It was all right there in front of us: the blood-soaked wildebeest and the panting lions. We could see the lions' stomachs rising and falling with each breath, look into their impassive eyes, study the details of their faces. They were just feet from our van, but paid no attention to us as they rested in the shade.

Off to the side were the still-warm bodies of the wildebeest, not even eaten yet. The lions had killed their prey and now apparently needed a rest before dinner. Further away was a group of vultures, waiting to dine on the leftovers. Zach said the vultures might sit there for hours, waiting for the lions to eat, but would never make a move as long as the lions were nearby. It was an incredible scene, the true circle of life.

On the way back to the lodge we saw another dazzling sunset, perhaps the best one of the week. It began with streaks of light shooting down from thick clouds. As if the heavens had opened and hundreds of golden Masai spears were thrust down into the pale green dusk of the plain. Then a sunset exploded across the sky in streaks of mango and purple. Zach stopped the van and we sat there for several minutes, admiring the magnificence of the scene as daylight slipped away on the Masai Mara.

Reflections Under a Mango Sunset

Some of those moments on safari had an almost mystical affect on me and I began to reflect on the alternate reality that we experience while traveling. As we sat beneath a mango sunset, I realized that Lisa and I were putting distance between ourselves and the tasks and worries of everyday life at home. It was already becoming all too easy to forget we had another existence, where at this very moment people were dealing with office meetings and to-do lists, traffic jams and electric bills. The constant movement of travel could obviously get tiring, but we seemed to be releasing stress rather than acquiring it. Out here on the road we were able to just be.

I soon found myself not only contemplating the alternate world of travel but also wondering about the worlds we all construct for ourselves at home. I thought about how my life, or anyone's life, might be considerably different but for those few key decisions that nudge us in a particular direction and influence the course of our future.

What was the likelihood, for example, that I would marry a woman who once lived on the same block as me in Tucson but only after meeting her several years later in Boston after we each made an independent decision to move to the same city on the other side of the continent? Was it all a quirk of fate, or did some larger cosmic forces manage to line up the right sequence of events for this to happen?

Then, what about my work? In the past, it always seemed that my career path was somewhat randomly dictated by the fact that certain opportunities presented themselves at a particular moment in time. Now, though, with more time to think, I began to discern a pattern to this job history.

My first adult employment was as a journalist for the *Woonsocket Call* newspaper in Rhode Island. I was in my early 20s and was thrilled to be making a living as a writer, which was a goal I'd had through high school. However, after a few years of writing about school committee meetings, zoning board hearings and police reports, I discovered a yearning for more wide-ranging experiences in my life.

I surprised myself by turning away from writing temporarily to get involved with Up with People, an international student leadership program. I soon became enthralled by travel and cross-cultural topics and spent several years traveling in North America and Europe, making friends from dozens of countries and staying up till all hours of the night talking to host families. Some of my most memorable experiences were as an educational program manager, when I was on the road ten months of each year, overseeing learning activities for a group of 130 students.

Unfortunately, I couldn't maintain a job forever that required me to essentially live on the road. So I moved on to graduate school and earned a master's in political science, with some of my studies devoted to the intersection of culture and government. After this I went to work for a consulting firm that wanted my help in creating training manuals about the business cultures of various countries. I then spent the next seven years researching, learning and writing.

Throughout this career journey, although there were legitimate reasons for each of my decisions, I was aware there wasn't any sense of progression within one field and that I seemed to be dabbling in various occupations. Looking back now, however, I could detect recurring themes.

For one, it was evident that my jobs had all tended to revolve around writing or culture and that I was happiest when I was learning about the world or contemplating ideas. I was also struck by how my life seemed to loop through cycles of about seven years or so. The exact numbers varied—take away a year here, add two there—but there were clearly discernible phases. The first one, beginning in high school and continuing through my first job, was devoted to journalism. The second period centered on international student exchange. The third cycle was devoted to cross-cultural training for businesspeople. Now, I sensed that my current work path was narrowing once more and I could only conclude that another trail was waiting to be uncovered.

As I considered this, I realized Lisa had similar cycles in her own life. She was intent on working in the health care field, so she got a master's degree in public health and worked on an academic clinical trial. When that job ended, she took a corporate position that entailed less research but more managerial responsibilities. These cycles also lasted seven or eight years each and, interestingly, she had recently expressed the belief that it might be time for her to move on to something new.

I wondered if I would have noticed these patterns had it not been for this trip and the opportunity to break from our normal routine. When we are engulfed by our daily schedule, after all, we rarely take the time to see how each moment and each decision fits into a larger patchwork.

As I breathed in the clear air and marveled at the boundless Kenyan sky, I came up with Life Lesson #1. *Our life as a whole can best be understood as a progression of smaller lives.* Just as the earth has its seasons, our lives consist of a series of cycles, each with its own strand of interests and opportunities. Perhaps, in the end, what we all really need is some type of sabbatical experience every seven or so years in order to reflect on our lives and refocus our energies.

"ARE YOU CRAZY? THEY DRINK BLOOD!"

Lisa and I wanted to experience more in Kenya than just game drives in national parks and so we arranged to spend parts of two days in tribal villages, visiting with the Masai and Samburu people. There are more than 70 tribes in Kenya and one's tribal identity is still important, but the Masai and Samburu are the only ones to have actually retained most of their traditional way of life. The Samburu live north of Mount Kenya, while the Masai reside in the southern part of the country and spill over the border into Tanzania.

Lisa and I first visited a Samburu tribe while staying at the Shaba game reserve. In exchange for touring the village, we were asked to pay $20 each and were told the money would be put into an education fund for children. A young man named Festus greeted us and served as our guide, as he was one of the few people in the community who spoke English.

As Festus took us around, it was soon apparent that he was putting us through the paces of a staged tour. But pre-planned or not, we reasoned, how many chances would we ever get to interact with tribes in Africa? The tribespeople seemed genuinely interested in teaching us about their culture and we were fortunate in that no one else was visiting the village that day. Hence, we had a lot of individual attention.

The tour started in the elder's hut, where the men were all engrossed in a board game. Not quite the first image I expected to see during my initial foray into an African tribal village, but it was unquestionably authentic, at least. All of the men had large holes in their ear lobes, which had been pierced when they were young adults and then gradually enlarged over time. Their ears were decorated with symbolic earrings that represented a particular status or stage of their life. When Festus explained that the hut was the province of male elders, I asked him more about how the community was governed.

"All Samburu villages have a chief," he said, "but most decisions are made jointly by the village elders. These are older men who are respected in the community."

"Is the chief elected by the other elders?"

"No. Our chief inherited the role from his father," he explained. "The medicine man also learned his job from his father."

Next, some village women performed a welcome dance, followed by male warriors who put on their own dancing show, which included an impressive demonstration of jumping abilities. Then they showed us how to make a fire without matches. Two sticks, pieces of hay, some donkey dung, and lots of friction. Lisa wanted to know if the tribe still made fires this way, since matches were so readily available in nearby towns.

Festus smiled. "It is our way of life," he said.

When the shows were over, Festus took us into one of the village homes. There were 25 of these, one for each family, and the entire community was surrounded by a fence of thorn bushes to keep out wild animals. The shelters were all built in the same way—a wood frame of logs and branches tied together, with dried cow dung used for the walls. The hut's living area was very basic, with just a small kitchen and two sleeping rooms, one each for the parents and the children. In the sleeping area, a cow skin covered the floor to serve as a mattress.

This is such a different, different world, I thought. Our cultures are so far removed from each other, it's as if we live in parallel universes.

Inside the hut, we sat down with Festus and talked about life in the Samburu community. The home was dark and smelled of smoke and earth. He told us that the villagers burn goat dung in the shelters to keep away mosquitoes and snakes.

"How did you happen to learn English, Festus, when other people in the tribe did not?" Lisa asked.

"When I was a child, my parents decided I should attend school rather than become a warrior," he told us. "They saw me doing puzzles in the sand, so they decided I should spend more time at school."

He gave us some insight, as well, into the stages of life for Samburu tribespeople. He said, for example, that males are circumcised sometime after their 12th birthday.

"Oh, that hurt a lot," he said, wincing at the memory.

The circumcision ceremony is meant to mark the passage from boyhood into warriorhood. In his early-to mid-twenties, then, a warrior becomes a junior elder and is allowed to marry. A man will always marry a woman from another village, said Festus, and the average marriage dowry was ten cows. Later in life, the men become senior elders and take on a more responsible role for making community decisions.

When we left the hut, Festus walked us again through the village, ending at a narrow lane in the sand, between two rows of women who were selling souvenirs. As numerous people looked on expectantly and the women pushed items in front of us, Festus explained that anything we bought would provide funds for education and health care for the village.

Lisa and I wanted to be supportive and we couldn't blame them for trying to sell crafts, but we didn't appreciate being almost shamed into spending additional money. After all, we had already paid $40 to visit the village, money that was also supposed to fund community needs.

It was easy in these situations to feel guilty for having been born in a richer Western country. We had a similar reaction one afternoon in Nairobi, when a Kenyan driver pointed out for us some slums on the other side of the highway.

"Yes, we see that also in some cities in the U.S.," said Lisa.

"No," replied the driver.

"Really, there are slums in the United States," she said.

He smiled at her knowingly, as if he knew that she was not being truthful.

We could only laugh at the absurdity of the belief that there were no slums or poor people in the U.S. But of course Kenyans only meet tourists, so in relative terms we were all affluent.

I always had difficulty in grasping that our modest means by American standards translated to such affluence in another country. I was not born into money, I was the first person in my family to go to university and I spent years paying off student loans. However, most people in Kenya could never in their life dream of visiting the West, so the very fact that we were able to take an international trip forced me to confront the fact that I was lucky to have been born in a country that afforded me certain opportunities.

I yearned to be able to explain all of this to our Samburu hosts, but I couldn't even begin to try. So Lisa and I each bought one item, her a carved rhino and me a small tribal mask, and moved on. We reminded ourselves that we'd still had a fabulous time in the village. We learned a great deal, had a unique cultural experience and otherwise enjoyed our interaction with the people.

Later in the week, we visited a Masai tribal village. The Masai are distantly related to the Samburu, with common ancestors having migrated many centuries ago from the region that is now Sudan. Both tribes speak a dialect that is part of the Nilotic language group. Although the Masai have similar traditions to the Samburu, we wanted to take advantage of this chance to visit another indigenous community, especially since the Masai are the Kenyan tribe that is most well known outside of their country.

We met Zach after breakfast and drove a short distance to a nearby village, where we paid another fee and were met by another guide who spoke English. As at the Samburu village, only a couple of young men in the community spoke English and so it often fell to them to greet tourists. Our guide Wilson told us that each day the parents, or elders, would decide which individuals would go out to tend cattle and which ones would stay back to meet guests.

Shortly after arriving, we were taken to a small market and once more asked to purchase crafts. Like the Samburu, it was obvious the Masai walked a fine line between holding on to their way of life and caving in to the lure of tourist dollars. I was certainly impressed that the tribes had maintained a traditional society, but I was also aware they were selling that image to visitors, giving guided tours in a foreign language and hawking their jewelry and souvenirs. It was a dichotomy that puzzled us and we brought up the topic with Zach one day. He told us he had a lot of respect for the Masai and Samburu. Zach is a member of the Kikuyu tribe and he bemoaned the fact that his people had not retained many of their customs.

"The Masai and the Samburu are the only Kenyan tribes who have kept their traditions," said Zach. "It's great—I love it! I love visiting with them."

I realized, finally, that while the tribes were perhaps overly aggressive in pushing their wares, they weren't different from anyone else in the world who made money from tourism. What made them seem different from, say, the Turkish carpet salesmen we had recently encountered was more our own perception of the situation. Simply because they were an indigenous people, we wanted to believe they were somehow uncorrupted by outside influences.

Ironically, we want to have the cultural experience of interacting with these tribes but don't want to believe that our interaction can change them. But if they had remained entirely pure and traditional, I knew, we would not be spending time with them. In the end, I decided to simply appreciate that these tribes were willing to teach outsiders about their culture and customs. The fact is, they have managed to retain much of their traditional way of life when other tribes have not and we were fortunate enough to be able to interact with and learn from them.

The Masai village experience was similar in many ways to the time we spent with the Samburu, although the particular community we visited was less polished. The show they put on—starting a fire, doing some dances—was less spectacular, but their sales pitch was also low pressure. In this way, then, it was a more enjoyable experience for being relatively informal.

Wilson told us the Masai lived a semi-nomadic existence and that each village only stayed in one place for about five years. By then, the shelters were less sturdy and so it was time to move on. He took us inside one of the huts and spent time talking to us about Masai life, as Festus had done in the Samburu village. Sitting on a log, Wilson explained how the tribes were polygamous. His father, for instance, had five wives. The rule was that each wife had a home for her family, while the father would alternate his sleeping locations. Whenever his father and mother slept in the same hut, he said, the children would sleep with one of their stepmothers in another home.

Arranged marriages were also common, although perhaps less so than they once were. Wilson said he would like to choose his own wife, even though he would then be obligated to pay his parents two cows for not going along with their wishes, in addition to whatever dowry he would owe to his bride's family. He also mentioned that he wasn't terribly interested in maintaining the tradition of polygamy.

"I think one wife is plenty! Don't you agree?" he smiled.

"Yes, but one husband is usually enough, too," said Lisa.

"Yes, yes, that's true," he laughed.

Lisa then asked him where he would get the cows to pay his parents and for his dowry.

"Every young boy receives cows from his parents," he explained. "They care for them, and the cows have babies of course, so eventually every man has a small herd of cows."

We learned that cows were important animals to the Masai and Samburu tribes. According to Masai legend, in fact, all the cattle in the world were originally given to them by God. Family or tribal wealth is usually measured in number of cattle, which is why cows are used for dowry payments. The tribespeople have many uses for these animals. Not only is cow dung used for walls and cowhides for bedding, but the cows also provide a staple of the tribal diet. The warriors draw blood from living animals by shooting a small arrow into the cow's neck and then mix this warm blood with milk for breakfast.

As we talked, I noticed that Wilson had pictures of soccer players on his sword sheath. I asked him about that, and he said that since he attended school in the city, there was television, so he was able to follow the sport.

"I watched the last World Cup and was rooting for Senegal, since Kenya didn't qualify," he told me. "But I also cheered for Brazil, especially because I like their players, Ronaldo and Ronaldinho."

I marveled once more about the wildly interconnected world we live in. Here I was, an American, sitting in a cow dung hut in Kenya, talking to a Masai tribesperson about soccer players from Brazil.

Afterwards, Wilson and some of the other Masai men walked us outside the village perimeter and down to the nearby river. We came upon a young boy and some goats. One of the goats was just two-days-old and they let Lisa hold it while we took pictures. Lisa, a baby goat and some Masai warriors, standing outside under the wide Kenyan sky.

At the end of the visit, our guides suggested to Lisa and me that the next time we visited the Mara, we should stay with them in their village and have the experience of sleeping on a cowhide in one of their huts. Obviously, the odds weren't very good that we'd come back to this exact place *and* they would still be living here, but it was an intriguing thought. When we walked back to the van, we saw Zach talking in Swahili with some of the other tribespeople whom he knew from previous visits. I asked him if he had ever stayed with them in one of their villages.

"Are you crazy?" he laughed. "They drink blood!"

Our time with the Masai and Samburu helped us appreciate something important, which is that we are all irreversibly shaped by our home culture. This is apparent wherever one travels, but nowhere was it more evident than in Kenya. It became especially clear one day when Lisa commented on how well behaved the Masai and Samburu children were, and how they obviously respect and defer to their elders.

"In the United States, there seems to be less respect in some cases between young people and adults," she said to one of our guides, "and more young people are likely to 'do their own thing.'"

Yes, that's true to an extent, I thought. But then again, it's all cultural, isn't it? One of the reasons young people do their own thing in the U.S. is because they're conditioned to do so. From a young age, Americans are taught independence and choice. In an African tribal village, there is no independence and little choice. Everyone has a role in life, and each person learns about this from parents and grandparents. There are always family members around and children are expected to respect and obey their elders.

When we see and admire these traits, what we're appreciating is an aspect of something that is quite foreign to us in cultural terms. We may appreciate the level of respect that we observe between young people and adults in these villages, but I also doubt that we, as Americans, would give up our freedom, independence and choice in the exchange.

Global Rule #2. *We are all silently and permanently molded by the assumptions of the culture in which we are raised.* We cannot change this about ourselves, nor can we change anyone else's cultural perceptions. This means, of course, that if we want other people to understand and appreciate our way of life, then we are obligated to understand and appreciate theirs.

On the final evening of our safari, we convinced Zach to have dinner with us. It had been difficult to carry on extensive conversations in the safari van, with Zach intently focused on spotting animals or avoiding road hazards, and we wanted to spend more quality time with him. Over a bottle of red wine, Zach opened up to us more. He told us about an experience he had with malaria, his two decades of safari experiences, some of the tourists he had met and his impressions of Americans.

"Kenyans like Americans very much," he said. "They are open and honest and are usually fun to spend time with. Of course, we don't always know what to think about your government. The U.S. is very powerful and we just have to stay on the sidelines. We sit here and watch America and wonder what it will do next."

I had flashbacks for a moment to our conversation in Selcuk, Turkey, with Mehmet. But Zach did not veer off into any radical directions. We had a pleasant and interesting exchange.

He did note that he was particularly perplexed by the presidency of George Bush. "Why does he need to flex his muscles so much?" he asked. On the other hand, he said that Kenyans loved Bill Clinton because he was "so open," a comment we heard with surprising regularity in almost every country we visited. And he didn't understand the Congressional impeachment of Clinton in the late 1990s over the Monica Lewinsky saga.

"What is it with Americans?" he asked. "Why did you make such a big deal of that? If Clinton were President of Kenya then, he would have been a hero. We'd see what he did (attract a younger woman) and cheer him. We'd say 'good for him!'"

That led into a discussion about cheating in a marriage. Lisa said she felt that what Clinton did with another woman was wrong.

"Yes, cheating is painful," admitted Zach. "Yes, very, very painful. But forgiveness is also important. You must be able to forgive."

Zach expounded on the family situation in Kenya. Although marital problems may arise, couples do not easily separate or divorce, he said.

"If I wanted to separate from my wife," Zach explained, "my mother might get involved and say, 'I like your wife. She's part of the family. You have to work things out with her.'"

Sadly, though, Zach didn't have any recent experience with even disharmony in his marriage, as his wife and young daughter had died in a tragic accident three years earlier. While walking on the street one day, they were hit by a matatu driver. The daughter was killed instantly, while the wife was in a coma for a month before she died. Zach said it took him more than two years to pay off the hospital bill. His one other child, a son, now went to school in a small city outside of Nairobi, near his extended family.

This was the first time that Zach allowed us to see some of his pain. Throughout the week, he had been a good-natured guide, quick to laugh, not easily disturbed by problems or challenges. Now, sipping the last of our wine, our eyes were moist listening to Zach talk about his loss.

"I spoke with my wife in the hospital before she slipped into a coma," said Zach softly. "She just wanted to know about our daughter. I said that she was fine. I didn't want my wife to know the truth. At least she was in peace about that."

Southeast Asia: Bali and Thailand

A Corner of Heaven

Bali is the most famous of the more than 17,000 islands that make up the Indonesian archipelago. Lisa and I trekked there after our Kenyan explorations with visions of unwinding on exquisite beaches in the middle of our journey and ordering tropical drinks while gazing in wonder at vivid, Crayola-colored sunsets. Although it didn't take long to see there was much more to Bali than sea, sun and sand, for the first few days we went into relaxation mode.

When we arrived, Lisa was congested and coughing and was bothered by a sore throat and headache. I wasn't sick, but was ready to slow down for a few days. We'd had a lot of early mornings in Kenya and had spent many hours bouncing along dusty, unpaved roads. So we settled into a small hotel in the southwestern corner of the island that was close to a beautiful stretch of Jimbaran Beach. Each day, we walked there and savored the sunshine and salt air, sometimes having whole stretches of coastline to ourselves. It was a long sweep of sparkling sand wrapped in a semi-circle around a cove of indigo water and there were moments when it was easy to believe we'd stumbled into a corner of heaven.

The chance to spend time at the beach and to also have lodging in a quiet hotel removed from the tourist commotion was the perfect prescription for replenishing our energies. We alternated time at the beach with time by the hotel pool, where we dozed in the sun, read, listened to piped-in Balinese music and sipped yummy concoctions of various fruit juices.

We also took advantage of some ridiculously low-priced massages, typically $6 for one-hour, including tip. The hotel allowed a local masseuse to work by the pool, where an open-air massage table was shaded by a roof and two walls. There, Lisa and I had our introduction to Balinese massage. I'd never had my body kneaded quite so thoroughly before and was surprised at the number of times I winced in pain, as knots in my muscles slowly dissolved.

After the first massage, I told the therapist, a short, fiftysomething woman, "You have strong hands."

I wasn't trying to be humorous, but for some reason this caused her to convulse in laughter. Whenever she saw me during the next few days, she'd smile, flex her arms and say, "Me strong!"

In addition to traditional massage strokes, the therapist used her thumbs or palms to perform acupressure on certain nerve or energy points and had a unique way of popping the joints on all 20 fingers and toes. Balinese massage is an extension of the Ayurvedic massage that originated in India and is not only meant to relieve tension, tone muscles and improve circulation, but also to unblock and increase the flow of energy through the body.

Well, something worked. Beaches, massages, sleep. In a few days, we had both regained our vigor and Lisa was feeling healthier. Before venturing too much further afield, though, we decided to spend more time at the local beach, which at the beginning and end of each day took on a personality that was far removed from the afternoon quiet we'd become accustomed to.

The northern end of the beach served as home to a fleet of colorful fishing boats, painted in bright blues, reds and greens. During one early morning visit, we saw dozens of fishermen returning from the sea and watched them unload their slippery catch for the daily market. Then, in the evening, it was time for numerous fish shacks and eateries to come alive on the beach's southern strand. These restaurants were mostly shuttered in mid-day but became beehives of activity at dinner, when tables were set up directly on the sand and tourists seemed to materialize out of thin air. At dusk, it was impossible to walk much more than 20 yards without people imploring us to eat at their establishment.

All of the seaside restaurants had similar selections of food, so the main differences were in the atmosphere, service and price. The idea was to arrive when the sun was still hovering above the horizon, choose a place to eat and then enjoy the meal as the sun set. An entire tradition had developed around this culinary event and every restaurant seemed to follow the same routine. Customers would first be shown a selection of fresh fish, with snapper, grouper, prawns and crabs all arrayed in big chests of ice. Each person would make a selection, pay according to the weight and turn the fish over to the kitchen staff for cleaning and grilling. The cooked seafood was then brought to our table with a plate of rice, potatoes, salad and fruit.

After dinner, guests would sit on the beach with a cool drink and watch the sun descend in a blaze of fiery glory, while meandering waves from the Indian Ocean lapped against the shore. When the sunlight was gone, waiters came around to light candles. Up and down the beach, all the restaurants were illuminated by these candlelit tables, giving the appearance that the sands had been adorned by a meadow of twinkling stars.

Monkeys, Temples and Black Magic

During our time in southern Bali, we met a twentysomething European couple, Marco and Petra, who were staying at the same hotel as us. He was Italian, she was German, and they were graduate students in Austria. They were delightfully personable and one evening, while talking over dinner at one of the fish shacks on Jimbaran Beach, we learned they had a similar geography dilemma to the one Lisa and I faced.

"Since you're from two countries, where do you see yourselves eventually living?" I asked.

"Italy," smiled Marco.

"No, no, not Italy," interjected Petra. "Well, I don't know. I don't mind not going back to Germany, but my preference is not to move to Italy. I'm pushing for us to stay in Austria. With the European Union now, it is easier for us to stay in someplace other than our home country. I guess we don't yet know the answer, though. We'll see."

"Yeah, that's our motto too," I said. "We'll see."

We also talked about our travels. They were on a two-week Balinese vacation, they said, what about us? We told them about our trip.

"Oh, I would love to take time to travel that much," said Petra.

"It's something that we talked about doing for a long time," said Lisa, "and we're happy that we were able to make it happen."

"When we are young,' said Marco, "most of us have the energy to take a long trip, but usually don't have the time or the money, and when we are old we may have the time and money but don't always have the energy. You have a good solution, I think. It's nice that you could take time off from work to do this."

"Yes, we did have some fear at first about leaving work and giving up some income," I said, "but we finally decided that the old saying really is correct, that no one on their deathbed ever said, 'Oh, I wish I'd spent more time at the office.'"

"You are lucky to have this opportunity," said Petra. "Many people would love to be able to do this."

"We do appreciate it," said Lisa, "and we try to remind ourselves not to take it for granted."

After getting to know Marco and Petra, we shared a ride with them to the Ulu Watu Temple at the southern tip of the island. A temple was first established at this location in the 11th century and it is dedicated to the spirits of the sea. The structure itself, though, wasn't nearly as impressive as its setting, perched dramatically on a cliff high above crashing waves.

In addition to its location, Ulu Watu is well-known for two other features: sunset performances of the Kecak dance and the bands of monkeys that roam the grounds. We went to Ulu Watu for the temple, the oceanside setting and the dance. The monkeys were an unexpectedly amusing warm-up act. Not to mention unexpectedly aggressive. At times, they would take food right out of the hands of a startled visitor. One monkey got hold of an empty camera case, took it up into a tree, and then turned it upside down looking for food. Another snuck up behind a tourist who was posing for a photograph and snatched a pair of glasses off the top of her head. At one point, Lisa even found herself engaged in a battle to keep her water bottle.

"Now that was a sight!" I said. "We're on a clifftop in southern Bali and I turn around to discover my wife playing tug-of-war with a monkey."

The monkeys were amusing, but it didn't take long for their act to get somewhat hackneyed. Luckily, by then it was time for the Kecak, a well-known Balinese dance that recounts a tale from the Ramayana. In the story, Prince Rama must rescue his wife, the kidnapped Princess Sita, from the evil King Rawana. He is aided in his cause by Sugriwa, king of the monkeys, and his monkey army. Naturally. Were we supposed to compare the monkey army in the story, I wondered, with the real monkeys that were running wild around us?

Actually, the dance was quite enjoyable. For one, the location was magnificent. The performance was staged under the open sky, with the ocean and the setting sun serving as a dramatic backdrop. The Ulu Watu Temple was beautifully silhouetted off to one side. As for the show, we were especially impressed by the 70-person bare-chested male chorus, which kept up a near constant chant of *chaka-a-chaka-a-chaka-a-chaka* for an entire half-hour, while the dancers swirled about in bright robes and exotic masks. At the end, a male performer was entirely surrounded by a ring of burning coconut husks and managed to extinguish all traces of the fire by running in circles and stomping on the flames with his bare feet.

We discussed this part of the show later with a local man whose brother was a Kecak dancer. He told us the person who smothers the fire must go into a spiritual trance beforehand. The performance, in fact, has its origins in the Balinese tradition of trance dances (*sanghyang*) in which individuals try to communicate with their ancestors or deities.

"The man must learn to see the fire as water," he said. "If he doesn't see it as water, if he still sees it as fire, then he shouldn't go through with that part of the dance because he will burn his feet."

The temple and the Kecak dance were an interesting introduction to the local culture and it whetted our appetite for further explorations of the island. In order to soak up more aspects of Balinese life, we moved on to Ubud, which is in the center of Bali and is considered the hub for cultural tourism on the island. Although this area has acquired some of the scars of the tourist industry and is now lined with hotels and souvenir shops, it's still more traditional and faithful to Balinese customs than are any of the beach resorts.

During our trip to Ubud, we were fortunate to have a driver, Ketut, who spoke English well and was happy to answer our questions about the island. Ketut, we learned, was a common name for a fourth born child in Bali. The ritualistic Balinese have a prescribed set of given names for their children, depending on where they fall in the birth order.

As we headed inland that day, we wound our way past sleepy villages and Hindu temples. We were awed by dazzling vistas of fertile rice terraces, which seemed to form long green staircases that rolled delicately over the sloping hills. As we drove through rural towns with names such as Batubalan, Sukawati, Celuk and Peliatan, we saw locals in their woven conical hats working in the rice paddies.

Ketut told us that the Balinese have a strong sense of belonging to a particular village and that, even if they work elsewhere on the island, they're expected to return to their homes for family events and important temple ceremonies.

"We do much ceremony in Bali," he said. "For us, time for ceremony is like holiday. We always go back to our village for this. If you do not always go back, if you miss three or four times, then the village may ask you to stay away. If you don't want to participate in the community, they will say, then you maybe should just stay elsewhere. But it's very hard to leave your home."

The people of Bali indeed have a strong, almost unbreakable, sense of community. Many aspects of life are governed by a *banjar*, a village association whose membership includes all of the local married males. One of the banjar's responsibilities is to organize local ceremonies for births, childhood birthdays, marriages and cremations. In addition, it may lend assistance in building a new village home or draw on a common fund to support financially needy residents.

Beyond this, the banjar ensures that individuals abide by traditional laws (*adat*). A person who doesn't work to support the community or who breaks the law, say by stealing from a neighbor, runs a risk of being banished from the village. This is a serious punishment on an island where so much of life revolves around family and community. Banishment also means that individuals are cut off from their ancestors and thus presumably from ancestral support after death.

We asked Ketut about the offerings to the gods that people prepared on a daily basis. The ones we'd seen most frequently were small trays of folded leaves, filled with flowers and rice. They were put out every morning and could be found in front of homes and stores, on street corners, at the foot of statues, on the dashboards of automobiles and even in the surf along the beach. It was also common to see women walking down a street with beautiful stacks of fruit on their heads, to be left at a local temple as a more elaborate gift. An offering that was put out in a home or a business was often accompanied by burning incense, which was supposed to help it float up to the gods.

This smell of incense is actually one of the lasting memories that we took away from Bali. It was interesting during our travels to notice how certain colors, smells or sounds became associated in our minds with particular places that we visited. In Kenya, as I've written, we were struck by the distinctive smell of a wild earth and by the colors of green and red. Turkey calls to mind the soothingly beautiful call to prayer. So now we could make an addition to our list of sensuous memories: the smoky and spiritual aroma of incense in Bali.

"These offerings are for many reasons," Ketut told us. "People ask for safety, for continued work and income, to please the good spirits, or to keep away the bad spirits."

What about the offering that was now on his dashboard? Did he replace this every day? Did he put it there because he hoped it would keep him safe while driving?

"Yes, every day, I put new offering in my vehicle. To ask the spirits to keep me safe. And also so tourists won't complain to me."

Huh?

"That is a joke, of course," he smiled.

"Oh, we won't complain, Ketut," I said. "As long as you give us a discount on the cost of the ride."

"Ah, now you make joke, yes?" he laughed.

Later, we mentioned to Ketut that we had recently seen the Kecak dance and were impressed with the dancer who was able to stomp out a fire. This led into an entire unprompted discourse about black magic and the casting of spells.

"Yes, dancers must practice long time to learn trance," he said.
"It's very impressive."
"Like people who do magic. They must learn for many years."
"Magic?"
"Yes, black magic. You know?"
"No."
"Oh, there much magic on Bali. Very hard to learn, but some people can cast spells and make another person sick. Maybe even make them die."
"Black magic? Here in Bali?"
"Yes, it's true."
"But how? Why?"
"How? I don't know. I no can do that. Many years it takes to learn. But it happens. I see it. Maybe a person steals something, or is bad to someone in your family. So you want revenge or want to put bad luck on that person. Then you can ask for a spell, for magic. Maybe it just makes them sick, or maybe it can be more serious."

This was the first we'd heard anyone talk about black magic, but it's apparently widespread in Bali and other Indonesian islands. Balinese practitioners are called *leyaks*. There have been instances of people who were targeted by a spell not only falling sick for no obvious reason, but also of individuals who reportedly had nails or other foreign objects mysteriously introduced into their bodies. To counteract black magic, there are ways to purify oneself or to ward off spells. This blends nicely with traditional Balinese beliefs about needing to balance the positive and negative forces in the universe, or the need to both please the good spirits and keep away the bad ones. Although acts of black magic are not exactly everyday occurrences, there is nevertheless a strong undercurrent of cultural belief in an unseen, supernatural world.

It's difficult for a Western mind come to grips with this. If we can't see it or touch it, how can we believe it's there? Is it possible that it's not the magic that is real, I wondered, but rather that belief in the magic creates a psychosomatic reality in which people fall ill because they believe they're under a spell? Even though I consider myself open to esoteric ideas, I still have difficulty grasping this concept. But it's a genuine component of some Asian cultures, where people have a great deal of faith in a mystical world that exists side-by-side with our physical one.

White Swirls on a Cobalt Sky

Our conversation with Ketut was one of several opportunities we had to learn about some of the unique facets of Balinese beliefs. This is one of the truly memorable aspects of any trip to Bali and, unless you spend your entire visit sitting by the ocean, it doesn't seem possible to avoid encounters with island spirituality, or at least with Hindu religious practices.

Hinduism has been a part of local life since sometime in the first millennium, having first arrived from India. Numerous Hindu kingdoms once existed in Indonesia, particularly on the island of Java, with the peak of the Hindu era coming during the 14th century reign of the Majapahit Empire. Soon after this, Islam began to make significant inroads into the region and within a century much of the archipelago had been converted to this new religion. As a result, the Hindu leaders moved to Bali and took with them their religious and cultural traditions. Today, although the majority of Indonesia's population is Muslim, Bali remains a Hindu island.

The Hinduism of Bali, however, has been syncretized with indigenous customs so that the people actually practice a fusion of Hinduism, animism and ancestor worship. The Balinese worship Hindu gods but also practice animist rituals meant to appease the deities and spirits that are believed to reside in nature. A sense of spirituality often appears to pervade the entire culture. Not only are offerings to the gods literally everywhere on the island, but Hindu temples are as much a part of the natural landscape as are mountains, lakes and trees.

In fact, every village in Bali has at least three temples. There is a temple of origin that serves as a main place of worship for the community, another which pays homage to local spirits, and a third to honor village ancestors. Beyond this, there are larger shrines devoted to the spirits of the sea or the mountains. Also, most family compounds have a small house-temple, where people pray, meditate and make offerings to the gods. In these Balinese sanctuaries, the most recognizable structure is usually the *meru*, a traditional multi-level, thatched-roof shrine.

Some of the most dramatically beautiful temples on the island are the nine sacred "directional" temples, which are considered to belong to all Balinese rather than to individual villages. We visited two of these. One was the Ulu Watu clifftop shrine on the southern coast, where we saw the Kecak dance. A second was Pura Ulun Danu Bratan in the mountains of central Bali, which was dedicated in the 17th century to the goddess of the waters, Dewi Danu. We stopped there one day during a trip around the island.

"Very beautiful," said our driver. "One of most beautiful in Bali."

The temple sits in a gorgeous, somewhat ethereal setting on a small slice of land in Lake Bratan. It is surrounded by clear blue waters that were as smooth as glass when we were there. At first, I took numerous photos, trying to capture the view as the lake mirrored the multi-roofed shrine and a nearby mountain. In the end, though, we just sat wordlessly and absorbed the silence, watching devout Balinese meditate in the grass while above us clouds of mist traced white swirls on a cobalt sky. At that moment, it almost seemed possible to detect the whisper of faith as it swept around us on a soft breeze.

As we rested there, I was lulled into reflection by the warmth of the sun, the rhythm of the lake and the sighing of the wind. I found my mind drifting back once again into the past and recollections from different phases of my life came flooding back to me. It was as if the further we got into our travels the further back into myself I was able to go.

I recalled, for instance, being six-years-old in Manville, Rhode Island, and making up games in my backyard with the girl next door. We'd pretend that we were adults and whenever it was time for me to go to work, I always seemed to end up as a writer and would start pecking away at an invisible typewriter. It was apparently an idea that never left me. There were times when I thought I'd be a sportswriter or a novelist or a political journalist, but the vision always centered on writing.

Likewise, I also had a long-time interest in travel and other cultures. I still have a poem I wrote in elementary school about the places I dreamed of traveling to. For as long as I could remember wanting to write, I also had a habit of staring at maps and globes and wondering about the people who lived in all of those other countries.

In fact, I was curious from an early age about learning in general and my mind often wandered off in random directions. In the seventh grade, for example, I did a research paper on meditation. I had no background that gave me a reason to be interested in this topic, but when ideas jumped out at me I usually delved into them. In retrospect, I can see this curiosity is partly what drove me into journalism (I would get paid to investigate and write about different issues), but ironically it's also what began to drive me away (newspapers report on the news, not whatever random topics a reporter happens to be interested in). I had nothing against the education beat, I was merely hungry for knowledge of a wider world.

Looking back now, I could see that different sections of my life fit somewhat obviously into a much larger puzzle. The strands of my life, I realized, all revolved around a desire to write, a need to continue learning and an interest in travel and culture. Those three characteristics are parts of my core identity and there is apparently evidence of this going back to childhood. If I wanted to be fulfilled, I was beginning to understand, I shouldn't lurch from writing to learning to culture and back again, as I sometimes seemed to do, but rather find a way to integrate these interests into my life all at once.

In front of a Hindu temple in Bali, these thoughts led me to Life Lesson #2. *Each person's life has a distinctive pattern and purpose.* Our lives often make more sense than we realize, but we rarely take the time to put all of our experiences into context. All too often, our gaze remains fixed on the current moment. We can see where we are, but we don't always perceive where we've come from or where we're going. The rhythm and meaning of our existence, however, becomes more comprehensible when we look at our lives with some detachment from our daily to-do lists.

Bad Fish

Ah, but even an island paradise can have its downside.

On our next to last evening in Bali, we stopped at a small restaurant near our hotel for dinner. We'd had good luck with food most every place we had been and there were a number of people already dining inside this restaurant, which is usually a good sign. I ordered fish satay with peanut sauce, which is essentially a shish kebab with pieces of skewered fish. It tasted fine, but by the time I was back in our room I was already experiencing painful stomach cramps. These plagued me all night and through the next day. I didn't sleep well and made multiple trips to the bathroom. The next day, I was tired and achy and still couldn't keep anything in my stomach. Never was I allowed to be very far from a toilet. Damn fish.

Or at least I hoped it was the fish. Could it be a black magic curse, I mused half-heartedly, as I doubled over in two from another cramp? Did I offend our driver, or not tip our waitress enough?

"You're delusional," said Lisa.

Yeah, I know. But, still, this island feels unusually mystical, I thought, as I ran once more to the bathroom.

I was still pretty run-down two days later, when we had a scheduled flight to Thailand. Well, it was appropriate, perhaps, that Lisa was not feeling well when we entered Bali and I was sick near the end of our stay. Sickness on the road is a part of the travel experience and these were the only times on our first trip that either of us was sick for several days in a row. They were ironic bookends to our experience on this gorgeous island.

Still, as I sat in the airport at our departure gate, trying to rehydrate myself by pouring Gatorade powder into a bottle of water, I asked myself, "Now, how did I get here? How long has it been since I've slept in my own bed? What exactly am I doing, dehydrated and with an upset stomach, sitting in an uncomfortable chair in an airport in Southeast Asia, waiting for a flight to take me to yet another country?"

Thankfully, with the help of fluids and antibiotics (courtesy of the supportive travel clinic we'd visited before leaving home), it only took me a few more days to fully recover. But if we ever take a trip like this again, I told myself, remember to pack the antibiotics and powdered Gatorade.

"Special Price, Just for You"

As we disembarked from our flight at Bangkok International Airport, Lisa and I walked past a group of smiling flight attendants who stood perfectly upright in a straight line and thanked all of the exiting passengers with a *wai*, a gesture that involves putting your palms together in prayer and bowing your head slightly. It was an interesting addition to the usual good-bye. Sort of like, "Thanks for flying with us and, by the way, we also recognize the divinity in you."

In moving from Hindu Bali to Buddhist Thailand, I reflected, we had evidently somersaulted from one spiritually-centered Southeast Asian culture to another. If anything, the spirituality of the Thais was even more obvious on a daily basis due to the constant repetition of the *wai* from almost everyone we met. It was a polite and enchanting reminder of the peoples' shared faith.

However, we also soon discovered that Thailand served up its spirituality with an attitude. Upon leaving the airport we were abruptly exposed to the other side of Bangkok life, which is its madcap freneticism. It's not so different, perhaps, from flying into New York for the first time, hiring a taxi for the ride into the city and then marveling at the controlled chaos and frantic energy of the city. Except for one thing. In Bangkok, when you get to the hotel and pay your cab fare, the taxi driver thanks you with a *wai*. Seriously, I can't see that ever happening in New York.

We had our taxi drop us off at a Chinatown hotel on Yaowarat Road that we'd booked in advance. It was mid-afternoon when we checked in, so we decided to go for a walk and get a feel for the city. And that's when Bangkok really hit us.

It may have seemed hectic through the windows of a taxi, but on the streets Bangkok was an exotic kaleidoscope of activity, bubbling over with sights, smells and experiences. The city swarmed with people and traffic and was drenched in pollution so intense that people wore scarves over their mouths and noses. Accompanied by the blare of honking taxis and the exhaust of gridlocked autos, we walked past glistening modern retail stores that competed with old-fashioned pushcart vendors, brushed shoulders with businesspeople in suits and traditionally dressed women who carried baskets of produce over their shoulders, and then followed a Buddhist monk into a temple and discovered a parallel world of colorful pagodas, the smell of incense and a surprising gust of silence. Bangkok was certainly no run-of-the-mill city.

We had just spent a considerable amount of time delving into culture and spirituality in Bali, so we chose to devote our initial days in Bangkok to discoveries of a more metropolitan nature. Like many visitors, we began our urban explorations at Khao San Road, which is perhaps the definitive backpacker's haven on the Southeast Asian travel circuit. There, however, we discovered a place that seemed to have almost become a caricature of itself. Bursting with cheap guesthouses, restaurants, bars, sidewalk food stands, discount travel agencies, retail stores and internet cafés, almost every sign was in English and few Thais appeared to spend time there unless they worked in a local business.

"This doesn't seem like Thailand," I said. "It feels more like an Epcot World version of Bangkok."

After this we began our adventures in Bangkok shopping. My limited tolerance for this activity was beginning to wear thin by this point in the trip, but Lisa never tired of exploring stores and markets. Now, some people reading this will understand Lisa's interest. They will think, "Bali? Istanbul? Bangkok? Why *wouldn't* I shop?!"

Others, though, will respond as I did. "Shopping? You went shopping in the last city. And the city before that. Aren't you *tired* of shopping?"

Hah.

It's not like Lisa was making major purchases. In fact, her efforts were mostly devoted to finding small mementos to bring home as gifts for family and friends. But she enjoyed the experience of shopping, even if she didn't buy anything, whereas I would have preferred to sit in a café and read, write in my journal or just watch people.

"Just think of it as early Christmas shopping," said Lisa.

I groaned, but I also knew that if I was going to spend this much time on the road with my spouse then I had to make a few compromises. So sometimes I begged off a shopping excursion and other times I tagged along. And, it pains me to admit this, but sometimes it was even interesting. Perhaps Lisa has always instinctively known something I didn't, which is that if you look at what's happening around you then even shopping can provide an entertaining snapshot of a culture.

In Thailand, for instance, as in many Asian countries, a trip to a local bazaar can be a peculiar experience for someone accustomed to American retail customs. In a typical Thai market we would negotiate narrow aisles crowded with other shoppers and listen bemusedly as vendors shouted at us to check out their products.

"Come look. Special price. Yes, special price, just for you."

Invariably, when we saw something interesting and asked the cost, the salesperson would quote a high price. It was just expected that people would bargain. Since we don't come from a bargaining culture, it's a game that took some getting used to. But we had now gone through this ritual in Turkey, Kenya and Bali, so we were beginning to see that it could actually be fun. Sometimes we'd respond to their inflated quote with an equally ridiculous lowball offer, causing the merchant to either feign offense or laugh noisily. But they would always make a second, third or fourth offer, sometimes even calling after us if we walked away.

At one shop, I took a liking to a small wooden Buddha carving and asked the shop owner for the cost.

"600 baht," she said. At the current exchange rate, that was just over $14.

"300," I said.

"500," she replied.

"400."

"No. 500. Final price."

"OK, thank you," I said and walked away. I believed I could find a similar item somewhere else, but never did see one quite like it and so found myself back at the same shop sometime later. I picked up the sculpture and turned it over in my hand. This time, the woman's husband came up to me.

"You like?" he asked me. "400 baht."

"300," I said, surprised at the suddenly lower price offered by a different salesperson.

"OK, 350 baht, then we have deal," he responded.

"Deal," I said, and went home with the wooden Buddha for about $8.

Added to this negotiating ritual was the whole concept of "lucky sales." Many vendors believe it's bad luck to lose their first sale of the day. Or at least that's what they say. So if we showed any interest in an item early in the day, we had to be prepared for a full court press.

"You my first customer. I lower price just for you. 400 baht. OK?"

"What about 250?"

"250? What, you want me lose money? 350 baht. Please, sir, you must buy. You first customer."

And on it went. I found it interesting that the Thai people combined this competitive bargaining culture with an extreme sense of politeness. Even after an animated bargaining session, it was common for shopkeepers to conclude a transaction by folding their palms in a *wai*. This was, I suppose, an apt illustration of the paradox in Thailand between compassion and spirituality, on the one hand, and a strong-willed determination on the other. For despite their smiles and kindness, the Thais are also an independent people who live in the only country in Southeast Asia that was never colonized. Various colonial powers made inroads into Vietnam, Cambodia, Laos, Malaysia and Indonesia, but never into Thailand.

WHO SAID GLOBALIZATION COULDN'T BE FUN?

In the end, though, the quintessential symbol of Bangkok's contradictions has to be the city's Patpong district. In many ways, Patpong is the urban counterpoint to Khao San Road. The two areas are equally well-known but represent disparate ends of the tourist experience. One is a mall for Western backpackers and the other is an amusement park for sex tourists. In their own distinctive ways, each is similarly unreal.

Patpong derives its notoriety from being the home of various go-go bars and sex clubs. A few decades ago, the area was fairly seedy and catered mostly to businessmen or soldiers who needed an erotic pick-me-up. Over time, the district became more fashionable and evolved into a tourist attraction that now accommodates a wide audience and offers all sorts of unusual entertainment options. There are the standard strip shows and topless dancing acts, but there are also clubs that offer such circus-like attractions as women who shoot ping-pong balls from a place you never knew they could shoot them from and even venues that stage live sex shows.

Curiously, this all exists now in the middle of one of the largest shopping districts in Bangkok. There are several blocks jammed with stores and street vendors, selling jewelry, T-shirts, designer watch rip-offs, music CDs, artwork and miniature Buddha statues. There is also an abundance of places to eat, from local Thai restaurants to American fast food joints. And interweaved with all of this are the sex clubs, most of them with touts and attractively dressed women out front, trying to entice tourists inside by distributing flyers that offer a restaurant-like menu of their shows.

"Welcome, please. You want see ping-pong show? Come in."

No, thanks. We'll stick to the street show.

"Yes, come in. Discount tonight. Very good show."

No, really, we're having enough fun out here.

"What about live sex? Come back nine o'clock, you see sex. Here, take flyer."

It's a bizarre yet fascinating place, although not representative of the rest of Thailand, and it prompted an outburst of dismay from Lisa.

"It's so degrading to these women," she said. "Why do they put up with it?"

"Well, it's not the only place in the world with activities that are degrading to women," I said. "It doesn't make it right, but I'm kind of more curious as to why these activities are acceptable here. There has to be something in the culture that allows people to tolerate this."

"It's still degrading," she said.

I never did determine to my satisfaction why an otherwise conservative culture would put up with such overt sexual activity. Is it all for the tourism? Is it because many of these young women send their money home to families in rural areas? Is it more of a "to each his own" attitude, fueled by a Buddhist desire to not judge others? This is far from the only city that allows open sexuality, of course. Amsterdam has its red light district, Tokyo has go-go bars in Shinjuku, and even Nevada in the United States has legal prostitution. It's just that no other place has such an abundance of outrageous sexual expression displayed in such a public manner.

How does this fit, I wondered, with the whole cultural concept of *greng jai*, which compels the Thai people to act with a certain level of courtesy and respect toward each other? So strong is this national attitude, in fact, that the syndicated television show *The Weakest Link*, which a few years ago was a hit in the United States and Britain, raised the ire of many people for its callousness when a local version was aired in Thailand. In the game show, a group of contestants voted to eliminate the weaker members and each defeated individual was typically mocked by the hostess and dismissed with a brusque comment, "You are the weakest link. Good-bye." The contest reduced some participants to tears and observers claimed it went against the Thai spirit.

It was difficult for me to comprehend how the same culture could be outraged over the heartless nature of a game show and yet be accepting of a sex industry that demeaned individuals in a different way. But that, I imagine, is precisely why Bangkok is such an alluringly contradictory city.

If these urban attractions weren't enough to capture our interest, we were also lucky enough to receive a small glimpse of Bangkok from a resident's perspective when we hooked up with Sean, an Irish expatriate in Thailand whose brother, Kieran, is a friend of mine at home. We emailed him before traveling to Thailand and then called him once we were in town.

"Yeah, I'd love to show you around the city," said Sean. "Kieran has told me about you and, in fact, my wife and children just recently went back to Ireland for a while so it'd be fun to have someone to go out with."

Sean suggested on our first evening together that we go out to an Irish pub. Hmmm, an Irish pub in Bangkok, another one in the Dubai airport. Just goes to show, I suppose, that the Irish have learned a thing or two about exporting their idea of fun throughout the world. So we went out, tipped a few pints, then sat back and enjoyed the show as a Canadian fiddle player, his girlfriend, and some local Thai musicians entertained us with Irish folk music.

Lisa asked Sean how a town planner from Ireland came to be living in Thailand. He told us that he had begun his career working on local projects at home before deciding to take a leave and do some development work in South Africa. One thing had turned into another and that stint eventually led him to new assignments in Jakarta, Indonesia, then East Timor, and now Bangkok.

"At different steps along the way, I thought I was engaged in something temporary and that I would then go back to Ireland," he said. "But every new opportunity I was offered just seemed too interesting to pass up and at some point it became difficult to imagine returning to my old work. I do miss Ireland at times, but this is such great chance to live in different countries and see the world."

"Do you think you will go back someday?" asked Lisa.

"Sure, I imagine that I'll eventually go back to Ireland. But maybe not for a while. I was able to keep extending the official leave from my old job for a number of years, but finally I was forced to make a decision to give it up. So that's when I decided to devote myself to these international projects for a while longer."

We also met Sean a second night in Bangkok. After dinner that evening at his favorite local restaurant, we headed to a jazz bar where we heard a singer perform a rap song in Thai, backed up by a jazz band. They called it "big band rap." Let me tell you, you haven't really lived until you've heard big band rap in Thai.

These nighttime excursions were not only fun, but they also afforded us another view into the surprises that were around every corner in Bangkok. We could visit a backpacker's haven where everyone spoke English, buy coffee at a Starbuck's that was just steps away from a nightclub that staged live sex shows, go to a pub and watch Canadian and Thai musicians team up to sing Irish folk songs, or see a Thai jazz group perform rap music that has its roots in inner-city America.

Who said globalization couldn't be fun?

TOUTS, TUK-TUKS AND TAXI DRIVERS

During our days in Bangkok, it sometimes seemed as if a mild state of bewilderment and adventure always hovered over our shoulder. This was partly caused by the way the city assaulted our senses with diverse attractions and frenetic movement, but it was also the result of several run-ins—exasperating, but ultimately harmless—with local touts and taxi drivers.

One morning, after disembarking from a boat ferry near the Grand Palace, I made the mistake of pulling out a map to see in which direction we were supposed to walk. We knew, of course, that to appear lost in a prime tourist area would attract unwanted attention, so looking at a map was the equivalent of hanging a neon sign on my chest. Before I could even get the map unfolded, people swarmed at us, giving us directions or trying to sell us food and souvenirs.

"Looking for the Grand Palace? Over this way."

One trustworthy-looking person said the palace was just a block away—"come, I will show you the street"—and then he proceeded to lead us through two quick turns that conveniently deposited us at the door of his tourist business, which sold sightseeing trips around Bangkok. After rolling our eyes at him and circling the block again, we came upon a tourist information desk.

"Walk straight for two blocks," they said, and so we did, studiously ignoring all touts and hawkers in our path.

Two blocks later, there was the Grand Palace. Naïvely, perhaps, we believed we were home free when we saw the entrance. There was a soldier standing there, and a man in a suit. To our dismay, the suit came over and said there was a Buddhist ceremony going on inside and the palace was closed to the public until 1 p.m. He suggested that we visit some other temples and Buddha statues nearby for a few hours. We had no reason not to believe him (he was dressed in a suit and standing next to a soldier, after all), but then he overplayed his hand by becoming a little too helpful. He began circling places on a map where we should go—mysteriously in the midst of all those Buddhas he seemed to mention something about a "Thai factory," but I thought I misunderstood him.

And then a taxi appeared. From where, I wondered? Had the suit flagged him down? Was this just another one of those ever-present Thai drivers, always on the lookout for a new fare? When the suit started telling the taxi driver which attractions we wanted to visit, I became suspicious. This smelled too much like a setup, so Lisa and I started walking away.

A few seconds later, I was sure it was a setup, as the suit became persistent about our need to get in the taxi.

"No," I said.

"Why?" the suit demanded to know. "Tell me why not."

"Because I don't want to go," I said, walking further away.

And still he persisted, following us down the sidewalk. So I got angry.

"No!" I shouted. "I said 'no!'"

Well, there would be no *wai* after this encounter, I supposed. I regretted raising my voice, but I didn't appreciate his tactics. And, as it turns out, he deserved it. We walked further down the street, found another entrance to the Grand Palace and, of course, it was open. No holiday. No Buddhist ceremony. It was all just a scam to take us someplace where we would feel obligated or be pressured to buy something.

Well, one more lesson in avoiding touts. I never ceased to be amazed at the tricks that they unveiled in their efforts to make money from credulous tourists.

Eventually, after additional interesting encounters, I figured that I could only laugh at the education we were getting in dealing with Bangkok's touts and taxi drivers.

Another day we decided to utilize a traditional mode of Bangkok transportation, which is the tuk-tuk. This is a small open-air taxi, really a motorized rickshaw. We had seen them all over the city, dodging traffic and speeding past larger, less maneuverable vehicles. One of the things about tuk-tuks, though, is they are not metered. This can be either good or bad, for you must bargain for each fare with the driver before you get in.

In this instance, after we settled on a fare, the driver asked if we wanted to make a stop first, at a great club that he knew about.

No, we said.

Yes, yes, he insisted, it's right on the way to where you are going. I'll show you on the map.

Here we go again, we thought. So we got out of the tuk-tuk and started walking away. Now it was his turn to be upset.

"Hey!" he yelled. "OK, OK, no stops. Jeez. Get back in."

We hesitated, but decided to trust him. He took off with a jolt and we flew through the streets, weaving between other cars and through the madness of Bangkok traffic, wind blowing in our faces, holding onto the seat, wondering what we had gotten ourselves into. We did finally arrive in one piece and, as promised, without any stops along the way.

Later that same day, we were on our way to meet Sean, our Irish expat friend. Sean had given us the address to his apartment when we arranged a time to meet. No boats went in that direction and we weren't ready for another tuk-tuk just yet, so we flagged down a real taxi.

Unfortunately, this taxi also wasn't metered, so we again had to bargain for the fare. The driver said that Sean's apartment was a long way and would cost us 250 baht. I knew from looking at a map (in advance, this time) that it wasn't all that far, so I said I wouldn't pay that much.

"How much you give me?" he asked.

"100 baht," I said, figuring I should start at less than half of his asking price.

"OK," he agreed immediately, and so I knew even then that I was paying too much. Still, 100 baht came out to about $2.50 in U.S. currency, so it's not like the cost was breaking us. And, regardless of cost, this taxi ride was actually kind of fun. The driver's name was Noi and he spoke limited English but managed to be quite funny with just a few words.

When he heard we were American, he asked if we liked George Bush.

"Only sometimes," I said.

"Me, too," he laughed. "Only sometimes."

Then he asked about the person whose apartment we were going to. "Where your friend from?" asked Noi. "Thailand? America?"

"No, Ireland."

"Ireland? You been Ireland?"

"No," I admitted. "Have you been to Ireland?" I asked, figuring that I knew the answer but trying to have some fun with Noi.

"Me? No!" he laughed uproariously, as if I had just told the funniest joke. "No, only travel Thailand. Hahahaha!"

Later, he heard we were considering a day trip to Ayuthaya, a site an hour or two north of Bangkok where there were centuries-old ruins of an old Thai kingdom. So he offered to take us. He quoted a decent price, although we weren't really sure we wanted to spend that long in a taxi. But, just in case, he wrote down his name and phone number for us and asked for my name.

"Bob," I told him.

"What?"

"Bob."

"Oh, Bom," he said. "OK, Bom," he wrote on a piece of paper. "Bom, just call me. Say, 'Hello, Noi. This Bom. We go Ayuthaya.' And I come taxi." Then he roared laughing again.

We eventually made it to the street where Sean lived.

"Where he live?" asked Noi.

"Where?" I asked, confused. "I don't know the actual building. It's the address I gave you."

"OK, this the street," said Noi.

This was an oddly common occurrence during our time in Bangkok. We'd give an address to a taxi driver, who would navigate us to the correct street and then either try to drop us at a random place or ask us where the building was. Typically, we'd end up pressing our noses to the window, searching for building numbers until we found the right place.

In this case, though, we forgave Noi. When we arrived at our destination, he asked us where in the U.S. we were from.

"Boston," we said.

"Boston?" he asked, confused.

"Near New York."

"Oh, I sorry," he said.

Sorry? We thought he was sorry that we lived near New York. After all, being a Red Sox fan, that's not a sentiment that I'm unfamiliar with. But then he made a gesture with his hands that mimicked a plane hitting the World Trade towers.

"I sorry," he said again. "I sorry."

What could we say? Maybe these guys weren't so bad, after all.

Monk Chat

Despite the intense and somewhat fantastic urban aura that hovers over Bangkok, the most deeply felt part of Thai life arises from the country's religious faith. About 95 percent of the population is Buddhist and most men spend time in a monastery at some point, if only for a few weeks.

Lisa and I were introduced to Buddhism in Thailand at numerous temples (*wats*) in and around Bangkok. Our most interesting explorations were at the Grand Palace and its adjoining shrine, Wat Phra Kaew, known as the Temple of the Emerald Buddha. There is a long practice in Thailand of having palaces and holy sites attached to each other because it enables the monarchs to more easily perform their ceremonial religious duties. This temple was dedicated in 1782, the year Bangkok became the Thai capital.

Wat Phra Kaew was a feast for the eyes and quite different from any churches or temples in the West. It was vibrant and colorful, decorated in shades of gold, green and orange with a dizzying array of sculptures and pagodas. At each of six entrances were statues of mythical guardians—15-foot tall, multihued and outlandish-looking demon giants, called *yakshas*.

At various carvings of gods or goddesses, small groups of Thais crowded around to make offerings. Some lit candles, others prayed or meditated and still others went through a ritual blessing with lotus flowers. Inside the most sacred building at Wat Phra Kaew, the *bot* that housed the Emerald Buddha, we were instructed to remove our shoes and sit on the floor. This space serves as the king's private chapel and the walls were painted with murals portraying scenes from the life of the Buddha. In the front of the room was the revered Emerald Buddha, seated serenely above the crowd on a gold-covered wooden throne.

The exact origins of the Emerald Buddha are unknown, but it settled in Bangkok in the 1780's, moved there by King Rama I to serve as a national symbol at his new royal palace. The two-and-a-half foot tall statue, which is actually made of green jade, still has its robe changed three times each year by the king, with specific robes designated for each season. There is a diamond-covered robe for the hot season, a solid gold robe for the cool season, and a gilded robe for the rainy season.

We sat there in the midst of a group of praying Thais who had come to venerate the Emerald Buddha and I felt myself gently yielding to the hushed reverence of the surroundings. I recalled visits to other sacred sites, including the contemplative beauty of the Blue Mosque in Istanbul and the natural serenity that surrounded Pura Ulun Danu Bratan in Bali. I thought of past experiences amidst the quiet holiness of Notre Dame Cathedral in Paris or the medieval splendor of Westminster Abbey in London. And I remembered the awe of once stumbling across worn stones into the musty lower level of an ancient church in Florence, Italy, and watching a dozen robed and sandaled monks chanting their daily prayers.

As the memories flashed before me, I reflected again that the same sublime calm was evident in the holy sites of every religion. Did the palpable sense of spirituality in all of these locations, I wondered, arise from the sacredness of the buildings and the holy relics they contained? Did the sacredness of Wat Phra Kaew, for example, emanate from the Emerald Buddha statue? Or, rather, did these feelings emerge from within the people who had come to worship in the presence of the Emerald Buddha? There couldn't be much doubt as to the answer. This sense of transcendence has to arise from deep within each person in the room. It isn't the physical building that makes the people holy, but rather the worshipers and the rituals that make the site sacred.

Thus, Global Rule #3. *Religions are different because cultures are different, but at heart they are all seeking the same thing, which is an understanding of the transcendent.* Each faith seems to undertake the same search, ask the same questions, and perhaps even arrive at the same answers in different forms and different words. All of humanity is longing to touch the divine and we find inspiration wherever we believe we will, in whatever place or faith we already believe is blessed.

After beginning our Thai education in Bangkok, we moved on to the northern city of Chang Mai, which has long been an important center of Buddhism in the country. This city of 200,000 people, which was founded in 1291, is home to scores of Buddhist shrines and a monastic university.

Although we engaged in further temple hopping in Chang Mai, our most memorable experience was some time spent conversing with a Buddhist monk. At Wat Chedi Luang, a young man wandered over and began talking with us. All of the novice monks were expected to spend time with visitors and at least once a week there was even a scheduled "Monk Chat" evening where visitors could interact with monks. This enabled them to practice their English and gave visitors a chance to learn about Buddhism and the monastic life. We were simply lucky enough to have our own private monk chat.

I was excited for this opportunity, since some of my most vivid memories of Thailand were the daily sightings of monks wandering the streets. They are so omnipresent that public buses and boat ferries even have special seats reserved for monks. In Chang Mai, due to the presence of the Buddhist university, these saffron- and orange-robed young men were especially plentiful. They could be seen walking the streets, reading at an outdoor table or praying in a temple.

The monk that we met called himself James, because his father liked James Bond. Honestly. James said that he'd been studying at the Buddhist university in Chang Mai for five years. He appeared hesitant and nervous at first over the prospect of conversing in English, but his language skills were better than he realized.

"What is a normal day like for you?" Lisa asked.

James said his typical day was to get up before dawn, walk the streets to collect alms before breakfast, participate in morning prayer or meditation, spend the bulk of his day in classes or studying and then take part in an evening prayer session.

"Is it true that monks are only supposed to eat twice a day?"

"Yes," he smiled, "but when I study hard I get hungry, so sometimes I have to eat more."

He also confirmed that monks are not allowed to have any physical contact with females. Because of the "different feelings" that arise from touching a woman, he said, it would "distract the mind" from focusing on spiritual activities.

Later, I questioned him about meditation. Did it ever become easier? After doing this every day for five years, could his mind now slip more easily into a state of emptiness?

"It is still difficult," he admitted. "It is always easy to become distracted, to think about other things."

Later, a group of novice monks came into the sanctuary with an instructor and took a seat on the floor. James said they were learning about meditation. The young monks took notes as the teacher spoke and occasionally goofed around with each other. They didn't look very different from any other group of teenage boys in a classroom elsewhere in the world, save for their shaved heads and saffron robes.

Would any of these young men, I wondered, devote their lives to monasticism and Buddhist study? A majority of them, of course, would re-enter what they call "common life." Most Thai men become a monk for a period of time, but it is voluntary. They usually serve for a period of three months, although some enter a monastery for as little as a few weeks and others remain for several years. I recalled a conversation with Pravat, a local guide who had spent 11 years in a Buddhist monastery, six years as a novice and an additional five years as a full-fledged monk, before leaving to get a paying job.

"By becoming a common person, I could make some income and then send money home to my parents," he said. "They are still farmers and make little money."

The practice of serving as a monk is a rite of passage in this culture. Some have likened it to a Thai version of a sabbatical, giving young males the opportunity to remove themselves from their normal routine for a period of time in order to reflect on their lives before they take on the full role and responsibilities of being an adult. In its own way, it's comparable to the ritual transition that Masai tribesmen undergo on their way to becoming adult warriors, or the Australian Aboriginal tradition of the walkabout.

This reinforced to me the incredible influence that Buddhism has over the lives of the Thai people. Everywhere in the country are men who have spent from a few months to a few years as a Buddhist monk. It has to significantly influence how Thais view their lives and the world. How different would my life be, or the life of my friends, if we'd spent our teenage and early adult years focusing on spiritual growth in a monastery?

"James, can I ask what attracts you about being a monk?" I said. "Why have you stayed in the monastery for five years? Many of your childhood friends must be doing other things in their lives."

"I believe Buddhism speaks to the true reality of our life here on earth," he said. "I am interested in learning more about that, in trying to understand it if I can."

"Do you know yet if you will remain a monk, or if you will eventually leave the monastery?"

"I don't know yet," he admitted. "I will see. But it is good now, I am happy."

It was a pleasant and enlightening chat. Unfortunately, we couldn't get away without a question about George Bush. Even in the relative quiet and obscurity of a Buddhist temple in northern Thailand, surrounded by centuries-old carvings, the smell of incense and several meditating monks, James quietly asked us why the American government was so intent on throwing its military might around the world.

"I am afraid that maybe George Bush will end up starting World War III," he said sadly.

The fact that we couldn't seem to avoid these questions caused me to spend a lot of time thinking about my country and its reputation in the world. Many people, unfortunately, feel threatened by the U.S. government, even as they are simultaneously fascinated by the American way of life. In part, this derives from the inescapable contradictions that come with being a superpower. Other nations welcome American strength in particular situations, but also resent the country for possessing such outsized power compared to the rest of the globe.

That said, though, I do think the reasons for the world's conflicting feelings about the United States go one step deeper. This is because most people in other countries idealize America not for its power, but for its freedoms and its optimistic view of life and the future. Even a European friend of mine once said that she envied me for living in a country where people believed anything was possible, where the future was wide open and our options were only limited by our skills, our desires and our nerve.

This vision that others have of the United States consequently means that people put the country on a pedestal and believe it should be a force for good in the world. That's why they are disappointed when we don't seem to live up to our own ideals. That helps to explain why so many people we met were angry with George W. Bush. It goes without saying that other nations have had disagreements with American presidents for decades. However, President Bush seemed to exacerbate the situation, partly by his unilateral ways and go-it-alone stances on international issues and partly because he expressed little curiosity about the rest of the world's people.

Flip this explanation over and it explains why so many foreigners had expressed to us such admiration for Bill Clinton. Over and over again, individuals would say that President Clinton was "open" and "tolerant" and "interested in the world." Surely it's not a coincidence that these identical words and phrases popped up in conversations in pretty much every country that we visited. In fact, I sometimes felt as if I were following in the wake of a Bill Clinton world tour. In numerous locations, there were pictures of Clinton's visit, of the time he spent at local tourist sites or interacting with local residents.

To people in other countries, President Clinton was able to deliver a message of both optimism and interest. He implied that we were all part of one globe and that Americans were interested in the world. The Bush presidency, on the other hand, represented almost a rebuke to the planet. People began to fear that America would go it alone, that we didn't care what other countries thought or, even worse, that we weren't all that interested in other people or cultures. For a world that often looked up to the U.S., there could be no worse message to send.

Phuket Beach Encounters

Lisa and I couldn't leave Thailand without experiencing the country's world famous beaches, so we set aside time to visit the island of Phuket (we were there prior to the tragic 2004 tsunami). We booked a room on the north side of town, on a hill overlooking the ocean, and had a beautiful view of Patong Beach as it curved in a sandy arc and hugged a crystal bay. A perfect place, we thought, to relax before ending our trip in Beijing and Tokyo.

But we soon discovered that Phuket had a split personality. In less than ten minutes, we could walk from a fairly serene stretch of beach into the middle of an entertainment district on Bang-La Road that pulsed with some of the craziness of nighttime Bangkok. The streets were lined with bars and the sidewalks were crowded with Thai women trying to lure visitors into their establishments.

Inside these open-air taverns we discovered a peculiar cocktail of people, from tourists having post-dinner drinks to older, overweight Caucasian men with their arms around beautiful young Thai women. It wasn't quite the overt sexuality of Bangkok's Patpong district, but more of a party wonderland for foreign tourists who wanted to balance a sunny day at the beach with a shadowy night in a bar.

If drinking wasn't your thing, there was plenty more to occupy visitors, with dozens of restaurants, clothing shops, discount souvenir stands, bookstores, travel agencies, internet cafés, and the ever-present Thai massage centers. And all of it just two blocks away from a pristine coastline. It was a twilight-zone blend of laid-back beach resort, garish tourist town and frenzied entertainment district.

So what did Lisa and I do on our first night in this flamboyant bazaar? We went to McDonald's, of course.

For a while we thought we might get through the entire journey without frequenting a Western-style fast food place. But we gave in. It felt like a failure at first, but after bombarding our digestive tracts with the varied cuisines of several other countries, McDonald's offered the promise of comfort food. I found it disconcerting that a place we only rarely frequent at home was now a source of solace on the road, but such is the nature of travel. I could go back to spicy Thai noodles tomorrow, I told myself. For one night, McDonald's fries and a vanilla shake sounded pretty good. And I felt less bad about our choice when we walked in and saw that it was filled with Thais, making it seem almost like a local restaurant, after all.

The next morning, I wanted to sleep in late and Lisa wanted to go to the beach early. Lisa loves the ocean and whenever she gets near the coast her personality changes. She enters a happiness zone that causes any tiredness or discomfort she may feel to magically disappear. Evidently, she was even like this as a child. Her mother tells the story of a family trip when a four-year-old Lisa refused to get out of the ocean even though she seemed to be turning blue and was shivering with cold.

Although I see Lisa's passion for the ocean as a charming trait, I admit that on those days when I don't share a need to join her at the beach I'm more likely to think she's been possessed by some sort of crazed obsession. That's how I felt on this particular morning:

BOB—"Can't we just sleep in? The beach will still be there in a few hours."

LISA—"We're in Thailand! The beaches are supposed to be beautiful here. We need to get there early."

BOB—"Just two hours, then we can go."

LISA—"No, this is the rainy season. What if it rains this afternoon and we miss going to the beach? We have to go this morning."

BOB—"Argghh."

I was going to listen to my body's plea for more sleep and let her go on alone for the morning, but I decided to tag along. Truth be told, I enjoyed myself. The beach was quiet, the scenery was gorgeous and I stood in the turquoise water and let the surf pound over me. I asked myself, why was I even upset about getting out of bed for this?

Well, as it turned out, I ended up leaving the beach that day with a painful sunburn. Strange, because I'd put on sunscreen. Apparently, though, it had washed away in the water and I hadn't been sufficiently diligent about re-applying it. The sunburn on my shoulders was bad enough that I had trouble sleeping on my side for the next several days.

This became an important development soon thereafter, when we contemplated a day trip to the island of Ko Phi Phi. Lisa was particularly excited over a boat ride and the opportunity to go snorkeling, but I was suddenly feeling allergic to the thought of being in the sun for an extended period of time. In the end, I finally decided to go for it and we booked a trip for the following morning. Unfortunately, it was after midnight when we went to bed that night, and I tossed and turned on my still tender shoulders for two hours, turned on the light and read, then finally fell asleep at 4:30 a.m. When my alarm went off at 6:00, I wasn't in the best of shape.

Over breakfast, Lisa saw how tired I was and suggested that she go on the snorkeling trip by herself while I stay behind. I could rest, let my sunburn heal further and catch up on my writing, she said. It was my own classic travel dilemma—I knew it would be best for me to pass on the boat trip, but I've always been plagued with this perhaps irrational fear that whatever activity I skip might turn out to be a once-in-a-lifetime missed opportunity.

In the end, I decided she was probably right. Lisa left and I went back to the hotel room thinking, "if only I hadn't gotten so damn sunburned, I'd be on that boat with her." I let myself be depressed for a half-hour, but then I fell asleep, woke up in late morning, wrote in my journal while drinking coffee on our balcony and felt better.

Lisa had a wonderful time snorkeling at Maya Bay and visiting the nearby islands. She came home with stories of beautiful coves hidden among jagged green islands and translucent blue waters that were home to colorful schools of fish. She also came back raving about a twentysomething Japanese couple she had met, Yumiko and Hiroshi.

"You know how most of the Japanese we've met are too quiet or shy to spend much time talking with us?" asked Lisa. "Well, Yumiko approached me first. She began hanging out near me and feeding the fish close to where I was snorkeling. Then after lunch she offered to take my picture because I was alone. She later said that, because she is Japanese, she had to work up her courage for more than an hour before she could initiate conversation and she told me that if you were there she never would have approached both of us."

Lisa also showed me some notes Yumiko gave her with ideas on what to do during our upcoming visit to Tokyo. Good, I thought. Lisa had fun and now we have more travel tips for Tokyo.

"Really, she was wonderful!" raved Lisa. "I had so much fun with her."

A few days later, we took one more stroll along the beach during our last afternoon in Phuket. With just Beijing and Tokyo in front of us before returning home to colder weather, we reminisced about the different beach scenes that we'd experienced during our trip. We had enjoyed lazy afternoons, watched stunning sunsets and even had some pretty good oceanside meals along the coastlines of several countries.

While wandering, we stumbled across a parasailing operation on Patong Beach and I spontaneously decided to inquire about the service. To be honest, I hate heights. But I've been skydiving twice, in fits of either extreme bravery or insanity, and parasailing seemed fairly tame compared to that. So I went up to the Thai men who ran the business and within minutes I found myself being hooked to a harness and parachute.

"I guess I'm going through with this," I said, glancing over at Lisa.

I looked at the speedboat that was idling in the water at the end of a long cable that ran directly to me and had a bout of jitters over the fact that I was about to be lifted into the sky and twirled through the air above the ocean. Before I had a chance to think more about it, though, a diminutive Thai guy grabbed the parachute behind me and told me to start running. I took some quick steps across the beach, the boat sped off in a burst of acceleration, and about three seconds later I was off the ground and climbing toward the clouds.

The Thai male who grabbed the parachute rose into the air with me. They called him the "monkey man" and he was responsible for steering. We made a run down the length of the beach, floating at a moderate height. Then, as we made a wide turn at the end of a cove, the wind swooped in and lifted us up quite high. It's not the same as skydiving, but we got plenty high enough to make it exciting. And the other aspects of parasailing were at least similar to the experience of floating down to earth after jumping out of a plane—hanging in the sky by just a rope and a parachute, hearing nothing but the whoosh of the wind, and drifting in the breeze with a bird's-eye view of the coastline below.

My only regret is that it was over too quickly. Once I was up there, I wanted to float in the air for as long as possible. But soon we were back approaching the beach and I could see Lisa in the sand below, waving. The monkey man then climbed down to my shoulders, put his legs around my chest and reached backward to pull down on the parachute. Now I understood the monkey man moniker. He steered us to a soft landing on the sand and several of his colleagues descended on me to unbuckle the harness.

Before I could even say thank you, I heard a voice call out: "Lisa? Lisa?"

It was Yumiko, who was out walking the beach with her boyfriend, Hiroshi.

It turned out that Hiroshi spoke minimal English, but Yumiko had been an exchange student in Canada and was fairly fluent. They had outgoing, happy-go-lucky personalities that were not so common among the Japanese we had met. We talked for a while on the beach and then invited them to our hotel pool, where we spent more time together. Later in the day, we lightheartedly brought up the possibility of them coming to visit us in Tokyo, since we were going to be there fairly soon.

"Or maybe you can come to Osaka, where we live," they responded.

"We'd love to, but it's too late to change our flights and unfortunately our time is running our before we have to be back home and at work," Lisa said.

"Actually, my sister lives in Tokyo," said Yumiko. "It would be fun to see her and you at same time. But I don't know if it can work."

We left it at that. It would be fun, but we didn't really expect to see them in Japan. Perhaps on a future trip we could visit them in Osaka, we said. Little did we realize this was just the beginning of our adventures with a new Japanese friend.

Northeast Asia: Beijing and Tokyo

Art Students

All Communist nations are not alike.

I learned this within hours of arriving in Beijing. Lisa and I had booked a hotel on Wangfujing Street that was located near a pedestrian-only district filled with shops and restaurants. After checking in, we went for a walk and saw the area was crowded with high-rise office buildings and modern department stores that could as easily have been found in London or Singapore. Comfortably juxtaposed with the local businesses were such Western staples as McDonald's, KFC, Pizza Hut and Starbucks, all overflowing with locals. We watched in fascination as young Chinese adults attired in fashionable clothing sauntered through a retail paradise.

I was strangely surprised by this contemporary setting. Although China's burgeoning, fast-growing economy has certainly been well-publicized in recent years, this is somehow still not the image I had of Beijing from afar. After all, China is not only a Communist state of more than a billion people, but also an ancient land that has traditionally been somewhat closed off to the rest of the globe. Individual travelers have only been allowed to visit the country since 1982, so for many years the only way to glimpse China was to join a tour group that was closely regulated by the government. In a sense, the entire country has often been one big Forbidden City.

Perhaps my expectations were influenced by the recollection of a 1980s visit to East Berlin, in the old Communist-controlled state of East Germany. My memories of East Berlin were of a dreary, colorless city. The cars were old. The clothing styles were old. The store shelves were bare. And in order to get into and out of East Berlin, I had to pass through a Berlin Wall checkpoint that was manned by armed soldiers. It felt as if I were entering a police state that had been frozen in time a few decades earlier. Beijing, though, evinced no such drab sense of being left behind the rest of the world.

When we ventured away from the pedestrian-only avenue, we discovered not only hundreds of people, but also swarms of bicycles and surprisingly chaotic traffic. In a society where individuals were expected to conform to the expectations of the group, I never imagined there would be such disorder on the streets. But the automobile drivers seemed to expect others to stay out of their way, acting as if they'd hit you without blinking if you dared to cross their path. The pedestrians, however, were not cowed. Rather than standing still at corners to wait for a red light, people would cross a street whenever they desired.

This was obviously not a society, I mused, with an abstract notion of order. Confucian ethics may prescribe certain behaviors and create a certain sense of conformity, but Confucius didn't seem to hold much sway over Chinese traffic patterns.

As we took in the sights and sounds of the city that evening, we were approached by two female students.

"Can we talk with you?" asked one of them. "We are university students and our teachers ask us to speak with foreigners so we can improve our English."

That seemed like a reasonable request, since it was the same explanation given to us by James, the young Buddhist monk in Chang Mai, Thailand.

"My name is Li Ming, and this is Xia."

"Li Ming and Xia?"

"Yes. We are art students."

As we talked, they explained to us what they could about Beijing, gave us directions for walking to Tiananmen Square and even went into a lengthy explanation about the Mid-Autumn Festival (*Chung Chiu*) that had recently taken place. Also known as the Moon Festival, it began centuries ago as an occasion for farmers to mark the brightest harvest moon of the year. These days, millions of people take time off during the celebration to visit relatives. It's traditional for people to exchange moon cakes—sweet pastries in the shape of a moon that are filled with red bean paste or jam.

After conversing for a while, the two women asked if we'd like to visit an exhibition of their work that was just two blocks away.

"The gallery is nearby," said Li Ming. "Next year, we are going to have the opportunity to travel to Europe with our paintings, and we would like to show you our work."

We hesitated, since we'd by now programmed ourselves to remember that we were more vulnerable to tourist traps on our first day in a new city. But we had a nice time talking with Li Ming and Xia and they seemed so sincere that it was difficult not to trust them. So we followed them through a shopping mall and into a university building on a nearby street. There, they did actually show us several rooms full of artwork and gave us a brief introduction to Chinese painting. Li Ming explained that almost every object in a picture had a symbolic meaning.

"For instance, the seasons can show the stages of our life," she said, "and different flowers can be used for each season. A plum for winter, an orchid for spring. Or a picture of a boat may be used to represent a family."

"Almost all of these paintings are of landscapes or calligraphy," I said. "Do you paint many pictures of people?"

"No, not so much. Landscape is more important for Chinese painting."

Landscape and calligraphy, we learned, are considered the most important forms of Chinese art. In fact, after our lesson in landscape painting, the students introduced us to a professor, Mr. Wu, who taught us about calligraphy. In the Chinese system of writing, a visual image represents each word. There are more than two hundred "base" characters and these combine to form several thousand compound characters. For instance, the word for landscape is Shan-Sui, which literally means mountain-water. The word for computer, meanwhile, can be translated as electric brain. Knowledge of about 3,000 characters is considered necessary to read most books or newspapers, while a more educated Chinese might be conversant with as many as 6,000 to 8,000 characters.

Lisa and I quickly discovered, though, that calligraphy is an art form that can only be honed with years of practice. Mr. Wu gave us a brush and demonstrated how to paint some basic characters. The brush, he said, should move from top to bottom and from left to right. Every Chinese word is expected to be written with a specific sequence of strokes.

Watching the professor glide through his own work, it seemed like an easy task. But it was much more difficult than it looked and we failed miserably. Not a single one of my strokes came out as I envisioned and I felt clumsy with that calligraphy brush in my hands. Mr. Wu was gracious about our efforts, though, and at the end of our lesson he drew "Bob" and "Lisa" in calligraphy and gave us the two parchments as gifts.

Then, of course, came the inevitable sales pitch. If we would buy a painting, they told us, it would support the students and help finance their trip to Europe the following year. I groaned, but it was difficult to feel too badly about this particular ambush since we'd benefited from the transaction in other ways. Li Ming and Xia were sociable, we'd learned a few things and we even had two original pieces of calligraphy to take home with us. So where was the harm in buying art from a couple of students, we figured, even if they had befriended us under slightly false pretenses?

We finally agreed to buy a scroll that was painted in calligraphy with the character for "love." Li Ming said that all Chinese characters have multiple layers of meaning, so although the simple meaning of this character was "love," the deeper meaning was to "use your heart to love your family and your friends."

Of course, they could have been selling us a scroll that said "Brooklyn Bridge" for all we knew. So we later showed the scroll to a Chinese friend, along with the two parchments with our names in calligraphy. Happily, she translated them exactly as Li Ming had. So we could hang them on our wall at home, after all.

BREATHLESS AT THE GREAT WALL

In the popular imagination, the Great Wall of China has acquired almost legendary characteristics over the years. As with all legends, these traits tend to be a mixture of fact and myth. Yes, the oldest sections were built as early as the 7th century B.C., the wall was initially meant to be a defense against foreign invaders and it is a very long and spectacular piece of work. However, the wall is apparently not visible from space, it wasn't built as a single contiguous structure, and even today no one seems to know its exact length. In the end, though, these are facts for historians and tour guides to quibble over because once you're standing on the wall none of these disputes truly matter.

Unfortunately, it's a complicated proposition to get to the wall without booking a ride through a travel agency. The distance from Beijing makes public transportation a challenge and it wasn't possible for us to rent a car. So we resigned ourselves to a day tour and boarded a minibus early one morning with two men from Spain and a husband and wife from India. Although our ultimate destination was a section of the Great Wall at Badaling, about 50 miles away, the tour dictated that we first had to make several other stops.

One of the more entertaining of these extra activities was a visit to a school for Chinese medicine. We were provided with a brief overview of acupuncture, reflexology and herbal medicine, then a few doctors came into the room and offered to examine us. After feeling my pulse and looking at my eyes and tongue, a doctor told me I had back problems. This is actually true, although it's something that comes and goes. He then told Lisa she had trouble digesting food and told the Indian woman she was chronically tired.

I was intrigued by this, but Lisa was more skeptical. She said the doctor could have picked out anybody in the room, given that person a diagnosis of back problems and stood a reasonable chance of being correct. Well, OK, that was true enough. But why, then, was I the only person who received this diagnosis? If there was no medical basis to it, then it was a lucky coincidence. My interest in the school, however, declined rapidly when the medical staff put on a sales pitch for their herbal medicines. They prescribed two bottles of pills for me. At a cost of $100! I had to say "no" several times before they finally relented and let me leave.

Jeez, art students, medical doctors, everyone wanted us to buy something from them. Who said the Chinese weren't capitalists?

Back on the bus, I asked Zhen, our guide, about local perceptions of Chinese versus Western medicine. She said many Chinese people utilize Western practices for emergency care and surgery, but Chinese methods for general health or chronic long-term conditions. This made sense, as it seemed to blend the strengths of each culture. The West has a technological focus that has produced significant advances in surgery, emergency medicine and fast-acting pharmaceuticals, but the East has a more personal, holistic philosophy that enables physicians to treat the entire patient and possibly see connections that a Western doctor may miss.

This led us into a longer conversation with Zhen. We were now in the habit of asking people for their impressions of America and Americans, so we put the same question to her.

"I usually enjoy my time with tourists from America. I think Americans are open people, very honest," she said. "We don't always like the U.S. government, but the American people we like."

"What about the U.S. government?"

"Well, U.S. always thinks it can tell other countries what to do. And China is mad at U.S. for bombing of Chinese embassy."

"In Serbia? But that was several years ago."

The incident took place, in fact, in May of 1999, when a U.S. B-2 bomber with satellite-guided weapons dropped several bombs on the Chinese embassy in Belgrade. The intended target was reportedly an import-export agency for the then-Yugoslavian government, which was located one-third of a mile away. An address mix-up was blamed for the mistake.

"Many Chinese are still upset over this," said Zhen. "The U.S. has still not told China why it bombed our embassy."

"Why? But, well, it was an accident, wasn't it?" I said.

"An accident?! Hah!" she said, laughing derisively.

I was taken aback by her response. Although there were a few whispered suggestions that the bombing was deliberate, the most-accepted conclusion was that it had been a bureaucratic mistake. From an American perspective, the event was relegated to history and there seemed little doubt it had been an accident. But the Chinese evidently had a different take.

It's interesting, I reflected, how the military and economic power of the United States can lead to a sense that America is almost omnipotent and couldn't possibly have made such an error. Occasionally, a conversation abroad will remind us of this different lens through which other nations view America.

Like the vendor I met one day in Beijing who asked me where I was from. "England?" he asked.

"No, United States," I replied.

"Ahhh, USA. Most powerful country in the world."

Now, it should go without saying that I don't skip around the globe thinking, "Hey, I'm from the most powerful country in the world." In fact, it never really crosses my mind except when I find myself in these conversations abroad. But the fact that this is the first thing a street vendor can think to say to me upon hearing where I'm from—well, it says a lot, I imagine, about how the world looks from this person's vantage point.

That led me to Global Rule #4. *Our perception of the world depends on our perspective of the world.* If you live in India, you embrace uncertainty; if you live in Germany, you embrace order. If you live in New York, you're in the center of the world and anything is possible for those who take initiative. If you live on Easter Island, you're isolated from the world and have to rely on your community. If you live in Ushuaia, Argentina, you're looking up at the planet; if you live in Hammerfest, Norway, you're looking down. We may believe the world is an objective place, but our experience of it is still subjective and our perceptions are influenced by where we live.

Our tour bus finally made it to the Great Wall at Badaling, which is one of the sections that were refurbished in recent decades. This is one of many makeovers the wall has undergone in its long history. Much of what we now know as the Great Wall was built during the 3rd century B.C. during the Qin dynasty. Several sections, though, are believed to pre-date this construction by several hundred years and some of the work done by the Qins was meant to link several walls that were already constructed by other kingdoms.

A modernization of the wall took place during the Ming dynasty of the 14th to 17th centuries. The Mings lengthened the structure and faced much of it with brick and stone, giving it the look it has today. After the Mings, the wall fell into disuse. Some sections collapsed, while other parts were removed by locals for building materials. The wall was "rediscovered" in the 20th century when it became a symbol of Chinese history.

Purists will tell you this historic structure is being ruined by tourism, with cable cars, entertainment arcades and souvenir stands clogging the grounds. We didn't feel overcrowded during our visit, though, perhaps because Zhen steered us to an entrance that was less busy. In any case, once we were on the wall we felt miles away from most traces of 21st century tourism.

Zhen gave us a few hours to explore on our own. She said we could climb to the highest point at this section, where we'd likely see other tourists coming from another direction, before needing to turn back. So the six of us in the tour group set off excitedly to begin our trek. We were disappointed that the sky was gray and a light rain was falling, but this turned out to be fortunate as the hike up along the wall was quite a workout. It didn't take long to realize this wouldn't be a Sunday stroll in the park and we were soon happy for the cooler weather. The wall was much steeper than any of us had realized and involved climbing hundreds of steps. Within five minutes, the Indian woman decided she was not cut out for the walk and turned back. Her husband also began drifting behind us, although he later walked on alone.

About ten minutes later, the heftier of the Spaniards gave in to his huffing and puffing. Standing at the top of a particularly steep flight of stairs with his hands on his knees, he waved us on and wished us well. We were just 15 minutes into the walk, but only Lisa, me and one remaining Spanish man were left to tackle the rest of the wall.

After 45 minutes of climbing stairs, sweating, stopping to catch our breath and holding onto handrails at the steepest parts to keep from slipping backwards in the rain, we finally reached the highest point. It was worth every bit of effort. We were breathless and the view was breathtaking. The vantage point and the foggy, wet weather combined to create a dramatic vista, with billows of white mist hugging the wall as it twisted through the jade-colored hills of the surrounding countryside.

We took in the sight of the Great Wall snaking up and down hills for as far as we could see in both directions. It's astounding to see the length and the scale of the structure and to realize that we were standing on just a small portion of a wall that would possibly stretch all the way across the continental United States. The Chinese call it the Wall of 10,000 Li (miles) and, although no exact measurement has yet been made of this twisting edifice, a common belief is that it would extend from Seattle to Miami if it were flattened into a straight line.

"This is one of those places that I knew people actually visited," I said to Lisa, "but somehow it was hard to imagine being here myself. And even now, standing here, it's a bit unreal."

Lisa and I were unusually exhilarated. Some people may go to the Great Wall and dismiss it as just one more site that has been overrun and diminished by tourism, and perhaps on another day if I were feeling more tired or world-weary I might have said the same thing. But I just couldn't bring myself to feel cynical.

"We're on the freaking Great Wall of China!" I shouted, as raindrops splattered around us and we stared into the distance at a wall that wound its way to the horizon and beyond the edge of the visible world.

We then trekked back down to the tour bus, making sure to stop periodically to admire the views and breathe in the moment. At one point, an elated Chinese tourist even stopped us to ask if we'd get in a picture with her to capture the occasion. Someday, even more people will travel to the Great Wall and it will lose some of its mystique. But China is yet untraveled enough compared to other major tourist destinations that it still felt like a big deal to be there.

"Our Home is Your Home"

On one of our final days in Beijing, we made plans to meet Xiaoqing (pronounced shaow-ching), who is the sister of one of Lisa's co-workers in Boston. Xiaoqing lived a few hours outside of Beijing, but she had graciously offered to come into the city to spend a day with us. We were thrilled to have time with her, of course, for one of the ever elusive experiences of traveling is to have encounters with local residents, with people who aren't tour guides or shop owners.

From the moment we met her, Xiaoqing was kind and welcoming. She was particularly excited to spend time with Lisa, I think, because of the connection to her sister, whom she hadn't seen in eight years. Upon arriving at our hotel, Xiaoqing presented us with a small gift and for much of the day made a point of walking arm-in-arm with Lisa in the Asian tradition of expressing friendship.

That morning, Xiaoqing suggested that we first take a taxi over to Liulichang, which is a street market famous for its handicrafts and art shops. There, we spent half the morning looking at paintings, calligraphy, sculptures, Mao pins and Buddha statues. At one point, a shopkeeper presented us with a lock that was tricky to open. She told us that most people couldn't figure out how it worked. Well, neither could I. The woman then had Xiaoqing try it, but told her that if she was unable to open it, she would lose face.

We've all heard the phrase "to save face," of course, but most of us don't take this concept quite as seriously as do the Chinese. It's not a stretch in China to say that face is akin to one's dignity and honor. It's a character trait that is jealously guarded and to "lose face" can be a source of considerable embarrassment to an individual. Because of this, the Chinese are usually careful about chastising others in public.

So, even though the shopkeeper challenged Xiaoqing's face in a joking manner, she managed to turn a seemingly inconsequential, fun exercise into a suddenly serious matter. Most people, when confronted with this trick lock, would probably react as I did. "Oh, well, I can't open it. Big deal." But Xiaoqing was bound and determined to get this lock undone once her face had been threatened—so much so that she even had the vendor give her hints until she was finally able to release it. I had read about the importance of face in China, but had never seen it demonstrated so plainly.

After our jaunt through Liulichang, we ventured over to Beihai Park. This is a beautifully landscaped area near the Forbidden City that once served as a recreational spot for emperors. Before that, it was the site of the Great Khan's palace and the center of the Mongolian Yuan dynasty that ruled China in the 13th and 14th centuries. All traces of the Khan's palace are gone, however, so our primary reason for going there was to arrange a tour of some nearby hutongs. These are the narrow streets and alleyways of old Beijing, which at one time housed much of the city's population.

The name *hutong* is of Mongolian origin and the first of these streets are believed to date to the Yuan dynasty. Along these narrow lanes generations of families lived in distinctive courtyard houses (*siheyuan*). All of the hutongs were laid out on an east-west axis, so the homes were built with a south-facing entrance. This is considered good feng shui since the south is the *yang* side and faces heaven, while the north is the *yin* side and is connected to the forces of the earth.

Many of these old neighborhoods have been razed in recent years to make way for high-rise apartment buildings and other projects, but a few of the traditional hutongs have been preserved. Some of these streets and homes date back several centuries and are an architectural link to the city's history and to a vanishing way of life.

For visitors who want to experience a hutong today there are only two ways to do so—by foot or bicycle. The streets are too narrow to be navigated by most vehicles, so the majority of tours are conducted by rickshaw drivers who pedal visitors through the ancient lanes. We found a group of these guides near Beihai Park and Xiaoqing helped to negotiate a price for an afternoon tour. Since each rickshaw had seating for just two people, we hired two drivers to take the three of us around the neighborhood. Neither of the drivers spoke English, so we certainly benefited from having Xiaoqing along to translate. Ironically, she had to miss an English class in order to spend time with us, but her professor agreed that real-life practice was more educational than anything she might have learned in a lecture.

Although the Great Wall was a stunning site, our visit to the hutongs was culturally more interesting. We wandered through the streets at the leisurely pace of a bicycle ride, with a warm breeze in our face and dust kicking up under the tires, and enjoyed the scenes of daily life in this old section of the city. The small neighborhood shops and the sidewalk food stalls. The teahouses. The men sitting outside around a portable table, intently focused on a game of Chinese chess. The children coming home from school in their identical uniforms. The adults bicycling to the store or home from work. The elderly man fishing in the river with a bamboo pole. The way in which everyone seemed to know each other, as evidenced by the number of people who shouted "hello" to our drivers, who were themselves lifelong residents of this hutong.

Then one of our drivers, Zhou, said he would be happy to show us where he lived, if we were interested. Yes, we said, we'd love to visit his home. So he drove us to a ramshackle two-room apartment, with a tiny kitchen and a cluttered living room-bedroom area. There was a television in the corner, two sofas that doubled as beds for he and his wife and, strangely enough, a picture of Mel Gibson on the wall. There was also a small pull-out sofa for their son, who lived with his grandparents and visited on weekends. This is common in the Chinese culture, where many children are raised by their grandparents.

Zhou sat us down in his living room and made us a pot of green tea. Then, without asking, he brought me a can of Chinese beer. He told us that he used to be a taxi driver, but that it's common for taxis to be fined by the police (a fact confirmed for us by another driver) and so it was difficult to make much money. As a rickshaw driver, though, he not only made more money but also had a more interesting time interacting with tourists.

As we were getting ready to end our visit, the second rickshaw driver, Chun, became caught up in the moment and asked if we also wanted to visit his home. Absolutely, we said. So we all climbed back into the rickshaws and drove to another small apartment, this one shared by Chun and his parents.

We completely surprised his mother, who was in the midst of cooking dinner and was somewhat shocked to see her son walk in the door with two Americans and a Chinese woman. But her personality quickly changed into that of a welcoming grandmother. She served us moon cakes and almond juice, then sat down and talked to us nonstop in Chinese. Thankfully, we had Xiaoqing as a go-between.

The mother told us that she'd lived in this same apartment for 58 years and said we were the first Westerners who had visited her home. She showed us pictures of her grandchildren and said the next time we were in Beijing we should stay with her. At this point, her husband, who had just come in from the other room, reminded his wife that they already lived in a small and crowded apartment that barely had room for their family.

But she laughed and waved him off. She was just thrilled by the experience of having Americans sitting there in her kitchen.

"Next time, our home is your home," she told us.

If this had been the end of our day, it would have been fascinating enough. But when the hutong experience was finished, we hopped into another taxi for a ride across Beijing to meet one of Xiaoqing's friends, Jiang. He was the manager of a Kung Fu dance show and he and Xiaoqing had made plans for dinner.

We met him at a restaurant that specialized in Peking duck, a local specialty in which slices of meat are wrapped in a crepe along with plum sauce and a few slivers of onions or cucumbers. After Jiang ordered the dinners, our hosts told us we wouldn't be allowed to pay for our meal. They explained that because we were Xiaoqing's guests, she should host us for dinner in the Chinese culture. However, since she was Jiang's guest, he was then obligated to pay for all of us.

"This is our culture," Xiaoqing told us. "We are your hosts and this is how we treat guests. You cannot argue."

After dinner, we went across the street to a theater and Jiang got us tickets to a show called "Hidden Dragon Crouching Tiger" that combined dance, music and acrobatic martial arts. The show centered on two rival schools that held a yearly fighting competition. When the two primary combatants, Tiger Girl and Dragon Boy, ended up falling in love, it dissipated the hatred that had existed between the schools for several generations. At the end, all of the students made a pilgrimage together to Shangri-La Mountain.

A variety of martial arts skills were showcased during the performance, including bare-handed, sword, stick and leg fighting. Lisa was especially agog over the abilities of the 11-year-old Tiger Girl. At intermission, we were allowed to go backstage to meet the performers. Although we couldn't communicate in Chinese, when we saw the young female star we clapped for her and she just stood there shyly and smiled, proving that she was just a little girl, after all.

At the end of the evening, after thanking Jiang profusely—and Xiaoqing even more profusely—we went back to our hotel room and collapsed into bed. It had been a long day of marvelous encounters. The hospitality and kindness of the people we met had brought the city to life. No longer was Beijing just the large and bustling capital of China or merely another tourist destination. The city, for us, had been transformed. It had become Xiaoqing, rickshaw drivers, a hutong grandmother who served us moon cakes, the gracious manager of a dance show who bought us dinner, and a charming 11-year-old female martial arts prodigy with a shy smile.

"Hill? Bank?"

The two policemen only spoke Japanese, but they were our best hope. They studied the piece of paper I had handed over with the name and address of our *ryokan*, a traditional Japanese inn, and then unfolded a large city map. Lisa and I waited patiently for their verdict.

After arriving at Tokyo's Narita Airport, we had taken a train to the northern suburb of Ueno, where we'd booked lodging. Upon arrival, though, we realized there was no taxi stand nearby and we didn't have a detailed enough map to show us the small side streets between the train station and our ryokan. We asked a woman in a ticket booth for help, but couldn't find the right words in either of our languages. Few other station employees were visible and no maps seemed to be available. This was unexpected. We were in Tokyo, the final city of our round-the-world journey, and we were stumped over how to get to our hotel.

Eventually, we discovered a small, two-person police post outside on the street. Although we couldn't communicate verbally, the officers were tremendously polite and helpful. After studying the map for a minute, one of the men nodded in recognition and began to mime directions for us.

He traced his finger along a street on the map and raised his other hand in a sweeping, upward motion.

"Hill?" I asked.

He smiled and shrugged.

The officer then pointed to an intersection on the map, while miming a large building and a person counting out money.

"Bank?"

Actually, I didn't know why I was saying anything, since they didn't understand a word. So I just began smiling and nodding. This went on for several minutes—him acting out instructions, me grasping for a meaning. Then he put away the map, smiled, bowed and sent us on our way.

"Arigato," I said, as Lisa and I set off in the direction he had pointed to. I could only hope that I'd understood half of what he'd tried to communicate.

"Do you know where you're going?" asked Lisa.

"What do you think?" I said. "I don't have a usable map, I don't speak Japanese and now I'm following directions that were given to me in sign language by a policeman."

And so we walked. Up a staircase, over a bridge, up a hill, down another staircase, and then just when it seemed we were going over the river and through the woods to grandmother's house, we found ourselves on a small shopping street in a residential area of Ueno. This doesn't look good, I thought. We walked on warily, fearing we were now just wandering disorientedly with our luggage through random neighborhoods in northern Tokyo. Suddenly, though, we came to an intersection that seemed to match our directions. There was a bank! We turned left and—yes, there it was—we were at the door of our ryokan.

What do you know, I said, I can even understand sign language directions in Japanese.

We checked in and were shown to our room. This particular ryokan was something of a cross between a small hotel and a bed-and-breakfast. It was run by a husband and wife team and our room was in the traditional Japanese style, with futons on the floor. We left our shoes at the door, as instructed, then Lisa entertained herself by slipping on a kimono that was hanging in the closet and we sat down to contemplate this final stop on our round-the-world adventure.

FROM GINZA TO BASEBALL

There are not a lot world-famous tourist attractions in Tokyo. No Acropolis or Great Wall to plan a trip around. In fact, when we met Japanese travelers on the road and asked them for Tokyo highlights, they would usually suggest Disneyland to us. Well, umm, thanks, but that's not quite what we had in mind.

We had gone to Japan in the first place because, in order to visit Beijing on our particular round-the-world ticket, we needed to fly back to the U.S. via Tokyo. That being the case, it seemed silly to not experience a few days of Japanese culture. We very much wanted to see Kyoto or other regions of the country, just as we'd wanted to see more of China, but there was simply no time. Lisa had made a commitment to be back at work on a specific date and our trip was using up almost every bit of clock that we had. So we contented ourselves with a short stay in Tokyo before ending our tour and returning home.

But with no must-see attractions clamoring for our attention, Lisa and I decided to give ourselves time to simply walk the streets. In truth, the city itself is the main attraction anyway. The shopping, the nightlife, the masses of people dashing through their daily lives, the hustle and bustle and energy of a metropolitan area of 30 million residents.

To experience Tokyo, though, it's first necessary to tackle the city's subway system. But one glance at the subway map of 12 train lines and 274 stations was almost enough to send us scurrying back to the safety of our ryokan. There are more lines and stops on the Manhattan subway, but while those trains are mostly laid out in straight lines that move in a north-south or east-west direction, the Tokyo system map looked more like a crumpled spider web and was strewn with such easy-to-remember names as Itabashi-kuyakushomae, Ushigome-kagurazaka and Bakuro-yokoyama.

On the other hand, the subway was certainly modern, clean and efficient, as was the entire city of Tokyo. The planners were thoughtful enough to color-code the trains and list the subway stops in Roman letters, as well as in Japanese script, for the benefit of travelers. Also, numerous vending machines were readily available to dispense tickets, via a system that priced fares based on how far one was traveling. All we had to do after deciphering the map was punch in the cost of the ticket we wanted to buy and add a few yen. But what *was* the cost of the ticket we needed? Good question, actually, because the list of fares seemed to be written only in Japanese.

"Uh, Lisa, can you figure this out?"

"Uh, Bob, there's a line of Japanese commuters waiting in line behind you to buy tickets."

Damn.

Luckily, a security person happened by and helped us to purchase our tickets on that first morning. From then on, we bypassed this dilemma by purchasing a metro pass that automatically deducted the cost of each ride from our card based on where we entered and exited.

That challenge behind us, we got on the subway and went to explore Tokyo. Or attempted to. We went to the Imperial Palace, where the Japanese emperor lives, but could only view it from a distance. Then we went to the famous and fashionable Ginza district, but quickly tired of window shopping for expensive clothing and art.

"I'm bored," I said. "Maybe we've seen too many cities, I don't know. But Tokyo has to be more interesting than this."

So, in search of something more vibrant and exciting, we hopped back on the subway and snaked our way to the Shinjuku district. As soon as we exited the station, it was obvious that Shinjuku would at least be a more fascinating place to roam the streets and people watch. Entire city blocks were mobbed with hordes of shoppers, young people with nose rings and spiked hair, video arcades, conveyor-belt sushi restaurants, electronics stores, camera shops and the omnipresent pachinko parlors, those brightly lit clubs where Japanese devotees spend hours chasing prizes in a distinctive pastime that blends a pinball game with a slot machine.

Nearby was also Tokyo's version of a red-light district, Kabuki-cho, lined with strip clubs and video booths, all mixed in among restaurants and discount retail stores. There, the sidewalks were crowded with tipsy, grinning businessmen who reeked of smoke and alcohol. The most memorable part of Shinjuku, though, was the neon. By evening, the streets were ablaze with dozens of neon signs.

Our tour of Tokyo continued another afternoon in Asakusa, a more traditional neighborhood that gave us a glimpse of Tokyo in its pre-skyscraper days. We meandered through pedestrian-only streets, saw women in kimonos out shopping, watched mothers on bicycles pick up their children at elementary school, and ate in a tiny, family-run noodle eatery. Strangely, though, the biggest attraction in Asakusa is Kappabashi-dori, which is a street of restaurant supply stores. Really. Who needs the Acropolis when there are restaurant supply stores to visit? OK, so the attraction isn't really the tables and chairs, pots and pans, silverware, glasses, tea cups and window signs that are sold up and down the street. The real lure is the stores that sell plates of plastic food.

Local restaurants, you see, are well-known for displaying models of food in a front window alongside their menu. A few of these replicas were so well made I swore they were actual meals. So plastic food is now considered by some to be a form of pop-art and Kappabashi Street is the place to ogle or order these replicas. Unlikely as it seems, this has made the district into something of a tourist attraction. There is even a song about the street that is played over and over again through loudspeakers on every corner.

This fixation on plastic food was one of several features of Japanese life that to me seemed both normal and odd at the same time. As travelers, we always expect a new country to be different and exotic, and so we're prepared for unusual sights. But it's perplexing to encounter a more commonplace object that seems to vary from the norm. That's how I felt about the plastic food.

A second curiosity was the vending machine hubs. Although we have vending machines in the U.S., the Japanese almost have a fetish for them. Lisa and I could pop out of our ryokan to a nearby sidewalk and purchase hot and cold coffee, soda, yogurt drinks, ready-to-eat noodles, rice, comic books, magazines, music CDs, stuffed animals, toys, toilet paper, pornographic movies, condoms and a wide selection of beer, whiskey and sake. It was like an automated version of a convenience store, liquor store and news stand all wrapped into one.

I pondered these things as we walked the length of Kappabashi Street. But I also began to question our decision to come to Tokyo. It was a lively city, but we hadn't had any truly memorable experiences yet and I was starting to think that our sudden interest in plastic food and vending machines was slightly pathetic. Was this truly all there was to Tokyo, I wondered, or had our travel batteries finally begun to run low?

Maybe a baseball game would help.

I had read a lot about Japanese baseball culture and had made Lisa promise that, while we were in Tokyo, we could go to a ballgame. Since I grew up with the Boston Red Sox, I always tried to attend several games each year at Fenway Park. So we headed to the Tokyo Dome and bought tickets for a contest between the Nippon Ham Fighters and the Chiba Lotte Marines.

Much has been made of the difference between the American and Japanese versions of baseball, but the game itself is similar. The variations in Japan center more on training methods and internal team dynamics, which are influenced by a group-oriented culture. When baseball was introduced to Japan in the 1870s by Horace Wilson, an American teacher, it seemed ready-made for a society that has always strived for individual prowess (sumo wrestlers or samurai warriors, for example) but has also insisted that the group is the foundation of society. Baseball features key battles of individual skill in the pitcher-batter confrontations, but a team is ultimately successful only when its players function smoothly as a unit.

When the rules of baseball are merged with the dictates of Japanese culture, the result is a sport in which the individual is expected to submerge his own goals or identity for the benefit of the team. This is different from an American sporting culture in which athletes are more exalted for their individual skills.

There is something else, though, about Japanese baseball that is almost worth the price of admission by itself. That is the fan experience, which was a spectacle unlike anything I'd ever seen in the United States.

In a way, the fan experience started even before the contest. Except for the higher priced seats closer to home plate, most spectators purchased a ticket based on the team they were rooting for. The left field seats were reserved for fans of the visiting team and the right field side for supporters of the home team. The fanatic fans who filled these seats were collectively known as the *oendan* and they began their descent into madness as soon as the umpire shouted "Play Ball!"

"Pure Boru!"

The visiting team was up first and so were their fans, who engaged in a series of coordinated cheering, jumping, shouting, flag-waving, drum-beating, whistle-blowing, trumpet-playing mayhem. And, no, coordinated mayhem is not an oxymoron, but rather a quintessentially Japanese way of rooting for a team. The cheers we saw were all choreographed, loud and non-stop.

Then, when the ballplayers switched from offense to defense after each half-inning, the other team's fans rose and launched into their own organized pandemonium. The first set of fans politely gave way, since it's not socially acceptable to cheer while the other team is batting. For the young students sitting behind us in their identical school uniforms, that meant it was time to return to their chopsticks and finish eating their boxed dinners. For many adults, it was time for a concession run to bring back noodles and sake. Or, even better, to order beers from the attractive young women who wandered the stands with lightweight kegs strapped to their backs.

Then, there was the entertainment sideshow. I was amused by the booming English-language rendition of "Who Let the Dogs Out" every time the visiting team made its final out of the inning, but most interesting was the "fifth inning sweep." This was introduced by the public address announcer much as the seventh inning stretch is in a U.S. ballpark. While the grounds crew ran onto the field to do their normal sweep of the basepaths, some cheerleaders and the team's mascot came out and danced to the song "YMCA." Then, when the basepaths were swept, the grounds crew joined in the performance, doing a choreographed dance number with their brooms! Yes, I can just imagine the groundskeepers at Fenway Park doing that.

Amazingly, the fans' enthusiasm never seemed to waver. In the game we attended, the Nippon Ham Fighters took a 9–0 lead into the ninth inning. I should note that this contest was being played near the end of the baseball season and both teams were hopelessly out of the playoff race. It was the equivalent of watching two of the worst American teams competing during the last week of the season, with both clubs more than 20 games out of first place. Despite this, and despite the fact that Chiba Lotte was losing by nine runs, none of the Marines' fans left the stadium and they remained just as loud and raucous in the ninth inning as they had been in the first.

When the game was over, the Ham Fighters' mascot ran onto the field and bowed to the fans, while confetti shot out of the upper deck and rained over the spectators. It was as if the team had just won the league title. Dramatic music blared from stadium speakers, a pedestal was set up on the field, and two of the star players came over and were interviewed live while the team's fans stayed to watch and cheer. Amazing.

My apologies to the Japanese plastic food industry, but I'll take a baseball game any day.

Naked in an *Onsen*

Our Tokyo experience may have gotten off to a slow start but it redeemed itself with a captivating finish, made memorable by a day that we were lucky enough to enjoy with some new Japanese friends. We hadn't expected to hear from Yumiko and Hiroshi after we left them in Thailand, so we were excited to receive an email after our arrival in Japan. Yumiko wrote to say that, although Hiroshi had other commitments, she'd decided to visit her sister in Tokyo and would like to spend a day with us. What we didn't know from reading the email, though, was that we were actually getting three Japanese hosts.

We arranged to meet Yumiko for a drink one evening and to spend the following day with her. We were suitably surprised, then, when Yumiko met us at our ryokan with not only her sister, Keiko, but also with her mother. It seems that when Yumiko mentioned she was going to Tokyo to meet Lisa and me, the mother decided to hop on a train from Nagoya so she could join us.

Our experience with this clan really began late the following morning, when we met them at the Ikebukuro subway station and headed to a nearby restaurant for a Japanese-style *okonomiyaki* lunch. *Okonomi* translates as "what you like" and *yaki* means "grilled," so it literally means "grill what you like." The batter is a mixture of flour, water, eggs and shredded cabbage, to which can be added a wide variety of optional fillings, such as noodles, shrimp, squid, pork, beef, onions, mushrooms or corn. The concoction is poured onto a hot griddle in the middle of the table and fried on both sides. The end result is a stuffed-pancake type of dish, which is topped with seaweed shavings, okonomiyaki sauce (kind of like teriyaki) or mayonnaise. It was quite tasty.

As we were cooking our lunch, though, Mom kidded me about not ordering a beer.

What?

"I love beer," she said, "but I can't order a drink if the man hasn't."

Hmmm, someone should have clued me in to this beer-drinking protocol, I thought, as I sipped my ginger ale. Interestingly, this was the first of several comments that Mom made during the day concerning gender differences. She noted, for instance, that she would have to ask her husband for permission to travel and said lightheartedly that Lisa should thank me for being able to take this trip. Although she provide little context to her comments, it was clear that for her generation men were the primary decision-makers.

Later, as we discussed careers and work opportunities for men and women, Yumiko noted that companies in Japan prefer not to hire women who have children at home, so that many Japanese females have short-term careers.

"But the situation is changing," she said. "More women go university now or marry later. But in our society, still, women expected to stop work after they marry."

On the other hand, Yumiko said, Japanese men had the opposite problem, since there was a perceived obligation to advance their careers through what might be called mandatory workaholism.

"Many businessmen come home at 11 or midnight almost every day," she said.

As we talked, all three women expressed interest in knowing whether husbands in America would change diapers or help out with the housework. This was almost unheard of among previous Japanese generations, they said, but was becoming more common with Yumiko's and Keiko's peers.

After lunch, it was off to an *onsen*, a Japanese hot springs bath. The best ones were in the countryside, we were told, which meant a drive of one-and-a-half hours. So we piled into Keiko's car and set off.

As we drove, we continued our conversation from lunch and talked more about some of the differences between Japanese and U.S. cultures. One of the more interesting topics concerned how children are disciplined. In the West we often punish children by grounding them, by confining them to the house for a period of time. In this way, we restrict an individual's freedom, which is a concept that Americans take pretty seriously. In Japan, however, the opposite happens. Japanese families punish children by sending them *out* of the house.

"Oh, yes," said Yumiko. "Mom always sent me and my sister out of the house. And we would cry and kick and bang on the door to be let back in."

The cultural tradition in Japan is that children are sent away from their group. That is a stern punishment, and children are as upset by this as Western children are by having their freedom restricted.

Later, Mom talked about her interest in traveling and in meeting people. She explained that she once hosted an Australian exchange student, Jane, and had later gone to visit the young woman's family. Jane's family had been very hospitable and made her visit to Australia a wonderful one.

"This is why I want to meet you," she said. "Jane's family is so nice to me, so I want to be the same and welcome people in my country."

"My mom is different from other Japanese mothers," said Yumiko. "She is more open and interested in meeting people."

"Yes, I'm Crazy Mama," she laughed.

Halfway to the onsen, we stopped at a rest area, where Mom bought us all cups of tea from a vending machine and we broke out some cake she had purchased earlier. It was raining, so we huddled in the car and drank tea and ate cake. I joked that when I got back to the U.S., I was going to tell everyone that it was a Japanese tradition to drink tea and eat cake while sitting in cars in the rain at highway rest stops. And that I learned this from Crazy Mama.

"No, no," she said, in mock horror. "People will think Japanese people crazy."

Eventually, we made it to the onsen. There are as many as 3,000 of these hot springs scattered across the country, a result of the churning volcanic activity that takes place underground. The bath's thermal waters are believed to have a curative effect and they serve as a relaxing sanctuary for many Japanese. At one time, these onsen were an integral part of the social culture but, as we'd also discovered in Turkey, the advent of modern plumbing has considerably lessened the role of community baths.

Initially, I was quite looking forward to this experience. I'd previously been to a Finnish sauna and a Turkish hamam, so I was excited to experience a Japanese onsen. After we arrived, though, it occurred to me that I had no idea what to do once I got inside and that my four traveling companions were all women and were therefore heading to the women's bath, leaving me to fend for myself among a bunch of naked Japanese men. Hmmm. This is one of those moments, I realized, where it's actually not a benefit to be the only man traveling with four women.

"It's not a problem," said Yumiko. "Just go in and follow what everyone else is doing. Meet us back out here in about an hour."

Just follow what everyone else is doing. Well, that's good advice for a sauna, where you merely sit there naked, or maybe run out and jump in cold water once in a while. It's even OK for a Turkish bath, at least when you have an attendant shepherding you from one station to the next. But there is a ritual to a Japanese bath. A ritual about which I had no clue.

Nevertheless, I gamely walked into the dressing room, ignoring the stares that came with being the only Western male at a bath in the Japanese countryside. I undressed and walked into the next room, trying to ignore looks from a dozen naked local men. (I considered doing a naked version of the chicken dance or the macarena, so they'd really have something to look at, but, well ... no.)

In the room adjoining the lockers, there was a row of stools next to some shower heads, with men washing themselves. There were also two tubs, with men soaking in them. Then there was a door leading outside to some hot springs. Two, maybe three, options. I searched my brain, for I knew that somewhere, someplace I had read about Japanese baths. I knew there was an order to the bath, just as there is an order to almost everything in Japanese society. Should I sit at a stool and start scrubbing? Should I lower myself into a hot tub next to one of those men? Should I ... Should I ...

Punt.

Yes, I cracked under the pressure of the stares. Not to mention the fact that contemplation time is severely limited when you are stark naked in a roomful of strangers. So I walked straight through the room and went outdoors. Except I couldn't very well stand outside naked for any extended period of time, either, and I still didn't know whether I could get into the hot springs without committing a social blunder. Soon, though, it became clear that the first thing the men seemed to be doing was washing themselves, and then soaking. Well, that made sense, I supposed.

For future reference, then, proper onsen etiquette is as follows:

1. Remove all pieces of clothing and put them into the basket or locker that is provided. No swimsuits should be worn.

2. Walk into the bath in the adjoining room and take along your wash towel. This towel is approximately large enough to cover your elbow and is used by many people as an interesting but not very effective means of covering their pelvic area. The pretense, though, is generally more important than the reality.

3. Find an empty stool in front of one of the shower heads that comes out of the wall at hip level. Proceed to soap and rinse your body.

4. Relax for as long as desired inside the tub of hot water, the outdoor hot springs, or both. Remember, the tub is where you relax after you are already clean.

5. Dry off and get dressed again.

So I went back inside, grabbed a stool, soaped up and rinsed off. Quickly. My ritual duty thus complete, I retreated back to the outdoor serenity of the hot springs. There, I sank into the thermal waters and found a resting spot against a rock.

Once I settled down, the hot springs were perfectly relaxing. A misting rain fell and there was a cool bite to the air that contrasted nicely with the hot water. I sat buried to my neck in the heat and let myself be hypnotized by the rising steam as it faded into a silver-blue sky. Now, I could chuckle over the experience of being naked and confused in a Japanese bath. After all, I mused, these experiences are at the heart of what travel is about. In fact, they're the essence of what life is about. Although this situation had been more humorously awkward than anything, the fact is we usually learn the most from situations that unnerve us.

Life Lesson #3. *If you want to grow, do something that makes you uncomfortable.* If public speaking alarms you, go do it. Or train for a marathon. Go skydiving. Disagree with someone who intimidates you. Go back to school. Drive cross-country by yourself. Get naked on a clothing-optional beach. Start your own business. Leave your job and travel around the world. Don't do anything stupid or unsafe, obviously, but the point is, once you stare down something that scares you, you become filled with a sense of confidence and freedom. The world feels lighter and less daunting.

For dinner, Yumiko and her family decided we should experience good Japanese sushi. They spent a lot of time debating among themselves about the perfect restaurant. This was actually a theme of the day—they constantly talked and debated their options for what to do next. They said it was because they were indecisive, but I think there was a deeper reason, namely that the Japanese seriously value consensus. It would have been unthinkable for them to make a decision without first hashing out an agreement that all of them were comfortable with.

In the end, they settled on a small restaurant in the Ikebukuro section of Tokyo, which was operated by a husband and wife team, and it turned out to be a perfect choice. I had no idea that sushi could ever be so succulent. The *itamae* (expert chef) told us that he'd been making sushi for 48 years, since he was 19.

On this evening, we were fortunate to be the only diners in this restaurant. That, combined with our status as foreign visitors, entitled us to special attention from the chef. The *itamae* made each piece of sushi individually just before he served it and then presented it to us as if it were a gift, always following a particular order in the serving—first Lisa, then me (as guests), then Mom (the most senior person in age), and finally Yumiko and Keiko. He watched us eat every bite, beaming like a proud father with each taste that we enjoyed.

We were treated to an assortment of dishes that ranged from eel and flounder to tuna and shrimp. The only selection we didn't enjoy was *natto*, which was made with fermented soy beans and distinguished by an incredibly pungent smell and taste. Unfortunately, we had to eat our sushi before everyone else and they all watched for our reaction. Poor Lisa did everything she could to smile as she ate it, but it was all too obvious that was struggling not to gag and was using all of her willpower to swallow.

"Oh, I sorry," said the chef. "I sorry."

Not that it was his fault, of course, but he still felt the need to apologize. After this, I figured that I had no choice but to eat my own portion, so I held my breath and swallowed as quickly as I could.

"Actually," said Yumiko, "even many Japanese not like natto. Some of my friends tell me I am crazy to eat it. Some German friends visit us last year and they refuse to eat natto after they smell it. So you do well, really, because you eat it."

Now you tell us.

Well, the taste of natto was at least drowned out by the sake, which I ordered with my dinner. Mom finally got to order her beer, which made her happy. And they all insisted that Lisa pour my sake throughout the evening, partly because that's what women do for men in Japan, they said, but also because it's considered impolite for people to have to pour their own drinks.

For some reason, it was also a big thing for all of these Japanese women to see me drink alcohol. Mom seemed to want me drunk. I don't know, maybe as Japanese women they weren't supposed to drink very much and so it was a way to live vicariously through me, but Mom was definitely interested in promoting this. At one point, she noted a Japanese word that indicated some state of drunkenness and said she wanted to see me in that condition. Yumiko used a dictionary to translate.

"My mother wants to see you 'roaring with laughter,'" she said.

I see.

At the end of the evening, we tried to pay for the meal but they wouldn't let us.

"You don't understand," they said, when we insisted. "You are in Japan and you are our guests. We have to pay."

After our previous experience in Beijing we at least had been prepared for this eventuality, so Lisa thanked them with a few souvenir gifts that we'd collected during our Asian travels. A piece of lace, a miniature fan with a painting on it. The gifts were small, but we were aware that the social reciprocity involved in the exchange was important in the Japanese culture. As Lisa passed out the gifts, we thanked them again for dinner, and before leaving we took group pictures with the chef and with all of us together shouting "Kampai!"

But then it was time to return home. Yumiko would go back to Osaka the following day and Mom to Nagoya. Lisa and I would soon be winging it back to the United States. Our trip was about over.

Dancing Lessons from God

As Yumiko, Keiko and Mom drove us back to our ryokan, I basked in the glow of a sake-induced warmth as we twisted through the streets of Tokyo, past a maze of angles and signs and bright lights.

"See!" said Lisa, "it was a good thing, after all, that you skipped that snorkeling trip in Phuket. If you had been there, Yumiko wouldn't have approached me. But because you weren't on that boat, now we were able to spend today with Yumiko and her family in Tokyo."

"Yeah, yeah. Easy to say when you had the best of both worlds. You experienced the snorkeling in Thailand *and* this day in Tokyo."

Still, I had to concede her point about the strange synchronicity that led from my sunburn to her meeting with Yumiko to these experiences with our Japanese hosts in Tokyo. To my true surprise, then, a few moments later, our newly adopted Japanese mother turned and looked at us from the front seat, then said something to Yumiko in Japanese. Yumiko translated:

"My mother says that she believes in reincarnation," said Yumiko. "She says that before this lifetime we were all old friends, and this is what brought us all together now, so that we could spend this day together."

Ummm. Uhhh.

"Well," I finally said, "I guess that's why we're so comfortable with each other."

I sank back into my seat and watched as the reds and blues and yellows of Tokyo's neon landscape continued to rain through our windows. Could she be right, I wondered? Did we all recognize, deep down, that we knew each other? Was it possible that, beyond time and space, we were actually old friends?

My mind flashed back through our travels, from Turkey and Kenya through Bali, Thailand, Beijing and Tokyo. I recalled the insights I had gained into myself, my life goals, and my perspective on the world. Perhaps, I thought, by trusting our instincts, by opening ourselves up and taking this trip in the first place, Lisa and I were merely leading ourselves to the encounters we most needed to have.

For some reason, I was reminded of a quote by Kurt Vonnegut. In his book *Cat's Cradle*, he wrote: "Strange travel suggestions are dancing lessons from God." I'd read that sentence years ago, and had even written it down and saved it. Thinking about it now, it seemed to sum up as well as anything what these travels were about. This journey was about chasing our intuition and following through with our desire for a life sabbatical. It was about encountering the world and ourselves, knowing there was something to learn from all the people and experiences that crossed our path. And it was about listening to whatever the universe, or God, had to say to us. That's what we'd been doing during these travels, I realized. We'd been taking dancing lessons from God.

Eventually, we arrived back at the ryokan and we all got out of the car to say our good-byes.

Mom bowed and went to shake our hands, but then said through Yumiko that she really wanted to give us a hug. So I leaned over and gave her a hug and Lisa did the same, which pleased her.

"I'm not supposed to do this because I'm Japanese," smiled Mom, "but it's good to give you a hug."

"Today was a great day," I said. "Maybe you're right and we did know each other at one time. If so, then it's good that we were able to spend this day with our old friends."

"Hai," said Mom, smiling, "yes."

Part II

Traveling West Around the World

"That knowledge, which only travel can give, is worth, it seems to me, all the trouble, all the discomfort and expense of a circumnavigation."

—Aldous Huxley, *Jesting Pilate*

Interlude

When Lisa and I returned home after completing our first round-the-world journey, we went through a mix of feelings. There was a sense of relief at once more being able to sleep in our own bed, have the newspaper delivered to our front door in the morning and not have to figure out a new currency, language or transportation system. But it also felt strange to be home and it was hard to adjust to the fact that life was going to be "normal" again, without the constant rush and adrenaline of being in new places and having new experiences.

In time, of course, the sadness passed. Our sabbatical idea had been a good one—we not only had the memory of many amazing experiences, but we'd also gained insight into ourselves and had a renewed sense of excitement over beginning the next stage of our lives.

About two months after settling back in Boston, we started looking for a house to buy. The plan was to move into our own home within a few months and then hopefully start a family. But the universe, alas, had other ideas. The real estate market in greater Boston at that time was ridiculously inflamed. Even with two incomes, there was nothing in our price range but shoebox-sized condos and crumbling fixer-uppers. Still, we dutifully searched the listings and went to open houses all through the winter and spring. We were convinced there would be a bolt of lightning and we'd find the perfect deal, or the market would finally soften. But it didn't happen.

So we decided it was illogical to put off having children just because we hadn't found a house. For some reason, though, we kept finding reasons to delay our plans. Meanwhile the calendar pages flipped past and before we knew it another summer was fading into memory. At that point, we decided to take advantage of some unused vacation time and frequent flyer miles. We booked a trip to Peru, reasoning that it was inexpensive and the break would do us some good.

In Peru, we wandered from the coastal capital of Lima to the beautiful Andean city of Cuzco. We traipsed through Inca ruins and bartered in colorful marketplaces. We took a bus through the Andes to Lake Titicaca, the highest navigable lake in the world, and visited man-made reed islands that are still inhabited by indigenous peoples. Most memorable, though, were the two days we spent in the tiny town of Aguas Calientes and at the nearby site of Machu Picchu.

On our second day there, when the tour groups had melted back into their buses and the mystical, mountaintop ruins of Machu Picchu were suddenly, eerily quiet, Lisa and I sat amidst the stones of Inca temples in the soft light of late afternoon and talked. We admitted to each other that we both wanted to travel some more and that we felt our first trip had ended before we'd experienced and learned everything that we were supposed to. Perhaps, we thought, that's why we couldn't bring ourselves yet to start a family.

So we began to speak in the abstract about the possibility of embarking on another trip, although it didn't seem at all realistic since Lisa certainly couldn't take another leave of absence from work. There was an obvious answer to this dilemma, we knew, but it would mean a more drastic split from our current lives. The solution involved two suppositions: (a) Although we couldn't afford a house in Boston, we could more easily do so in Arizona, where Lisa was from and where her family still lived; and (b) Since my work could be done from anywhere, if Lisa had reasonable job prospects in the Southwest then we'd be able to move cross country and take time off during our move.

Lisa was initially more enthusiastic about this possibility than I was. I love Boston and New England and I didn't want to leave. Still, I had to admit that other parts of the plan were attractive, since it was the one solution that would enable us to buy a home and it had the added benefit of giving us more time to travel. Eventually, I agreed to at least consider the possibility and Lisa began to put out job feelers. Remarkably, in the spring she found a position that was ideal for her skills and career level—and which didn't need her to start until late summer. This, needless to say, helped clinch the deal. I began to ponder the possibility that this was all a sign from the cosmos telling me not only that I needed to travel more, but also that it was time to stir up my life a bit.

After putting our belongings into storage and winding down our time in Boston, we had a four-month window before Lisa needed to begin her new job. We used the first few weeks to drive cross-country, visit some family and see a few new states. Then we left our car in Arizona and embarked on a second round-the-world journey.

Southeast Asia: Vietnam and Cambodia

WALKING INTO ONCOMING TRAFFIC

So it was that two-and-a-half years after ending our first trip we found ourselves back on the road, standing on a corner in Hanoi, Vietnam, trying to gather courage to cross the street.

In Hanoi, it turns out, as in much of Vietnam, crossing a street is not the simple exercise we're accustomed to at home. That is because few stoplights exist and every major road has a constant, almost unbroken, flow of traffic. At any given moment, dozens of motorbikes are streaming past, along with a few taxis and buses, none of which have any intention of stopping for pedestrians.

The scene is certainly unusual. Few of the drivers wear helmets but many people have scarves over their faces, making them look sort of like bandits on a motorbike. Moreover, a number of these one-seated vehicles manage to carry father, mother and one or two children, not to mention pieces of luggage or bags of groceries. Perhaps that is why they don't make sudden stops—everyone and everything would go flying. On top of this, there is a steady symphony of honking horns. The Vietnamese honk to tell others to get out of the way, they honk when they approach an intersection, and they honk as a warning to anyone who might not see them coming.

Surprisingly, none of this is a problem for the locals, who nonchalantly cross the road by casually weaving their way between the moving vehicles. This state of affairs does, however, pose a challenge for Westerners, who are used to waiting for traffic lights and who have been taught since childhood to never, ever cross a street in front of a speeding mass of metal.

That day, we stood on the corner for several minutes, surveying the scene. We saw that the Vietnamese seemed to inch out a few steps, serving notice that they were about to cross and giving drivers time to adjust their route. Then they marched straight through the wave of traffic, ignoring the near collisions with motorbikes and taxis, which miraculously seemed to surf around each individual. It was fascinating to watch, but nerve-wracking to endure, for there is a rhythm to the movement of vehicles and people that locals innately understand but which foreigners can easily disrupt. Truly, it was like being inside the old video game Frogger, except that backing up was not a realistic option. The trick, we were told, was to keep moving slowly and just trust that the traffic would find ways to maneuver around us.

Trust. No matter how many times I repeated the word, trust is just not easy to come by when you have to walk through a swarm of streaking motorbikes. What

Lisa and I quickly discovered, though, was that we had no choice but to step in front of the oncoming traffic. There was simply no other way to cross the street.

So we took a deep breath and stepped off the curb. We walked a few steps, and then a few more. Before we knew it, we were in the middle of the traffic and there were dozens of motorbikes and a few scattered taxis whizzing by on both sides. Hurtling vehicles just inches from our bodies. I gulped. It would really be unfortunate, I thought, if we ended up splattered on the pavement at the very beginning of our round-the-world journey. But at this point there was no turning back, so we kept walking—and praying—until we finally reached the sidewalk.

That we had made it across the street was good news. Unfortunately, this was but a single street crossing and we had to repeat the procedure several times each day, every day, for our entire stay in Vietnam.

Eventually, though, I began to see this activity as a metaphor for travel, or even for life. Life Lesson #4. *Life is all about taking that first step, even if it seems risky, and then the next step and the step after that, until we finally reach our desired objective.* Every person who crosses the street in Vietnam has to overcome a fear of walking into traffic, every traveler has to conquer a fear of the unknown, and most everyone in life has to deal with a fear of failure or rejection. In each case, all we can do is trust our inner self and have the nerve to take that first step. Sort of like walking into traffic in Hanoi, if you take it one move at a time, go with the flow and allow space for adjustments, it often turns out fine.

"Waiting for Mistah Right"

For those whose only impression of Vietnam is from old television images of bomb-strafed villages, Hanoi quickly puts those visions to rest. It's not Paris, but this Vietnamese capital of more than three million people is a city of wide boulevards lined with trees and cafés. The street scenes are a blend of the traditional and the contemporary, as teenagers talking on cell phones walk alongside middle-aged women in conical hats carting shoulder baskets filled with fruits and vegetables.

It was a pleasant place to wander on foot—at least once we learned the basic Vietnamese survival skill of crossing the street amidst a flock of motorbikes—and we enjoyed our daily jaunts through the avenues of Hanoi. We made the requisite tourist stop at the Ho Chi Minh Mausoleum, roamed the ancient walkways of the 1000-year-old Temple of Literature and, when we needed a breather from the buzz of people and activity, it was an easy saunter from our hotel to Hoan Kiem Lake, an oasis-like park in the center of the city.

There, lush green trees and purple flowers shrouded the murky emerald waters. The sounds of the city seemed buffered by the greenery and we felt protected from the piercing horns of motorbikes and the growl of nearby construction work. During the day, dozens of Vietnamese sat peacefully in the park, while in the early mornings they jogged, walked and did tai-chi along the water's edge.

We found it to be a delightful spot, not least because of the enchanting names and legends that envelop the lake. The translated name of the pond, for instance, is "Lake of the Restored Sword," because of a story that a magical sword from the spirit of the lake had been used to repel Chinese invaders. Later, a giant tortoise seized the sword from the emperor, sank back into the water and restored the weapon to its rightful owner. Meanwhile, on a small island in the center of the lake was the Ngoc Son Temple (or "Temple of the Jade Mountain"), which could be reached by crossing The Huc bridge ("Flood of Morning Sunlight Bridge").

Not far from this park is Hanoi's most historic and interesting neighborhood, the labyrinthine Old Quarter, where the timeless, narrow streets also have unique names, though they're derived from the guilds that originally set up shop in the district. One can while away the hours on Silk Street, Wooden Bowls Street, Blacksmiths Street, Paper Street, Bamboo Street and Incense Street.

When we were there, the Old Quarter brimmed with atmosphere. Families sat outside their homes in plastic chairs and cooked noodles on busy sidewalks, vendors hawked clothing, pirated movies, jewelry and artwork, women sold fresh produce on the street corner, bicycle rickshaws pedaled through crowded lanes, and aromatic coffeehouses provided a welcome respite from the steamy heat and the near 100 percent humidity that clung to our bodies.

"I think we're going to like Vietnam," I said.

"Yeah. I actually wasn't sure what I would think of the country because I enjoyed Thailand so much on our last trip and I was afraid Vietnam wouldn't live up to that. But, at least judging from Hanoi, Vietnam is unique in its own way and just as enjoyable."

"And besides," I added, "any culture that can come up with names like Incense Street or Flood of Morning Sunlight Bridge has to be interesting."

Although we enjoyed our time in Hanoi, the highlight of our visit to northern Vietnam turned out to be a two-day trip to Halong Bay. A World Heritage site off the country's northeastern coast, it encompasses nearly 2,000 limestone islands that jut out of the waters of the Gulf of Tonkin. The name Halong Bay means "Bay of the Descending Dragon" and the Vietnamese also have a noteworthy legend about this site. The story is that the bay was formed long ago by giant dragons that descended into the area to help the Vietnamese fight off an attack. The dragons spat out thousands of pearls, which turned into islands and formed a barrier that stopped the enemy's advance.

Halong Bay today is a uniquely beautiful and tranquil spot, with a forest of tree-topped stone pillars rising from the sea. We spent two days sailing through this extraordinary seascape on one of the many wooden boats (or "junks") that cruise the bay. We visited caves and inlets that were hidden among the islands, jumped off the side of the boat to swim in the sea and fell asleep in our cabin to the gentle rocking of the waves. There were also times when we floated silently and could hear nothing but the lapping of water against the boat and the cry of nearby birds.

Our fellow passengers included couples from Australia, France and Israel, as well as a single woman from Switzerland. We became particular friends with two of the Australians, Peter and Barbara from Sydney. We also spent time talking with Linh, a 23-year-old Vietnamese woman who was on the boat as a guide for Peter and Barbara. But there was little guiding to do once we were onboard and she was amiable and easy to talk to, so we had a long conversation with her in the evening. As the sun set in a stunning blend of purples and oranges, we sat on the deck with a bottle of wine and talked with Linh about her job, the people she met through her work, and Vietnamese culture.

She told us that, growing up, she used to think Americans were "demanding," but once she began working as a tour guide, she saw that many Americans were actually "very friendly, more friendly than I thought."

"But, some are still demanding," she laughed. "Of course, so are tourists from many places."

"What about the war?" Lisa asked. "Do the Vietnamese people have hard feelings toward Americans because of this history?"

"For older generations, maybe still some feelings about it. But for younger generation, it is just in the past," she said.

"There's something I've been wondering about," I said, "which is sort of connected to the war. In Hanoi, we heard the legend of Hoan Kiem Lake, about the sword that was used to repel the Chinese invaders. And today, when you were telling us about Halong Bay and some of the caves here, you repeated other legends that also were about fighting off foreigners. Is this a common theme of stories in Vietnam?"

"Yes, I think there many stories about stopping foreign invaders. Some are myth, yes, and some are true. Like the story of the Trung sisters, who lead the Vietnamese against the Chinese in the 1st century."

"Hmmm. So, are many of these stories popular? Did you hear about them growing up?"

"Oh, yes. Vietnamese people like stories and legends. But about many different things, not just fighting."

"Like what else?"

"Well, do you hear story about birth of Vietnamese people?"

"No."

"OK, I tell you the story, so now you will know more about Vietnam, yes?"

"Yes. Please."

"Long time ago, there was dragon king. He ruled the sea. And there was a fairy queen who lived on land. One day the dragon came on land and saw the fairy queen. They fell in love and got married, then had 100 children. But later, the dragon and fairy had to go back to their own homes. So 50 children go with father to the sea and the other 50 go with mother to the mountains. And these are the first Vietnamese people."

"That's interesting. So it shows that the Vietnamese are from both the sea and the mountains?"

"Yes, Vietnamese belong to sea and mountains, and we say also we are descended from dragon and fairy. Dragons also important in our culture."

"Ah, like the dragons that formed Halong Bay?"

"Yes, you see? There many legends like that in Vietnam."

We looked out at the sunset and drank some more wine. Then Linh changed the subject to relationships. She asked us why we thought there was so much divorce in the West.

"In your country, you are allowed to live together before marriage, but there is still much divorce. In Vietnam, there are many arranged marriages, we are not allowed to live together first, but it is less common to divorce. Why you think?"

I suggested that it might be because the West was more individualistic and more interested in self-fulfillment, whereas Vietnam was still more of a traditional society bound by certain customs or by a desire to satisfy the needs of the group or the family.

"Yes, our culture very strong Confucianism," she said.

Near the end of the night, Linh admitted to us that she is somewhat unusual for a Vietnamese female. Many women, she said, find a husband and begin raising a family in their early 20s and they rarely have jobs after getting married.

"If I do not marry in a few years, then maybe men think I am too old," she sighed. "I like my work. But if I marry and have family, then I probably not work and will just take care of husband and children. And I will be always with mother-in-law. In Vietnam, women always with mother-in-law. So I still hope to find man who say I can work. That is my dream."

We wished her luck in her choices.

"My parents say I am 'problem child,'" she said, "but I am waiting for mistah right."

Look, No Helmet

In planning our trip through Vietnam, Lisa and I charted a route by land down the length of the country, from Hanoi to Saigon. Hence, two days after our peaceful sailing excursion through Halong Bay, we awoke on a train to priceless early morning views of rural Vietnam. As we rubbed the sleep from our eyes, we watched people plow fields with oxen, wade through rice paddies and pedal bicycles along lonely red-dirt roads.

That morning, we were halfway through a 14-hour, overnight train ride from Hanoi to Hoi An in central Vietnam. On the train, we shared a four-berth compartment with a local man who got off at a 4 a.m. stop, and an American high school student who went to an international school in Hanoi. He had lived in Vietnam for two years, he said, as his father worked for an international nonprofit, and he and some school friends were on their way to the Vietnamese beaches for a senior trip.

The ride itself was tolerable enough. Well, OK, the train was noisy, the food was unappetizing (sticky white rice with lukewarm, scary-looking green vegetables for lunch), and the beds weren't very clean (we discovered in the morning that they simply re-folded and re-used the sheets), but we were at least prepared with our own snacks and sleeping liners. More importantly, we got some rest and enjoyed the views.

When we finally made it to Hoi An, we found it to be an agreeable place to loaf for a few days. The town was more touristy than Hanoi, but also more laid back. A few centuries ago, Hoi An was a prominent port for trading ships from Asia and Europe, which carried shipments of tea, spices, porcelain, silk and other goods. By the late 1800s, though, the Thu Bon River, which is the city's connection to the sea, silted up and became impassable for larger ships. Now, Hoi An was more of a large fishing village that had ended up on the tourist circuit.

One of the reasons the town is still popular is that many of its architectural gems—centuries-old homes, temples, pagodas and bridges—have survived the ravages of age and war, giving one the sense of having stepped back in time to a relaxed and picturesque version of old Vietnam. In Hoi An's Old Town, the narrow lanes were lined with green trees and pink flowers, while an assortment of antique wooden buildings squeezed onto the sidewalks. The structures almost all had second floor porches with carved railings and shuttered windows that were thrown open to the sunshine. Bamboo and silk lanterns hung in doorways all up and down the street.

This historic district is a pedestrian zone filled with art galleries, craft shops, cafés, bars and restaurants. Thus, it was easy to lose track of time just walking the streets, having lunch, looking at art, stopping for a drink and then wandering some more. If we ever got tired, one of the great places to hang out was by the riverfront, where an abundance of restaurants had sprung up and it was possible for us to have a full dinner for $3 or just relax at an outdoor table with a 60 cent bottle of local beer.

It was at one of these restaurants that we took a cooking class with Giang, a 20-year-old Vietnamese woman with an infectious spirit. Our decision to take the class was a spontaneous one, but the deal was too good to pass up. For $4, we were allowed to pick any three items on the menu, which we cooked with an instructor and then ate for lunch. That day, we feasted on shrimp spring rolls, sour soup with pineapples, and fish fillets sautéed in ginger and onion.

Equally enjoyable as the food was the chance to converse with the cooking teacher. Giang spoke excellent English, which she claimed to have mostly picked up from working at the restaurant. She had a vivacious personality and spent half of her time laughing and singing. She was also very tolerant of our cooking efforts, particularly the task of rolling vegetables and shrimp into the delicate rice paper sheets.

"Yes, you do excellent. You make great Vietnamese cook!"

She was very kind.

Because she was so fun to be around, though, we went back to the same restaurant for dinner. When there were few customers, Giang sat and talked with us for a while. She told us that she had come to Hoi An three years earlier and that her parents lived in a rural area a few hours away with her younger sister and brother.

"What do you do here when you're not at work?" Lisa asked.

"I have some friends, we go out, we listen to music, but I mostly work," she said.

"What is your normal schedule?"

"I work every day. I come in the morning at eight and stay until we close, maybe at ten in the night."

"You work that many hours seven days a week?"

"Yes. Well, every few weeks I can take day off. Sometime my father come to visit me."

We added up the hours and deduced that Giang worked 98-hours a week, on average. And her wages? About $30 for the month, some of which she sent home to help support her family.

"My family not have so much money, so I can help them this way."

As Lisa remarked later, "it kind of changes your perspective when you feel overworked and underpaid."

That night, we ended up staying at the restaurant until it closed. When the evening was over, Giang offered us a ride back to our hotel on her motorbike.

"You don't want to walk back to hotel now. It is late."

We had vowed to stay off these vehicles in Vietnam, both because of the zaniness of the traffic patterns and the fact that few people wore helmets. But it was about a mile to the hotel and would be a much shorter trip on a motorbike, we told ourselves. Besides, she was so excited about giving us a ride that it was hard to turn her down.

"Yes, it will be fun," she laughed. "I give you ride, OK?"

Sure.

So Lisa got on the back of Giang's bike, and I got on a bike with another restaurant employee, and off we went—speeding through the streets of Vietnam without a helmet.

Traveling the Open Road in Southeast Asia

It used to be that a backpacking trip abroad meant traipsing through Europe. That, however, is no longer such an automatic assumption. Now, Asia—and specifically Southeast Asia—is on the radar of many itinerant travelers. These individuals have traded the beaches of Spain for the beaches of Vietnam. Treks through the Swiss Alps have been replaced by treks through northern Thailand. London pubs have given way to Balinese bars. The ruins of the Acropolis have been exchanged for the ruins of Angkor Wat.

It's true that the vaunted Hippie Trail of the 1960s and 1970s was well-trod across Turkey, Iran and Afghanistan into India, and today many people still go to India, or journey across China, or make their way to such out of the way destinations as Mongolia and Bhutan. But the most obvious analogy to the traditional summer trek through Europe is the travel circuit through Southeast Asia. Much of it is compact enough to be traversed by bus and train, and it's popular enough so that one is always assured of being able to meet fellow travelers. That is precisely what happened to Lisa and me as we traveled through Vietnam and found ourselves dropped into a whirl of Southeast Asian wanderers.

Leaving Hoi An, we booked an eight-hour, $6 bus trip to Nha Trang, a coastal city further south. It was billed as a hop-on, hop-off tourist bus, but since we were apparently the only two Westerners who bought a ticket for that day it became a hop-on, hop-off minibus for locals. The vehicle's seats were worn and frayed, the air conditioner worked only sporadically and the driver smoked. However, any dismay we may have felt dissipated early on when we passed a larger bus that looked like it was held together with duct tape. As it creaked along the road, we saw that every seat was full and additional passengers were standing in the aisle, fanning themselves for relief from the oppressive humidity. Suddenly we felt guilty for traveling in comparative luxury.

Once we settled in for the day, we enjoyed the scenery, as the ride to Nha Trang traversed the gorgeous spine of Vietnam. For a good part of the journey, the coast was on our left and mountains were to the right. We drove past long vistas of verdant rice paddies, through a dramatic coastal panorama of the South China Sea and along winding and hilly roads perched above the seashore. Some of the route was a paved, two-lane highway and some of it was along bumpy local lanes, where our driver twisted his way through a maze of roadway obstacles. Not only trucks, cars and motorbikes, but ox-driven carts, bicycles, pedestrians and streetside vendors.

After arriving in Nha Trang, we found a $12 hotel room—with air conditioning and satellite television—located just one block from the beach. Then we hooked up with one more global nomad when we called Elliott, who is my sister Patty's brother-in-law and happened to be working on a three-month project in Nha Trang as an English teacher. Elliott is from Utah but had spent a number of years abroad, both in Australia and Southeast Asia. Like so many people who work internationally, he was captivated by the opportunity to make a living while exploring other cultures and was perhaps apprehensive that he'd be bored at home.

"I think about going back home sometimes," he said, "but then I always find some other country or city that I want to spend time in. I know I'll eventually settle back in the U.S., but there are so many other interesting places to see right now."

For the next few days, we were able to visit several times with Elliott and his girlfriend, Huyen, who was from Hanoi, over dinner, drinks, breakfast and some time at the beach. One evening, while having a drink at a local bar, we had an interesting conversation about ideals of beauty when Huyen told us that it was desirable in Vietnam to have lighter skin.

"This is why you see women with scarves on their faces when they ride motorbikes," she said.

"Really? We thought they were trying to protect themselves from breathing the fumes," Lisa said.

"That's part of it, but more because they don't want to get sun. They don't want their skin to get too dark."

"A lot of times, you will see women wearing long sleeves in the sun," said Elliott. "They even sell shirts that come all the way down and cover their fingers."

This was similar in ways to what we'd seen in Tokyo, where lighter skin was also seen as an ideal. But whereas a few Japanese used skin lighteners to effect a different identity, the Vietnamese seemed more concerned in general with not looking as if they'd been out in the sun.

"But why the obsession with not wanting to look tan?" asked Lisa.

"A lot of people who have dark skin work outside, like on a farm or in construction," Huyen said. "So if you have dark skin, maybe people think you are poor or from a lower class."

"That's interesting," Lisa said, "since at home many people lay out in the sun because they think having a tan makes them look healthy or attractive. It's not healthy for their skin, for sure, but the ideal is to have a tan. That, and to be thin."

"Yes, that's another difference with Vietnam," added Huyen. "Most men prefer their women to not be too slim. She doesn't have to be fat, but not too skinny either."

"Wow, that is just the complete opposite of the way American society is."

"But I think not all Americans are thin. Yes? I was surprised when I meet you, Lisa, because I think most Americans are larger, but you are thin."

"Oh, thank you. But maybe not so much after all this travel food! About what you were saying, though—I think if an American has an ideal, it's to be thin. But you are right that many people are larger."

It was an interesting conversation and was one more chance to gain a tiny window into a culture from a local perspective. Even more, though, it was fun to spend time with someone who had a connection to home. The world always seems smaller when you can drop into a town in central Vietnam and have a beer with your sister's brother-in-law.

On our final day in Nha Trang, after spending time lounging on some of the city's three miles of beaches (yes, the Vietnamese go to the seashore, but they tend to spend more time in the shade than in the sun), we were surprised to run into Peter and Barbara, the Australian couple whom we'd met on the Halong Bay boat. They were having drinks at an open-air bar along the water, so we joined them and ended up staying for three hours.

It reminded us of the time we met a Scottish couple in Peru on the train to Machu Picchu and then ran into them again several days later on a boat on Lake Titicaca in a whole other part of the country. Travelers frequent many of the same places, but it's still a shock to see people hundreds of miles away from where you last saw them, particularly when you're traveling by different means and staying in different hotels. The chance nature of the encounter with Peter and Barbara, though, encouraged us to exchange contact information for Saigon, where we'd all be going later in the week.

In Saigon, then, the four of us had dinner one night and met for drinks another evening. During our second encounter, at an out of the way restaurant in a small alley, we also bumped into Dave, a British man whom we'd met in Nha Trang. Dave had a grown son, but was recently divorced and had quit his job in order to travel. He began his trip with six months in India and had planned to spend two years on the road. In the end, though, he didn't quite make it to the one-year mark, because he met a Swedish woman on the beach in Goa, India, and fell in love. So he was cutting his trip short in order to move to Sweden.

On and on the planet spins, like a giant multicultural tumbler.

Saigon—or, as it's officially named, Ho Chi Minh City—is a bigger, brasher version of Hanoi. There are obvious differences between North and South Vietnam, which became apparent as we traveled down the length of the country. The North has a more traditional, conservative culture, while Saigon is more commercial and the people are more direct. There are differences in history, geography and climate between the two regions, so it's not surprising there are also cultural variations. When one sees this up close, it's less confusing as to why the country once collapsed into a civil war.

Speaking of which, Saigon is perhaps the best place in the country to learn about the Vietnam War. It's not pleasant, but it's really not supposed to be. One day, we visited the War Remnants Museum (which used to be called the Museum of Chinese and American War Crimes until the name was toned down for the benefit of tourists). Along with the expected assortment of tanks and planes, there were numerous ghastly pictures of war victims: dead soldiers, dying villagers and the deformed victims of the Agent Orange defoliation efforts.

It was an unsettling feeling to be an American at that museum, particularly when an armless victim of the war tried to sell us postcards from a basket draped around his neck. Upon approaching us, he asked the question that all vendors ask in this country—"Where you from?"—but which had never before stopped us in our tracks as it did that afternoon.

Remarkably, though, there doesn't seem to be much animosity against the U.S. for the war, at least among the people we met. A large percentage of the population is younger than 30, so they have no memory of the fighting and simply want to move forward rather than reflect on the past. Almost everyone was friendly and not a single person expressed anything negative to us about America. Quite the opposite, in fact, as they were excited to meet foreigners in general, and Americans in particular. In Nha Trang, some locals even asked to have their picture taken with me on the beach.

Another afternoon, we made a half-day visit to the Cu Chi tunnels, north of Saigon. This nearly 100-mile underground network was dug in the 1940s for the war against the French colonial government and then expanded during the Vietnam War. Viet Cong soldiers hid and lived in a maze of passageways there, which extended several stories below ground in some places and incorporated sleeping rooms, kitchens, medical facilities and weapons storage areas. The entrances were so well hidden that the U.S. military was never very successful in preventing the surprise attacks that were staged from the tunnels and thus resorted to bombing and defoliating as much of the region as possible.

We took a guided tour of the area, which began with an English-language film about the war. Several decades old, it was a tattered black and white picture with muffled sound. The movie began with idyllic shots of adults picking fruit from trees and children skipping happily off to school. Then it suddenly switched to jarring shots of American war planes dropping bombs on these villages, before finally explaining the origin of the tunnels. I wrote down a few of the statements that I heard during the film:

- "Like a crazy bunch of devils" the Americans attacked villages, farms, schools, women and children, chickens, even Buddha statues.
- The local villagers stopped the mighty U.S. fighters by "using their own simple crafts of guerilla fighting."
- "The Americans wanted to turn Cu Chi into a dead village, but Cu Chi would never die."

Well, I couldn't begrudge the Vietnamese their propaganda. We *were* in Vietnam, after all, and this territory suffered a great deal from the bombing campaigns.

After the film, we were taken on a tour of the tunnels, with their narrow and well camouflaged entrances. The guides showed us jagged bamboo traps nearby that ensnared foreign soldiers, as well as bombs produced from recycled metals that were used in ambushing tanks. At the end, we were able to crawl through a 30-yard stretch of one of the passages. The opening was widened for tourists, but the experience was still awfully claustrophobic, as we crouched or crawled through a dim underground trail. The man in front of me was a large person and nearly panicked in the dark, confined space. Halfway through he wanted to get out, but there was a line of people behind him and he was forced to move forward on bended knee until he reached daylight.

The War Remnants Museum and the Cu-Chi tunnels certainly present a one-sided display of the Vietnam War. But the exhibits, whether they mean to or not, also offer a valuable awareness that transcends politics and history, for they poignantly drive home the point that war is hell, no matter the cause or the combatants.

Saigon is not all about the war, however. Far from it. It is an enthralling, energetic city that assaults the senses in the same way that Bangkok does. The dampness of the tropical heat clutches at your skin as you walk down the street through a clatter of blaring horns and buzzing engines. Exhaust haze hangs in the air and mingles with the smell of soups and meats being cooked along the sidewalk and with the scents of herbs and incense from a nearby market. Meanwhile, persistent vendors and street hawkers are always pushing goods in your face and endlessly repeating the same utterances.

"Hello, sir."

"Please, ma'am."

"Where you from?"

"What your name?"

Even the charming young girls who sell jewelry on nearly every corner, all of whom seem to be ten years old, have perfected the same lines.

"Happy hour, buy two bracelets, get one free."

Through it all, though, Saigon captivates. There is an agreeable ambiance there, amidst the curious mixture of new and old Vietnam, the remnants of colonial France, the visiting businesspeople who are drawn to an emerging market, and the independent travelers who want to see the country before it gets *too* discovered.

We spent hours drifting through the cacophonous streets and bazaars, or relaxing at the many cafés that have sprung up around town, particularly in the vicinity of Pham Ngu Lao Street, a prime congregating spot for backpackers. These cafés are where we met a number of other Asian wanderers, including Sarah from England, who had just spent seven weeks traveling by herself in China and had ventured overland to Vietnam; Steve, an American who hoped to be a documentary filmmaker and who carried a pocket-sized video camera with him through two months of adventures in Southeast Asia, and Nancy from Australia, who taught English for half a year in Thailand and now worked as a scuba diving instructor in Vietnam.

Here, we also indulged our newfound addiction to Vietnamese fruit shakes. These are still one of my favorite food memories from the country—banana shakes, pineapple shakes, mango shakes, papaya shakes. Even now, writing this, I want to return to Vietnam, sit at an open air café on a muggy morning, feel the early sun as it rises over the city, listen to the drone of motorbikes in the background, and sip a cold, fresh, creamy banana shake.

We actually had more of a chance to relax and drink fruit shakes than we'd originally planned, since we ended up extending our stay in Saigon after I came down with a virus. It began as just a sore throat, so I didn't think much of it at first. But then the throat pain became excruciating, to the point where I could barely swallow without moaning in agony. That was followed by mouth sores and blisters. Not one or two, but eight or ten, all over the inside of my lips and my palate. And then I awoke one morning with a rash on my chest, stomach and back, along with a fever.

Uhh, this can't be good, I thought.

These symptoms intensified the day before a scheduled bus trip to Phnom Penh, Cambodia, so we decided to stay in Saigon a while longer. At a local health clinic a French physician examined me and drew some blood, then diagnosed me with "hand, foot and mouth disease." It sounded alarming, but she said it was a common virus in the region.

"It's viral, so there's nothing I can give you for it. The worst of the symptoms will pass after four or five days," she said.

"So, this isn't like the hoof and mouth disease we hear about?"

"No, nothing of the sort. Just rest and drink fluids. You'll be fine."

At the outset, I at least thought it was a unique part of the traveling experience, that I'd contracted a Southeast Asian virus. But Dave, our new British acquaintance, reported that he'd once been diagnosed with the same illness in the U.K. Then a few friends from home emailed and told me their children had also come down with the ailment. So, really, all that happened is that I got sick in Vietnam. But with an exotic *sounding* virus, at least.

The symptoms did indeed subside after a few more days and there were actually some benefits to the down time. As I rested and caught up on my journal, I had a chance to reflect on our stay in Vietnam. It was easy to recall the stunning landscapes and the vivid blend of sounds, smells and tastes that had draped us in a cloak of memories. But I also found myself returning time and again to images of the many travelers we'd met.

Peter and Barbara. Elliott. Sarah. Dave. Nancy. Steve. The names and faces blended with those of individuals from our first journey. Kelly the American lawyer whom we befriended in Turkey, the Italian, French and Hong Kong travelers who endured an overnight bus ride with us to Cappadocia, Marco from Italy and Petra from Germany, who were traveling in Bali, and Yumiko and Hiroshi, the Japanese couple we met in Thailand.

This list is overwhelmingly Western, of course, which says something about who currently has the money and freedom to travel. But what struck me even more was that the majority of these individuals were not on a short vacation but in the midst of a longer journey. They were part of a subculture of people who thought nothing of taking off for several months on a shoestring budget, merely because they wanted to experience Asia, or another part of the planet. Like Walt Whitman, the 19th century poet, taking to the open road—"the world before me, the long brown path before me, leading wherever I choose"—there were countless independent travelers out there discovering the world.

What encouraged me about this was that a large number of people seemed to have a vibrant interest in life beyond their own borders. On the other hand, of course, there is also a parallel set of people who seem to evince no curiosity whatsoever about other cultures. Sadly, it appears that some individuals can even become leaders of countries while being part of the latter group.

These thoughts led me to Global Rule #5. *The world would be a saner place if more travelers went into politics.* Consider the different perspective government leaders would have if they'd spent months of their lives taking buses and trains through other countries, staying in local hotels and conversing with foreigners in bars and cafés. Envision a world where presidents and prime ministers had experience as private citizens wandering through Asia, Africa, Latin America or the Middle East simply because they found it interesting. Think of how their own personal experiences with different cultures, faiths and worldviews would influence policy discussions.

Ah, to dream.

"Eat Well, Grow Up, and Take Care of Family"

Although we did have more of a chance to relax and drink fruit shakes in Saigon after I came down with a virus, we unfortunately had to shorten our visit to Cambodia. Our intent had been to continue by bus to Phnom Penh, Siem Reap and then Bangkok before flying to India. Following the extra time in Vietnam, though, we reluctantly skipped southern Cambodia and traveled directly to Siem Reap so we could pick up our itinerary from there.

After having visited the Southeast Asian countries of Vietnam, Thailand and Bali, we were excited now to add Cambodia to our list, something that wouldn't have been quite so easy just a few years earlier. From the early 1970s into the mid-1990s, the nation was an unlikely tourist destination, as it endured a U.S. bombing campaign, a war against the Vietnamese, a civil war and the genocidal brutality of the Khmer Rouge regime. Today, though, peace has thankfully returned to the country and it's a fascinating, if occasionally disquieting, place to visit.

The Cambodians are a devout people and there is a certain spiritual charm that pervades the land. When we were there, the streets of Siem Reap teemed with monks, strolling through town in their orange robes and sandals. At various temples the monks would interact freely with visitors and answer questions about Buddhism or the monastic life. Cambodian Buddhism, in fact, seemed very much like what we'd experienced in Thailand. Perhaps for good reason, since Cambodia, Thailand and Laos were all historically affected by India and the traditions of Theravada Buddhism, whereas Vietnamese culture (which did not have the same palpable sense of faith) absorbed more influences from China.

We also found the Cambodian people to be open and sociable. Perhaps it was the elation of being at peace and of finally being able to welcome tourists into their country, but it seemed a genuine part of who they were. They greet visitors in the same gentle way the Thais do, which is to place their palms together at chest level and then bow slightly from the waist. This greeting (the *wai* in Thailand) is called a *sompiah* in Cambodia.

Additionally, there were enough captivating quirks about the country to make it obvious that we were in an alien and unfamiliar culture. We marveled, for instance, at the women who sold baskets of fried crickets, spiders and cockroaches by the side of the road. They apparently flavored the insects by putting a peanut in their bodies before frying. We also smiled at the incongruity of some cars being driven from the right side, while others were driven from the left. The traffic flowed along the right half of the road, but there was no pattern as to which side of the car the steering wheel was placed. If you're buying an automobile in Cambodia, apparently, you have to take what you can get.

As in Vietnam, we were also astonished by the dexterity of the motorbike drivers and the people and items they carried with them. I made a list of some of the more peculiar items we saw being transported around town by motorbike:

- A crate of chickens.
- A half-dozen pigs, tied upside down to the back of the bike.
- A piece of furniture strapped to the front.
- A large mirror, balanced between the driver and a second passenger.
- A bag of fish in water, hanging from a pole attached to the bike.

Then, of course, there was the one unique feature that interested only me. In Cambodia, I had my first experience spending Riels. Since the national currency is called the Riel, if you ever go to Cambodia you too can spend my last name.

On the other hand, not everything is gentle or delightfully different in Cambodia. The country has suffered greatly in recent decades and is quite poor compared to some of its neighbors. Thailand is the wealthiest nation in the region and Vietnam is making significant economic progress, but Cambodia and Laos lag further behind. This was evident just from wandering the streets of Siem Reap. The infrastructure was barely developed, there were few street lights, the roads were rough and scarred and the sidewalks were crumbling. The river, meanwhile, was a murky brown and there was trash and sewage floating in the water.

Equally distressing were the beggars, many of whom were amputees after having been victims of land mines. One evening, while having dinner at a restaurant in the center of town, Lisa and I sat on a second floor terrace and watched a particular one-legged individual silently but persistently hold out his hat for money. Wherever we went in the city, we were inundated by individuals who pleaded for cash. A few of the more enterprising ones would sell postcards and trinkets with a sign on their cart saying, "I decided to stop begging, please help support me." Whichever way you cut it, though, it's heartbreaking.

That night at the restaurant, after watching this person appeal for bits of change, Lisa went over and gave him a few small bills. As soon as she did so, several other people immediately descended on her and asked for assistance. So what to do? Does a single small donation really make a difference, we wondered, or does it perpetuate the cycle of begging? Are we giving these individuals a reason to not seek work, or merely recognizing that job opportunities (particularly for amputees) are severely limited in this impoverished economy? They asked for so little money compared to what we have that it seemed like an easy gesture to help a few people who were less fortunate. Then again, there were so many of them that it sometimes became overwhelming and we just began ignoring everyone.

The paucity of the local economy was also driven home to us by the way the tuk-tuk drivers would battle ferociously over small fares. One evening, leaving another restaurant, we were overwhelmed by at least ten drivers all vying for our business.

"I saw you first."

"You come with me."

"Sir, please."

"Ma'am, not fair. No go with him."

They encircled us and shouted for our business until we were finally seated and on our way. And what were they battling for? A $1 fare to our hotel. To be fair, it could have turned into more than that, since the drivers would often take customers on other days to local tourist attractions. But many times it was just for that $1 fare.

It was unsettling, frankly, to have individuals fighting so energetically for a dollar here and there, when we were thrilled that a multi-course restaurant dinner for two only cost us $10. What is more, although Lisa and I stayed in a locally owned budget hotel in Siem Reap because we had to keep expenses down for a longer journey, there was no shortage of five-star accommodations in the city. There aren't many greater contrasts between the Western and the developing worlds, since some of these high-end hotels, complete with luxurious bedding, spa services and gourmet meals, were literally situated next to rickety street stalls, unpaved roads and muddy fields.

We had a chance to put more of a human face on our Cambodian experience through some conversations with Jorani, a guide whom we hired for one of our visits to the Angkor temples.

One day, when she wasn't working, we invited Jorani to join us for lunch and she suggested that we eat at a small, family-run restaurant in town. We sat on bamboo chairs, at tables with pink and white checked tablecloths, next to maroon and gold walls that were decorated with artistic photographs of local scenes. The dish that I ordered, Khmer curry with fish, was the best meal I had in Siem Reap.

I was intrigued when part of our conversation with Jorani turned out to be remarkably similar to the one we'd had with Linh on the Halong Bay boat in Vietnam. That is, about the expectation that all women would get married and start a family by the time they were in their early 20s. As in Vietnam, the majority of married women in Cambodia did not work outside the home.

"When I begin work, I was the only woman in my class at tourism school," said Jorani. "And even now, there only five other female guides, I think, in Siem Reap."

Jorani had the same inner conflict that Linh did. She wanted to have a career but also recognized that she lived in a traditional society in terms of gender roles. Consequently, she was expected to choose between devoting herself to work or to family. That is, if it were even still possible for her to be married.

"I like to be married," said Jorani, "but I am 25, so I think maybe no one interested in me now. Men sometimes call me 'tough chicken' or 'left over food.'"

I was sad for Jorani, as I had been for Linh. I did realize, though, that the corollary to this, which she also noted, was that there is an evident value for the extended family in the Cambodian culture.

"Cambodians have three rules for life," she said. "Eat well, grow up, and take care of family."

Later, in talking about the way in which Cambodians viewed other countries, she suggested there was an historic dislike for both Vietnam and Thailand because of the battles between these three lands in centuries past. At the same time, she said there was much that Cambodia could learn from the Thais and Vietnamese because they were achieving an economic success that the Cambodians could at the moment only dream of.

She did say that Cambodians had a good view of the U.S., despite the bombing campaign of the 1970s because "we understand it was against the Vietnamese."

"The U.S. is a dream for most Cambodians," she said. "They think that in the U.S. everyone is rich and happy."

Of course, if my experience of Americans mostly consisted of seeing tourists eating gourmet meals in luxurious five-star hotels while outside local children ran barefoot in the mud, then I'd probably think that, too.

HINTS OF A VANISHED CIVILIZATION

In the forested terrain of northern Cambodia, the 800-year-old temple of Ta Prohm merges with the jungle. The snaky tentacles of giant roots embrace the moss-covered ruins, slithering into the crevices of giant pillars and twisting around ancient carvings. Meanwhile, enormous stones that have been dislodged by brawny tree limbs lie deserted in corridors and doorways. The trees have become one with the temple and, in an odd turn of events, now provide essential support for the very walls they have subjugated.

It is an eerie but strangely beautiful scene, particularly in the mornings when a blanket of mist throws an otherworldly haze over the foliage-draped architecture and one can see hints of a vanished civilization as it mingles with the enduring splendor of nature.

Ta Prohm is one of nearly 100 temples scattered across more than 200 square miles near Siem Reap. The most extravagant ones are clustered near the shores of Tonle Sap (Great Lake). These are relics of the Khmer civilization that ruled a large swath of Southeast Asia between the 9th and 15th centuries. With the demise of the empire, however, the once vital temples fell into disuse. The central shrine of Angkor Wat remained a pilgrimage spot, but most other structures were abandoned to the jungle until the mid-1800s, when they gained new attention from European explorers. Today, they are part of a World Heritage Site and are Cambodia's prime tourist attraction.

It was during our first morning at the Angkor Archaeological Park that Lisa and I explored Ta Prohm. The weather was so muggy we could practically lick the humidity out of the air, but we were almost too enthralled at first to notice our clothes sticking to our skin. Jorani was with us on this day and she pointed out some of the more interesting views and carvings while giving us a brief history of the site. It was built in the late 1100s as a temple and monastery, although she noted that today it may be most famous as one of the locations used in the 2001 film *Lara Croft: Tomb Raider*.

Later, we visited the huge compound of Angkor Thom, which for a while was the capital of the Khmer empire. It, too, was built in the late 12th century and was enclosed by a wall more than seven miles in length. Although many of the original wooden structures are gone, the main attraction is the former state temple of Bayon where, on an upper terrace, 54 large pillars of mysteriously smiling faces gaze down upon visitors. It is the Mona Lisa of Cambodia, carved in stone.

After visiting just these two sites, it was easy to be impressed by the achievements of the Khmer civilization. But they were merely a prelude for the most well known and spectacular Cambodian temple, Angkor Wat. Built in the first half of the 12th century, it's a marvel of design and is considered by many to be the largest religious structure in the world, although similar claims have been made for the Temple of Karnak in Luxor, Egypt, and for St. Peter's Basilica in Rome.

When approaching Angkor Wat, one first crosses a sandstone causeway that passes over a moat. Once through the entrance at the western gate, there is a quarter-mile walkway to the main structure. Along this path, the temple's central tower and four smaller towers loom over the landscape, giving the impression that one is walking ever closer to a range of hallowed mountains.

This design is intentional and embodies the geography of Hindu mythology, with the towers representing the peaks of Mt. Meru, home of the gods and the sacred center of the universe. The lower terraces and outer moat symbolize the surrounding land and ocean. This link to Hindu tradition is one of the unique characteristics of Angkor Wat. When it was constructed between 1113 and 1150, the Khmers were a Hindu empire. Some of the other shrines in the region, including Bayon and Ta Prohm, were built three to seven decades later and coincided with a conversion to Buddhism. Angkor Wat was thus later converted to a Buddhist temple, as well.

Near the front of the structure there is a small pond, and from here Angkor Wat casts an exquisite reflection in the shimmering water. Inside the main complex, there are three successive levels of terraces. At the top, an extremely steep set of worn stairs leads to the inner chamber. The precipitous ascent is meant to epitomize the difficulty of rising to the level of the gods.

Angkor Wat is a captivating temple, surrounded by the forest, awash in intricate carvings and topped by lotus-shaped towers that occasionally provide a glimpse of an orange-robed monk standing in an open doorway. While we were there, though, I couldn't help but wonder what sometimes happens to great civilizations. The Khmers once ruled the largest empire in Southeast Asia and the capital of Angkor at its peak served a population of about one million people. This was considerably larger than Paris, London and other European cities of the same period, so the civilization was evidently advanced for its time. Yet today Cambodia is a poor and developing nation.

I always find it fascinating to stand amidst the swirling, ghostly mists of ancient cities and to ruminate on the empires and peoples that have come before us. It's impossible not to wonder at these times about the ephemeral nature of our own societies. Over the course of centuries or millennia, after all, it's inevitable that life will evolve and that many of the ideas, faiths and even civilizations that we hold dear today will change or vanish.

Although the day we devoted to Angkor Wat, Ta Prohm and Bayon was the highlight of our temple explorations around Siem Reap, we did spend additional time exploring the region. We went back to Angkor Wat to see it in a different light and hired a tuk-tuk to take us to other local ruins. The best part of these other days, though, was our visit to Phnom Bakheng.

We actually did nothing more than join the daily spectacle there, since this temple is popular for its sunset views and usually attracts a large crowd. It's one of the oldest ruins in the area, having been constructed in the late 9th century. The temple has seven levels, which once held 108 towers. These numbers, of course, are not coincidental. The number 108 is sacred in the Hindu and Buddhist faiths, while seven is an important number throughout the world, as various spiritual traditions have promulgated a belief in the seven levels of heaven, the seven planes of existence or the seven chakras of the human body.

Late that afternoon, then, we joined the throngs of people who gathered at Phnom Bakheng. We followed a trail up a rocky hill, then climbed an almost vertical staircase. The view from the top was dramatic, and even more so when I found myself encircled by a half-dozen butterflies. I stood there silently, fascinated by the scene and trying to quietly appreciate its beauty. When dusk crept in we all sat down to face the setting sun, which burned in a blaze of colors over the pillars of this ancient temple.

As the day faded into a multihued twilight, I reflected on some of our other travel experiences in Southeast Asia. We'd found it to be a fascinating region, with historic temples, beautiful beaches, tasty foods and a distinct sense of spirituality. But as my mind skipped through Bali, Thailand, Vietnam and Cambodia, I also found myself reminiscing about the very first trip Lisa and I had taken together outside of North America.

By the time I met her, Lisa had already traveled extensively in the United States, with forays into Canada and Mexico. But she hadn't yet been to Europe, so we planned a trip to England, Scotland and France. The English and Scottish portion went well, but that was just a warm-up, for no matter how odd the Americans and Brits may sometimes appear to each other, the fact is we all speak English and share an Anglo culture.

Next on the agenda was Paris, which is a city people tend to love or hate. I myself have always loved Paris. I love the gardens, the wine, the public art, the chocolate croissants, the cafés, the walks along the Seine and the aroma of romance that seems to be on every corner. So with these thoughts of Paris waltzing in the air, I settled into a seat next to Lisa on a Chunnel train leaving London. As we left the British countryside and zeroed in on France, I could sense Lisa becoming quieter. As we approached the suburbs of Paris, she seemed ready to hyperventilate.

"What's wrong?" I asked. "You've traveled in Mexico before. We just left Great Britain. What's so scary about Paris?"

"It just seems so different," she said. "I'm afraid that I'll feel lost or won't be able to communicate with people."

Well, I thought, maybe she's not going to be a traveler, after all. But then my mind raced back to my own initial experience abroad. To that terrified uncertainty on my first day in Europe. And I understood. Thankfully, just a few days later, Lisa too fell in love with traveling. If I caught the travel bug in Bruges, she undoubtedly caught it in Paris.

Her epiphany seemed to come at lunch one day over a simple ham and cheese sandwich. "I don't get it," she said. "I've never had a sandwich that tasted so good. How do they do it?" That night at dinner, she had a mouth-watering meal in a neighborhood bistro. The next day, still more great meals, not to mention the pastries we snacked on in the afternoons.

"I think I love Paris!" she said.

Now, it oversimplifies things to say she just fell in love with the food. Not to mention that a Frenchperson may be horrified to know it was a mere sandwich that led to this epiphany. But the food is symbolic of what makes France so interesting. Lisa fell for the sensuousness and taste for pleasure that is as natural to the French as is breathing and which is difficult to duplicate outside of that country. Unless, that is, you happen to be in Italy.

With this trip as a springboard, Lisa wanted to travel more and I wasn't going to argue. We made other excursions during the next few years, but not enough to satisfy our wanderlust or interest in the world. There was, after all, a whole planet to discover.

Now, as I recalled our journey from that first European trip to this day in Cambodia seven years later, it almost seemed as if Lisa and I had become different people. Our perspectives about life had evolved and ripened, we were more at home in the world, travel was less frightening and we had gained confidence in our ability to handle unexpected situations. Obviously, everyone reading this can also look back in amazement at the different, more innocent person they were five or ten years earlier. But the particular manner in which we've all evolved is a result of our own distinct experiences.

And so, sitting amidst the dormant ruins of an 1,100-year-old Cambodian temple, I arrived at Life Lesson #5. *We are all engaged in a never-ending process of becoming, but the way in which we grow depends on the life experiences we select for ourselves.* No one's life is static and we are all perpetually evolving, whether we are trying to or not. So if we want to be better, more confident, more interesting people in the future, then we need to choose worthwhile experiences in the present.

The Journey to India

Some travel days are just more interesting than others.

When it was time to leave Cambodia, we needed to go from Siem Reap to Bangkok in order to catch a pre-booked flight to Calcutta, India. We had two options—$170 per person for a flight or $11 per person for a bus. We weren't thrilled about denting our budget by $340 for a one-hour flight, so the $22 option was an easy choice. This involved taking a minibus out of Siem Reap ("very comfortable and air conditioned," said the ticket agent) and then transferring to a bigger bus at the border for the journey to Bangkok.

The vehicle that picked us up at 7:30 a.m. had room for 21 people, which included some flimsy fold-down seats in the aisles. Luckily, we were two of the first people aboard and settled into a standard seat. The cover was a worn and tattered piece of vinyl, but the cushion was at least sturdy. Astonishingly, by the time we left town we'd loaded 22 passengers into this 21-seat vehicle, not to mention luggage, which was piled in whatever empty space remained. The final passenger, one of the bus company employees, sat on top of a pile of suitcases and backpacks between some seats.

Needless to say, we had little leg room and there was no easy way to exit in case of emergency. But it was cozy and we had a place to sit, so as we set off down a paved road out of Siem Reap it seemed that we could handle the ride for a few hours.

Or at least for 30 minutes.

That's how long it took to leave the pavement for a dirt road. A bone-jarring, jaw-shaking, "please God make it stop" kind of dirt road, which we then traveled on for three-and-a-half hours.

At a rest stop along the way, we disembarked at a village that encompassed one small store and a few wooden huts on stilts. When I exited the minibus, a young girl, perhaps eight or ten years old, approached and asked me my name and where I was from. She said her name was Jae, and she tied a bracelet to my wrist.

"No," I said. "No buy, no money." Which was partly true, in fact, since I had no small bills in my wallet other than a U.S. dollar.

"Free," she said.

Then Lisa came over. "Your girlfriend?" she asked.

"My wife."

She smiled. "Nice."

She asked me to buy some postcards from her.

"I no money for school, so I sell postcards for school money," she said.

My heart broke. She was obviously skilled in working the passing travelers, but she also seemed somehow more real than many of the kids we usually ran into selling items to tourists. Since I had nothing small in Cambodian currency, I gave her the $1 U.S. and she handed over a few postcards. She never did ask for money for the bracelet. When I left, she shook my hand.

"Nice to meet you," she said.

It was the sweetest moment of the day.

Later, we stopped for lunch at a lonely restaurant in rural northern Cambodia. Lisa and I ordered big, flavorful plates of rice and vegetables and I used the equivalent of a $6 bill to pay for lunch, which was the smallest piece of cash in my wallet. The waitress whistled because the bill was so large. As we ate, some of the staff laughed at a television show filled with young actors who spent all their time in trendy clubs and cafés. I couldn't help but notice the contrast between the scene on television and that around us, as we sat at splintering wooden tables in an open air restaurant with cattle wandering around an adjacent field and people working in a rice paddy across the street. At least, I thought, we were seeing a fleeting glimpse of the Cambodia that exists beyond the tourist brochures.

When we finally made it back to a paved highway, our shaken and stirred bodies breathed a sigh of relief. For a second or two, at least. Our driver screeched to a stop within a few feet of reaching the pavement, turned off the air conditioning and opened all the windows. Hmmm. Very comfortable and air conditioned, eh? Well, I suppose the ticket agent never promised the air conditioning would be on for the entire ride.

I tried to look on the bright side. We'd get some fresh air, it seemed, and the breeze would make up for the loss of air conditioning. Which would have been true, had we been driving down a quiet country lane. But we had now joined a well-traveled road, which meant that stomach-turning fumes from creaky old vehicles began pouring in through the open windows. The smell of exhaust was a real treat when mixed with the dust and sweat that were also accumulating within our cramped little minibus. And the paved road? Actually, it was a pothole-filled adventure, with the driver constantly swerving to miss the worst obstacles.

We finally made it to the border checkpoint at Poipet at 1:30 p.m. We unloaded our luggage and dragged our bags about one-half mile, through the Cambodian and Thai immigration windows, down a street for a few blocks and finally to a café on the other side of the border where we were met again by the bus company. We were told to sit and relax. The next bus would pick us up in 20 minutes.

More than an hour later, someone pointed us in the direction of a flatbed truck.

You're freaking kidding me, right?

No, no, they said. Only ten minutes to where bus is. Really.

So we all loaded onto benches on the back of this truck, with luggage piled at our feet and the sun beating down on our necks, and set off once more.

"I'm sure this will be a good story one day," I sighed.

Ten minutes later, they dropped us off again. This time, it was true—a real, 45-seat bus awaited us. Comfortable, cloth seats. Leg room. A toilet. And when we began driving to Bangkok, the roads were paved and smooth.

"Oh, I love Thailand," said a German girl in the next seat.

It was a remarkable contrast. Although we knew that Cambodia was mired decades behind Thailand in development terms, it was still startling how evident that gap was when crossing the border by land. It was also amazing to realize that a plane covered this same ground in one hour. Certainly, it's something to remember whenever I fly. The ease and comfort of air travel, yes, but even more so the sights and complexities of the world on the ground that zoom by unseen from the air.

The travel day itself was far from over, but everything else was a relative breeze. Four hours later, we were in Bangkok. We didn't even care anymore that we were dropped off in a different location than what we were originally told. We dragged our luggage through the humid streets of nighttime Bangkok for a while, hoping to find a local restaurant at which to eat some pad thai. After 15 minutes of walking, though, we gave in to the heat and the fatigue. We hailed a taxi.

"Airport, please."

There, we changed clothes in the bathroom, got some dinner at a food court, and finally went to the boarding area for an 11:40 p.m. flight to Calcutta. The scene there was mildly chaotic, as the Thai airline staff tried to steer everyone into a single file row for check-in, while dozens of Indian passengers stood three or four abreast, formed random lines and moved about arbitrarily.

"One line! One line!" yelled one of the female Thai flight attendants. "What's the matter, you don't understand English?"

I was startled to hear a Thai woman shout, particularly in English. Apparently, though, she had been through this before, as we would quickly discover there is rarely such a thing as an organized line in India.

We landed sometime after 1 a.m. and were soon in a car, being driven to our lodging place. Somehow, it seemed like an illusion. Eighteen hours earlier, we'd left our hotel in Siem Reap, then endured a long journey to Bangkok by minibus,

bus and flatbed truck, and now we watched as blurry reflections from the streets of Calcutta flashed past our window in the dark.

India

IMPRESSIONS OF CALCUTTA

"You'll love India."
"You'll hate it."
"India is only for advanced travelers."
"India is a breeze—it's not as bad as people make it out to be."

We'd heard it all. And, what's more, it's all true. India is every good thing that you've ever heard, and it's every bad thing that you've ever heard. The country is a mind-altering drug that will challenge the perceptions of anyone who thinks they understand life on this planet.

Lisa and I were excited to begin our Indian explorations in Calcutta, partly because we had a friend, Kate, who was an expatriate there. I first met Kate in the 1980s and she had since gone on to do a lot of international work. She happened to be based in Calcutta, the capital of the Indian state of West Bengal, when Lisa and I were passing through.

So, it was through Kate—and her driver, Vijay—that we received our introduction to India. We spent a few evenings and a weekend day with her and it was enjoyable to catch up with a friend while easing our way into the culture. We also benefited from being with Vijay during some of our weekdays in town. He talked to us about India and cheerfully drove us to several of the city's sights, including the Victoria Memorial, Marble Palace, Botanical Gardens and Pareshnath Jain Temple.

But Calcutta, we soon learned, wasn't about tourist attractions. It was about impressions. Almost everywhere we went in the city, the images kept slapping us in the face, yanking us from one extreme to the other.

First, and most obviously, the poverty is inescapable because it is so visible. As we traveled through the city, it was impossible not to notice the throngs of impoverished residents who slept on sidewalks. The people who bathed on street corners with a bucket of water and soap. The dilapidated, barely standing shacks that passed as homes. The men who urinated in plain sight against walls or in gutters. Or the heaps of rotting garbage on the side of the roads, some of it being eaten by dogs and birds.

But then, in the midst of this we walked into a sparkling, contemporary shopping mall that made us recalibrate our image of the city. Inside, fashionably dressed Indians shopped at Benetton and Levis, snacked on ice cream from Baskin Robbins ("vegetarian ice cream") and enjoyed Bollywood and Hollywood movies in a brand new theater.

The second notable impression of Calcutta was the sense that it existed in a perpetual state of movement, noise and confusion. Nowhere was this more evident than in the city's bewildering array of traffic patterns.

"Driving is not disciplined here," said Vijay, on our first day.

Actually, the driving was more like barely controlled pandemonium. There were no traffic lanes, every vehicle relentlessly strove to nose ahead of every other vehicle, and cars drove within inches of each other and squeezed into miraculously narrow spaces. I can't count the times I braced myself for the crunch of crashing metal, only to open my eyes and discover that no collision had occurred.

But again, just when we thought the city was in complete bedlam, we would see two women parading serenely down the sidewalk in stunning maroon and gold saris. Or a group of schoolchildren giggling contentedly on their way home from school. Or, most unexpectedly, a man sitting cross-legged on the sidewalk, silently lost in his thoughts and enigmatically pounding away on a manual typewriter. An unusual sight perhaps, but he was at peace amidst the commotion.

Finally, visitors to Calcutta must deal with the clamor of the streets. The sidewalks are a place of business for people who spend their days concocting novel ways to extract rupees from passersby. We were continually approached by locals asking for a tip or a payment. Some wanted to be paid for leading us on an unsolicited tour, or for providing directions, or even for taking our picture. I couldn't blame them, really, since there simply isn't enough work for the immense population and this is one way to make a living or supplement a meager income.

Nonetheless, it does take some getting used to, at least for a Westerner who is accustomed to having a zone of privacy on the street. At one market we went to, a young man offered to lead us to shops and carry around our purchases in a basket. A nice offer, maybe, but we politely declined his assistance. So he followed us anyway. For 40 minutes he walked alongside us and talked nonstop, telling us about products that were available in the various stores. We tried everything to deter him. We courteously told him that we were only looking and not buying, we sternly told him to get lost, and we even succeeded once in ditching him in a crowd, only to have him pop back in front of us like a jack-in-the-box two minutes later. Finally we just left.

When he saw us departing, he said, "Maybe tomorrow I help you."

And yet, just when we began thinking that perhaps everyone in Calcutta made a living by wringing tips from visitors, we'd walk into an internet café overflowing with young Indians doing schoolwork. Or see well-dressed businessmen talking shop in a café. Or find a dozen locals browsing in a bookstore.

It was all just part of the Indian paradox. Every impression had two sides. There was uplifting spirituality and abject poverty, technological know-how and confounding disorder, vivid beauty and dreadful filth, and all of it was blended together in a staggering mass of humanity. Ultimately it was this—the paradox of Calcutta, and of India—that made the strongest impression on us.

One night, we went out to dinner with Kate at a local Bengali restaurant. Located on a narrow side street, the eatery had a cozy dining area in a converted garage. The house specialty was *thalis*, or combination platters of different dishes, which were served in little bowls around a large serving of rice.

A lot of our conversation that night was spent just catching up and talking about our lives. But we also discussed India for a while and I told Kate that what most astonished me were the extremes that we saw.

"This is our first stop in India, but already it seems like no place else I've ever been. It almost seems illogical at times that such variations of poverty and wealth, or bedlam and serenity, can exist in such close quarters."

"When people first come here, it can be really shocking," said Kate. "But after a while I think you almost don't notice it. I'm not sure if that's always a good thing, but eventually it just becomes part of the nature of the city."

"I guess it's the sense of contradiction that mystifies me. That there can be such overwhelming poverty, but there also seems to be a pretty decent middle class here too, isn't there?

"Yes. It's easy to see the poverty on the streets and miss everything else here, but the Bengali culture is actually very interesting. There is a lot of focus on literature and the arts. And learning is also a big part of it. The Bengali people put a lot of effort into educating their children."

"Do you ever get used to the paradoxes or the sense of chaos here?"

"This is not a place where you're necessarily going to feel in control," said Kate. "Once you get used to that, and get used to the chaos, then you find yourself just going with the flow."

As the meal neared its end, our waiter brought out a small dish with *paan*, an Indian digestive. It contains ground betel nuts blended with a variety of spices, such as mint, cardamom and clove, all wrapped in a green leaf. The betel nut is a mild stimulant, sort of like caffeine, and is also supposed to be a breath freshener.

"Oh, you should try this while you're in India," said Kate. "It's a cultural experience."

"What do I do?"

"Just put the whole thing in your mouth and chew slowly. That allows the juices to escape. It's very popular to chew this after meals."

So I tried it. It did have somewhat of a minty flavor, but also a tinge of what I can only describe as soap. No doubt, it's an acquired taste. But then again, the same could be said of India. I was certainly curious about how the next few weeks of our journey would unfold and to see if we'd be in the country long enough to reach the point that Kate described, where we would find ourselves just going with the flow.

MOTHER TERESA AND TAXI DRIVERS

One other thing we did while in Calcutta was to visit the Mother Teresa House. It was only for part of an afternoon and so we can't claim credit for doing any real work there, unlike the selfless volunteers who spend weeks or months at the Missionaries of Charity homes. But it was nevertheless a moving and instructive visit.

At the Mother House, the chipped wooden sign at the front entrance still reads "Mother Teresa, In," though she died in 1997. Within the simple walls, nuns dressed in blue and white go about their work, while in a small room decorated with plants and candles Mother Teresa is buried. Her tombstone is inscribed with the credo that Jesus spoke to his disciples: "Love one another as I have loved you."

Attached to this building is an orphanage for 300 children, similar to dozens of homes throughout India and the world. The Missionaries of Charity now oversee 4,000 nuns in more than 100 countries who care for children, refugees, AIDS victims, lepers, the handicapped and the dying. In Calcutta alone, there are 19 such facilities.

Lisa and I first visited a ward for malnourished children and another one for the mentally and physically handicapped. We watched the nuns wander from bed to bed, tending to wounds or providing drinks of water. Later, in the orphanage, we played with some of the kids. We were especially struck by those children who latched onto us and just wanted to be hugged or rocked back and forth in our lap.

"They really seem to crave being touched and held," said Lisa. "But at the same time many of them are laughing or smiling. It's as if they're just so happy that they're finally receiving affection."

Indeed, one of the primary tasks of volunteers at these homes and orphanages is merely to spend time with the children or with the sick, to let people know they are loved. If there is ever any doubt about this goal, one need only return to the Mother House and re-read the clear-cut inscription on Mother Teresa's tombstone.

These homes, interestingly, are both beloved and disparaged by Calcutta residents. Mother Teresa is an iconic figure who has inspired awe and respect, but there are also those who fear that part of her legacy has been to scare off tourists who only know about Calcutta through images of the destitute and the dying. That's understandable, I suppose, since there is certainly more to the city than the poverty. But I did come away from this visit with tremendous respect for those nuns who have devoted their lives to providing shelter and care to people who have been abandoned by society.

In the end, it left us with one more lasting impression of Calcutta. This one, though, was of gentleness, compassion and unconditional love.

When it was time to depart Calcutta, we booked a ten-hour train journey to Varanasi. Outside, the day was stiflingly hot, but aboard the train we had to huddle under blankets for protection from an air conditioning unit that blew a non-stop stream of arctic air at us. Whenever we went to use the toilet or get a drink, we were drenched by the hot, muggy weather that poured into the train corridors, only to return and shiver in an icy seating compartment. Yet another Indian paradox, I suppose.

To keep my mind off the chill, I focused on vistas of the countryside that flickered past our window. Rural towns crisscrossed by dusty lanes. Farm workers dressed in white robes sweating through their labor in the mid-day heat. Skinny cows grazing slowly under the hot sun in thin fields of grass. And, at the passing stations, travelers who somehow slept on lightweight blankets laid out on the concrete platforms as trains whizzed past.

As I stared at the scenery, I also reflected on the vastness of the subcontinent. Lisa and I were unfortunately only going to see a fraction of India during our time here. When we mapped out this particular journey we decided to spend our time in Calcutta, the pilgrimage city of Varanasi, the national capital of Delhi, the Taj Mahal city of Agra, and finally the region of Ladakh in the Indian Himalayas. There was a lot we'd miss—the captivating desert towns of Rajasthan, the cities of Bangalore and Mumbai, the southern beaches of Goa and Kerala, and the hill towns of Darjeeling and Dharamsala. But unless we had six months to devote solely to India, choices had to be made.

Once we arrived at Varanasi in the evening, we found ourselves inexplicably caught in a train station scuffle. Two taxi drivers simultaneously spotted us disembarking, so they both rushed up and offered their services. Since there was no obvious way to determine which one was there first, they began to bad mouth each other.

"He not reliable."

"He cheat you."

They almost came to blows over our fare, while a few locals joined in and vocally urged us to go with one driver or the other.

"He better driver."

"No, he more honest."

India. We were only one-quarter of the way through our visit to the country, but already we were astounded by the surrealism of the place. Mother Teresa on the one hand, and taxi drivers fighting over our fare on the other. Finally, we just pointed to one of the men and set off for our hotel, wondering what awaited us now in Varanasi.

Morning Light on the Ganges

It was five o'clock in the morning. The gray sky was turning gold at the edges as the sun prepared to rouse another day. We sat silently and listened to the squeaky wheel of our rickshaw as it spun along the dusty street, to the shuffling of cows as they meandered along the road and to the rustle of pots and the opening of windows as a neighborhood stirred. We were disoriented in the maze of this ancient city, watching in bewilderment as our driver twisted and turned down increasingly narrow, bumpy lanes.

The rickshaw finally stopped and we got out. Our driver pointed to what looked like an alley between two buildings. We entered it warily, but soon emerged from the shadows of the labyrinth to find ourselves at daybreak standing atop one of the ghats that overlook the Ganges River, gazing at one of the oldest and most dramatic panoramas known to man.

The sun was just emerging over the curvature of the earth and the early rays painted the water with an ethereal, silvery-orange glow. As the light rose, it imbued everything with radiance. The temples and pale pink buildings that lined the Ganges and reflected back into the shimmering waters. The weathered stone steps of the ghats. The musty row boats that bobbed in the water. The vivid red, green, blue, orange and purple saris of the Indian pilgrims on their way to bathe in the river. The vermilion dots on women's foreheads. As I took it all in, little chills slid up my spine.

This luminosity has been renowned for millennia. Varanasi was once known as Kashi, or City of Light, and is believed to be the oldest continually inhabited city in the world with a past that stretches back at least 3,000 years. Mark Twain alluded to this when, on a lecture tour in the late 1800s, he said the place was "older than history, older than tradition, older even than legend, and looks twice as old as all of them put together."

This is one of the most quoted lines about Varanasi, but Twain also made other interesting observations about the city, which was then known as Benares. When describing its spirituality, for instance, he wrote:

"Benares is a religious Vesuvius. In its bowels the theological forces have been heaving and tossing, rumbling, thundering and quaking, boiling and weltering and flaming and smoking for ages."

This is not only a typically humorous Twain line but it's also a fitting portrayal of Varanasi, whose vortex of energies has weaved extraordinary ties to several of the world's great religions.

Most prominently, according to Hindu legend, the city was founded by the god Shiva. A popular tale suggests that when the Ganges rolled down to the earth from the heavens, the impact had to be borne by Shiva, who cushioned the force by letting the water flow through his matted hair. Shiva then came to live on the banks of this river and a city was born.

Varanasi also has a celebrated bond to Buddhism, for it was at nearby Sarnath in the 6th century B.C. that the Buddha delivered his first sermon to disciples. This is one of four pilgrimage sites associated with the Buddha's life, along with the cities where he was born, gained enlightenment and died. A stupa marks the site in Deer Park where he first expounded on Buddhist philosophy. It is situated within pleasant grounds that contain a bodhi tree reputed to be a descendant of the tree under which the great teacher first reached enlightenment.

There are additional ties to Jainism and Islam, but even more fascinating is the theory, believed by many Indians, that Jesus spent some of his so-called lost years in India, both at Varanasi and in the Himalayas. Add it all up and it's obvious that Twain was on to something when he wrote that the sacred forces of Varanasi have been seething since the dawn of time.

The most striking scenes in the city are those of the Hindu pilgrims who come to bathe in the holy waters of the Ganges. Every day before dawn, thousands of people make their way to one of the city's 100 or so ghats and clamber down steep steps to the shore. Then, as the sun rises in the East, they bathe in the river to cleanse their souls and wash away sins.

At this time of day, numerous small boats stand ready to ferry visitors along the river. So, after arriving at the Dasashwamedh Ghat, Lisa and I made arrangements for a one-hour trip with one of these boat owners. Dasashwamedh is a popular bathing spot since it is centrally located and is one of the five most sacred ghats in the city. If possible, pilgrims try to bathe at each of these sites in order to complete a route called the Panchatirthi Yatra.

Before we boarded our ride, a young boy approached us, selling small bowls shaped from dry leaves which held candles in a bed of orange marigold flowers. The tradition is to light and then release these into the Ganges. At sunrise, the water shimmers with dozens of floating candles, tiny flames of prayer drifting heavenward.

As our long, thin rowboat silently plied the sacred river, we watched as hundreds of people bathed and prayed along the water's edge. Soothing music drifted over the scene from loudspeakers along the ghats. Men stripped down to loincloths or underwear and women dunked themselves while dressed in a full sari. A few individuals ritually poured water on themselves from a silver pot, brushed their teeth or even drank the water. Some openly prayed while standing in the river. Others sat silently and meditated under the rising sun. One elderly gentleman, adorned with a white beard and dressed in a white loincloth, was intently engaged in a series of yoga poses.

Then, about 15 minutes into our journey, the view changed. "Cremation," said our oarsman, nodding in the direction of the shore.

There, lying atop a simple wooden funeral pyre, was a body wrapped in a red robe. It was being watched over by family members. We had evidently reached one of the two burning ghats, Manikarnika and Harishchandra, that are used for cremations.

It is a Hindu belief that to die at Varanasi allows the soul to achieve *moksha*, or a release from the cycle of birth and rebirth. Some suggest that Shiva still resides in the area and whispers into the ears of people at the moment of death. Hence, thousands of Indians journey to Varanasi at the end of their life in order to die in this sacred city. There are hospices in the old town specifically to serve these individuals and several hundred people are cremated each day along the shores of the Ganges.

The tradition is for the corpse to be carried from the city down to the river, where it is immersed in the waters one final time. The body is later placed atop the pyre, where the cremation is attended to by a caste of people called the Doms. As we floated slowly past the ghat, a man used a torch to light a fire beneath the body. Half an hour later, on our return journey, we saw a flame and a plume of smoke rising from the same spot.

It struck me how natural it all seemed. People are born, they live, they die. Indian families grieve and mourn as much as anyone else in the world, but they also seem to better accept death as part of the life cycle. In Varanasi, perhaps, this is even more accentuated, if only because death and faith are such public acts.

Praying, bathing, and dying. In Varanasi, the rituals of life are conducted out in the open, for all to see.

Two Aspects of the Same Reality

If Varanasi were all about the rituals of faith, it would be a can't miss city. But there is another, less attractive side to the place, which makes it somewhat more of a challenge than your average tourist destination.

The most obvious downside is the city's uncleanliness. It's not that other Indian towns are paragons of spotlessness, but Varanasi is still a cut below. The biggest source of problems, ironically, is the Ganges River itself. Not only do hundreds of people bathe there everyday, but sewage flows into the water from open pipes, the ashes and unburned bones of cremated bodies are thrown in, and families who don't have enough money for cremation sometimes just opt for a river burial. It's not uncommon, apparently, to see a corpse floating in the water.

After our boat trip, Lisa and I walked along the ghats that line the Ganges. It was impossible to avoid the putrid whiffs of raw sewage, urine and feces that hung in the air. Yet, just feet away, people bathed in, fished in and drank from the river. These individuals were apparently so absorbed in their faith that they were oblivious to the pollution and filth. Or perhaps it's because they had such immense faith to begin with, since many Hindus believe that the Ganges purifies whatever it touches. Scientists, however, tell a different story and tests indicate that the levels of coliform bacteria in the water are several *thousand* times higher than what any health organization considers acceptable.

Needless to say, we didn't have much of an urge to bathe in the river ourselves. One local man, however, did threaten to toss Lisa into the Ganges.

The incident began innocently enough, when I took a photo of her standing along the walkway atop one of the ghats. There happened to be a group of five women coming down a staircase in the distance behind her. A few minutes after I snapped the picture, a young man approached us, appearing very polite and concerned.

"Excuse me, sir. The women you take photo of, they are on way to cremation. You know it not allowed to take cremation photos here."

"Actually, I just took a picture of my wife."

"But there are women going to cremation. This very upsetting to family. Some Japanese tourists here last month, they take cremation photos and end up in jail for one month."

"But there is no cremation taking place anywhere near here, so how could I be taking photos of a cremation?"

"You should not take these pictures. I tell you this so police don't arrest you."

The conversation seemed a bit ridiculous. Tourists are understandably asked not to take pictures of cremation ceremonies, but this was hardly a case of me photographing a dead body while the family mourned. We were not close to either of the burning ghats and, in any case, people on their way to a cremation tend to follow the corpse there, which these women were clearly not doing. Something was obviously up, which is even more apparent now when I look at the photo and can see that the women were carrying purses and plastic shopping bags. At the time, though, I decided not to push the issue. I politely thanked the man for his concern and promised to be more careful.

"You welcome," he replied. "Now, it good if you give me donation for family."

"What?"

"You give me donation, then I don't call police."

"You want me to pay you so you don't call the police? Are you going to report me for taking a picture of my wife?"

"You think this not serious, but it is." Now he raised his voice, trying to scare us by attracting attention. "What you do is illegal! You want to go to jail?"

At this point, Lisa chuckled slightly. The ridiculousness of it all was too much.

"This not funny!" he screamed. "You think this funny? I throw you in river! That not good for you. Then you see if it funny!"

OK, I'd had enough. I shoved a ten rupee bill in his hand, about 25 cents.

"You must give more. This not joke, you know. I call police on you."

"Fine, call the police," I said.

After this, we decided it was time to get away from the ghats and so we headed to the streets of the old town. There, we thought, we could shop, we could eat, or we could simply wander and soak in the ancient atmosphere of Varanasi.

Or, we could dive headlong into a circus.

In the gritty, twisting streets of the old town, we wandered through a fantastic montage of cars, buses, trucks, rickshaws, bicycles, people, flowers, jewelry, fruit, vegetables, cows, donkeys, dogs, weeks-old garbage, men bathing, children playing, men urinating and dogs defecating. As we strolled, we were followed and pestered incessantly by rickshaw drivers, touts for local businesses and homeless beggars. On one street, a man holding a snake in his hands appeared out of the corners and asked us for money. Nearby, a drifter with gangrene hands waved black fingers in our faces.

Then a seemingly affable man befriended us as we walked.

"Where you from?" he asked.

"America."

"Ah, America," he smiled broadly. "Welcome to my country, my friend! I am Rajeev."

"Nice to meet you, Rajeev. My name is Bob."

Finally, a glimpse of sanity.

I reached out to shake his hand and was surprised when he didn't let go. So I squeezed his palm again. When I relaxed my grip for a second time, however, he still didn't release me. In a flash, then, he switched his grasp to my forearm and began squeezing, as if he were going to cut off circulation to my right hand.

"I give good massage," he said.

He began massaging my forearm with something approaching a death grip. I yanked on my arm but couldn't release it from his hold.

"No, thank you," I said. "No massage."

"No? What about shave then? I also barber."

"Uh, no. No shave, either."

Finally, with a mighty tug, I was able to forcibly remove myself from his clench.

"OK, maybe later then," he said, and walked away.

Or maybe not.

Ultimately, I decided that I loved Varanasi and I detested Varanasi. Part of me wanted to spend more time there and absorb its spirituality and part of me never wanted to see the place again. It was ironic, I thought, that this grimy, polluted, chaotic setting was also one of the most sacred cities in the world. A dwelling place of Shiva, one of the Hindu trinity of Gods, and a spot where the soul is believed to instantly dissolve the bonds that join it to the cycle of birth, death and rebirth.

Once again, though, this is simply the contradiction that pervades India. In Varanasi, a sense of holiness and a sense of madness exist, even thrive, side by side. They are two aspects of the same reality.

Perfect Symmetry

When we, as travelers, enter a new country for the first time it is usually with some amount of anxiety. Stepping off a plane or crossing a border, we wonder about the first person we're going to meet, the first taxi or bus ride we're going to experience, or the first cultural blunder we're going to make. But eventually we're able to reach a minimal level of comfort, as the surroundings quickly become more familiar and the customs more identifiable. At that point, our confidence level rises and we slowly exhale.

In a country that has strong similarities to our own, this level of comfort can be reached within hours. In a more unfamiliar culture, it will take days. In India, I'd venture to say that many travelers spend weeks finding their bearings. The place is simply unlike any other nation in the world.

By the time Lisa and I reached Delhi we may not have been exhaling quite yet but the culture was at least more recognizable to us. We traveled to the Indian capital primarily for its flight connections and proximity to the Taj Mahal, but were still rather pleased with the time we spent in the area. It was no less chaotic than the rest of India, but we did manage to walk the streets and interact with locals without constantly looking over our shoulders or wondering what was around the next corner.

One day, we roamed the markets of Delhi and had some nice exchanges with store owners and artisans. We bought a tapestry from a woman who sold her wares from the sidewalk and a small sculpture of Shiva from a genial merchant who took time to explain to us the Hindu mythology behind various carvings in his shop. Admittedly, we did later have to sidestep a scam set up by an enterprising young man on the street, but that was par for the course by this point in our travels regardless of the country we were in.

This particular episode took place when we stopped to pull out an umbrella during a summer shower. Vikram walked up to us and joked about the weather, asked where we were from and acted like an all around good guy. He was well dressed and well spoken.

"You are heading to the market that is two blocks ahead? Yes, it is a popular place. Unfortunately, I am very sorry to tell you this, but there is a big labor strike today so that market is closed."

It sounded fishy, but we did once have a long bus trip in Peru delayed because of a strike, so it does happen.

"I am a journalist—see my identification card—so I would never lie to you. I am from Delhi and want foreigners to enjoy the city as much as I do."

Well, he seemed honest enough.

"There is actually another market that perhaps you should visit instead. It is further away, but for me I think it is better. Let me show you on a map where this other market is."

Now it sounded suspicious again.

We couldn't fully bring ourselves to believe him, but it did cross my mind that perhaps, just maybe, there was an iota of a chance he was legitimately telling the truth. Until …

"Oh, look, here is a taxi. It's pulling up next to us. I will tell the driver where you want to go."

Uh, huh.

See ya.

As we walked away, I wondered if he had learned his lines in the same place as the suit in Bangkok who tried this identical ploy with us outside of the Grand Palace.

Once you've been in India for a while, the country starts to lose its ability to shock. Cows wandering through the middle of a busy intersection in the nation's capital? Yawn. Men urinating in the street? Been there. Cruising down the wrong side of a two-lane highway, with our driver honking at the truck coming straight toward us? Didn't really *need* to go there again. Dancing bears asking for tips at a roadside toll booth? Well, OK, that was a new one.

We saw the dancing bears on a day trip to the city of Agra. Our driver stopped to pay a road tax when he crossed into the state of Uttar Pradesh and, as we sat in the vehicle and awaited his return, dancing bears suddenly appeared at our window. Really. Dancing bears! Who knew there were so many ways to rummage for tips on the street?

Thankfully, we soon left the bears in our rear view mirror and continued on to Agra, whose historic sights are the jewel in India's long list of tourist attractions. Frankly, Agra itself is a pigsty. But once we made it past the cow dung, the piles of trash, the smell of human waste, the incessant dust, the goats, the barking dogs, the performing monkeys, and the legless beggar who crawled to our vehicle and tapped on the window, well, the monuments and ruins of Agra were utterly stunning.

We began by visiting the ghostly ruins of Fatehpur Sikri, a 16th century capital of India's Mughal Empire, and the impressive red sandstone Agra Fort. But the main attraction, of course, is the Taj Mahal. The history of this magnificent structure has been told many times, but it's still heartrending to reflect that it was built by the Emperor Shah Jahan as a mausoleum for his wife, Mumtaz Mahal, who died in childbirth. It was said at the time that the emperor was so grief stricken his beard turned white almost immediately.

Construction of the complex took place between 1631 and 1653, using the labor of 20,000 workers. Ironically, shortly after its completion an ill Shah Jahan was deposed by his son, Aurangzeb, and was imprisoned at Agra Fort. There, held captive in an octagonal tower with a view across the Yamuna River to the Taj Mahal and the tomb of his beloved wife, the emperor lived out his remaining years. Because of this saga, the Indian poet Tagore has called the monument "a drop of tear on the cheek of history."

The mausoleum rises to a height of nearly 200 feet at the top of its onion-shaped dome, or the equivalent of a 15 to 20 story building. It was built during the era of India's Mughal Empire, which was a Muslim dynasty, and so the architecture incorporates a blend of Indian, Persian and Islamic design elements. Constructed of white marble, the symmetry and detail of the edifice is striking, with matching arches, domes and minarets on either side. Up close, one can see the marble is etched with elaborate decorations, including intricate geometric patterns and Koranic verses carved in calligraphy.

The monument sits at the end of a well-manicured garden and a long pool that is lined with cypress tress. Beyond this, there is a raised platform with another reflecting pool that mirrors the image of the Taj Mahal. Overall, the feeling is one of calm, despite the throng of visitors. In fact, everything is so clean, bright and serene that the reality of the outside world seems to fade away momentarily. It's an oasis of peace amidst the chaos of Agra and of India.

Interestingly, as we walked around the grounds numerous Indians asked to have their photo taken with Lisa and me because we were Westerners. One family even asked Lisa to hold their baby for a picture. It was a whole other side of the country—middle class families, Indian tourists—which we had glimpsed all too briefly to that point.

But perhaps this was fitting. The most important design feature of the Taj Mahal is its perfect symmetry. Now, the tranquility of the site and the people we were meeting provided us with sort of a balance to the mayhem we'd experienced in other cities. It wasn't an even trade yet, but it was an apt way for us to glimpse both sides of the soul of India.

We actually attained a little more balance in Delhi, during a pleasant stay in a family guesthouse. The owners, Deepak and Ramani, did their best to make it a comfortable place, with home-cooked meals, a sitting area with reading materials and even two young daughters who made an occasional appearance.

Ramani did most of the day-to-day managing of the pension, while Deepak was involved in a variety of other business projects around Delhi. One evening, though, Deepak sat down in the living area and had a long conversation with me.

"So what is your impression of India?" he asked.

"It's a very interesting place," I said.

He chuckled. "Yes. That is the careful answer, of course. But it's not exactly what I asked. What are your impressions?"

"Well," I said, after a pause to consider how honest I was supposed to be, "my impressions are all over the map. It's colorful, it's fascinating, there is a profound sense of spirituality. But it also feels like it's crumbling and disorganized and dirty, and it can be exhausting to travel here."

"Yes, yes, that is India!" he said, laughing more heartily now. "It is a captivating place, but it's also frustrating, is it not?"

Just a bit.

"Many people, you know, are disturbed by their first visit to India. The filth and the pestering and the craziness. Many Indians, too, are troubled by all of this. But eventually, if you are in India long enough, you begin to feel these things as mere annoyances and you see deeper into the culture. People who return for future visits often enjoy themselves more the second time."

I had a flash of Kate in Calcutta telling us that one eventually learns to just go with the flow.

"I can see that, I suppose, because this country does take some getting used to."

"Yes, that is why Ramani and I try to create a comfortable atmosphere in our guesthouse. People can come back after a difficult day and feel at home here. Sometimes, when we sense guests are particularly tired or frustrated, we try to send energy to their heart chakra and they begin to feel better."

He stood up to get some tea and poured me a cup.

"We are glad to provide a place where travelers can rest. But I am also glad for my daughters to have this interaction with people from all over the world. Travel is a great broadening experience. When I was fourteen, you know, my father took me on a summer trip around the world."

"Really? What a great experience for your father to give to you."

"Yes. Yes. I still remember vividly one day in Paris. I am fourteen, you see, and Paris seemed so magnificent to me. So magnificent. I was standing on a street corner, and a French woman walked by. She smiled kind of flirtatiously, and then she pinched me! Hah! I said, 'If this is travel, I want to experience more of this!'"

He laughed noisily and slapped the table.

"Oh, that trip opened my eyes. So marvelous, this world we live in! So many people and cultures."

He shook his head pensively and smiled, his thoughts lost in faraway lands.

"I want to give some of that understanding to my children," he said. "In our guesthouse, they are able to meet travelers from all countries. It is good for them. We try hard to teach them about the world. Not only about travel, though. We introduce them to spiritual ideas, and to such practices as yoga and chanting. And we also encourage them to venture out, to try new things. At the moment, they are working on their own tourist pamphlet about Delhi, written from a young person's perspective. It's a worthwhile project for them, because they will learn what it takes to have a success, or they may also learn about failure, which is an equally valuable lesson. Many people are not successes in life because they do not know how to deal with failure."

It was an absorbing conversation and I was delighted by Deepak's perspectives and by the broad-based view of life he tried to impart to his children. In fact, he even reminded me of an important lesson that is all too easy to forget. Life Lesson #6. *A successful person isn't one who never fails, but one who knows how to persevere in spite of setbacks.* We all learn from our successes, but we often learn more from our failures. So whether you're trying to do well in business, athletics or just life, it helps to know that you can pick yourself up again whenever you get knocked down.

And perhaps Deepak even sent energy to my heart chakra during our talk. Either that or he was just such a composed and captivating individual that I couldn't help but relax. I went back to our room, wrote down notes in my journal and drifted off into a peaceful sleep. Perhaps India wasn't such a bad place after all, I thought.

"Om Mani Padme Hum"

The heavens were colored a passionate blue and the earth below was draped in a jagged blanket of white. We were in the midst of one of the world's most breathtaking plane flights and I lost track of time as we glided in a dream world through shimmering skies above the snow-capped Himalayas. I snapped out of my trance when our aircraft rolled to the right, banking around a stony peak that seemed close enough to touch, then emerged into a valley and began a precipitous descent. Almost before we had a chance to prepare ourselves for a landing, we abruptly tapped the ground and skated to a stop on the runway of the Leh airport.

Back on terra firma, we stepped off the plane and into the sun-soaked but oxygen-deprived air of Ladakh, at almost 12,000 feet. The airport consisted of a landing strip and a small building, just large enough to handle two arrivals and departures per day. We collected our luggage and hired a taxi from the crowd of drivers awaiting our flight. A quick 15 minutes later, we were checking into a hotel on Old Leh Road.

"Julé!" said the desk clerk, mouthing the all-encompassing Ladakhi greeting that can mean hello, good-bye, thank you or please. "Welcome to Ladakh."

Lisa and I looked at each other in mild wonder. The hotel was only a few blocks from the center of Leh—Ladakh's biggest city—but it was bordered by trees and had a flower-lined terrace with a clear view to the snowy mountaintops in the distance. We were still in India and our flight here had not been a long one, but this seemed about as far from Calcutta, Varanasi and Delhi as one could get.

Which was, of course, the purpose of this little jaunt. We wanted to experience a different side of India and, by this point in our trip, were also ready for a break from the sweltering, crowded cities that we'd been traipsing through of late. So we arranged our itinerary to include Ladakh, a Tibetan Buddhist culture in the Indus River Valley of northern India, wedged between the Himalayan and Karakoram mountain ranges. This area was once on the crossroads of the overland trading route that linked Lhasa, Kathmandu and Kashgar with the cities of Central Asia.

Today, the Ladakhi landscape and customs remain strikingly different from other regions of India. The heat and humidity that we'd been putting up with were replaced by a bracing coolness, so much so that we often wore a sweatshirt in the early mornings or evenings. As we walked around town, the stone buildings seemed to blend into the slate colored mountains that ringed the city. In restaurants, the rice, lentils, curries, chutneys and tandoori roasted chicken of India had given way to Tibetan dumplings, noodles, stews, beef and mutton. Even the clothing was different. The colorful saris on the women, for instance, had been exchanged for long dresses, shawls and woolen caps.

In short, Ladakh appeared very much like the Himalayan kingdom it had once been. It has more in common with the mountainous Buddhist cultures of Tibet, Nepal and Bhutan than to the rest of the Indian subcontinent. Ladakh, in fact, is often referred to as "Little Tibet" and some have suggested that it resembles the Tibet of several decades ago, before years of Chinese control began to dilute the distinctiveness of that society.

Leh itself is a small and pleasant town. There are Tibetan craft markets, shops that advertise the sale of carpets and Pashmina shawls, galleries devoted to Himalayan and Buddhist art, and a variety of cafés and restaurants in which to linger. There, we met numerous Indians who were themselves seeking a respite from their homes or trying to learn more about this diverse corner of their country.

One of these individuals, Sanjay from Bangalore, had studied in the U.S. at the University of Virginia and worked for a while in Washington, D.C. He was vacationing for a few weeks in northern India, taking in the lakes of Kashmir and the mountains of Ladakh.

When he heard we were from the U.S., he quipped, "You have better infrastructure in your country and we have more culture in ours. Too bad we couldn't combine the best of both!"

An even more interesting conversation was with Shanti, from Bombay, who had come to Ladakh to live on a farm for a month or two. When we met her, she was sipping tea and had just been reading Gabriel Garcia Marquez' *One Hundred Years of Solitude*.

Shanti said she was going to spend part of her summer doing farm labor in exchange for room and board. It was a program developed by a nongovernmental organization and was meant to provide Ladakhis with the help they needed to sustain their farms while giving young men and women the opportunity to immerse themselves in a different culture.

Interestingly, Shanti had recently spent four years living in London, the last two of them working for a major bank there. But she'd recently decided to leave her job in England in order to return to India and was now debating what to do next in life. This summer job on a farm was a diversion while she considered her future.

"Wow, this is quite a switch for you," I said. "From a bank in London to a farm in Ladakh."

"I wanted something different," she responded. "I needed a change of pace, and also wanted to have new experiences in my life. And this is a good cause. I can feel I'm helping these villagers, but it also gives me a chance to learn about the Indo-Tibetan culture and how the lives of the indigenous people here are being affected by the economy and tourism."

I asked Shanti about her experiences living in England.

"Oh, I loved London. I loved the buzz and the culture. It was sad to leave, but I felt it was time for me to come home to India. There was one aspect of London, though, that I never quite adjusted to, which is that I felt isolated there. In India, you know, there is less privacy, people are together more, friends drop by your house. But in the U.K., that wasn't the case. Everyone respected each other's space, yes, but I'm used to the Indian way and I was often lonely."

"That's interesting," I said, "because I think Lisa and I feel the other way here in India. To us, it seems as if there is almost no zone of privacy and we miss that. I know part of it is just being a tourist and having to deal with street vendors who want to sell you their products, but it's still quite different from walking the streets in most Western countries. This sense that our space is being encroached on is something we've had to adjust to."

That night, sitting on the terrace of our hotel, I drank a cup of masala tea and ate a slice of butter cake that we'd bought at a Ladakhi bakery. I stared at the black Himalayan sky, which was filled with more stars than I ever knew existed, and thought about our chat with Shanti. Two things occurred to me.

One, that our conversation provided more support for Global Rule #2, which I'd written about in Kenya. That is, that "we are all silently and permanently molded by the assumptions of the culture in which we are raised." Shanti had been uncomfortable in England because others respected her space, whereas she preferred to be around more people. Lisa and I, though, were sometimes ill at ease in India for the opposite reason, because we weren't always given enough space, not even when walking down the street. In the end, we were merely products of different cultures and missed the comfort zone of the worlds we knew best.

Second, I reflected that Shanti was engaged in her own version of a life sabbatical, just as Lisa and I were. It was a different choice of activities, but she was also taking time off from work to have new experiences and gain new perspectives on the world, which she would then carry with her to a new chapter in life. I gazed up again at the stars and silently wished her an interesting summer.

As much as we enjoyed our time in Leh, the more interesting attractions of Ladakh are at the region's many Buddhist temples, or gompas. The biggest challenge in exploring these sites is that many of them are perched high above local villages and require a hike uphill. That isn't the easiest activity in the thin air of Ladakh, so visitors tend to do a lot of slow walking, one unhurried step after another.

One of these shrines, the almost six-century-old Namgyal Tsemo Gompa, is located above Leh and is visible from almost anywhere in the city. To reach it, Lisa and I first walked back in time through the winding, muddy streets of the old town. The lanes there were barely wide enough to accommodate three people and a cow standing side-by-side and the mud brick homes almost teetered into one another. In the absence of any street signs or a discernible path out of the neighborhood, we kept turning to and fro, striving to maintain an uphill course, until we finally found our way out of the maze and spotted Leh Palace above us. This nine-story fortress is halfway up the hill to the gompa. It was built in the 17th century and was once the home of the Ladakhi royal family, though it now lies in disrepair, its walls crumbling and its floors pockmarked by holes.

From the palace, the gompa is clearly visible up a steep path worn into the rocky mountain and so we trudged upward. It may not have been the wisest choice of our trip, because by the time we reached the top Lisa was feeling faint and I was marginally dehydrated. Ladakh is not only in the mountains, you see, but it's also a high desert. The Himalayas block monsoon clouds from reaching the region, meaning the area gets little rainfall and relies on the melting snowcap for its water. For visitors, the increased dryness intensifies the effects of the altitude because dehydration is already a risk at higher elevations. We learned this the hard way. When we reached the temple, high above Leh, Lisa sat down and put her head between her knees and I guzzled water.

Once we recuperated, though, we were treated to a stunning panorama of Leh and the surrounding villages, which were sprawled across a valley between two mountain ranges. The view was framed magnificently by colorful lines of prayer flags that were strung downhill from the gompa. These patches of blue, white, red, green and yellow cloth are imprinted with prayers and mantras. They are a common sight in the Buddhist Himalayas and locals believe the wind carries the written prayers up to the heavens.

On another day, we hired a driver to take us to a few of the many temples that are strewn throughout the Indus valley. The most memorable experience we had was during a dawn visit to the Thiksey Gompa, a monastery about ten miles south of Leh, where it's possible to observe monks performing their morning *puja* (prayer ritual).

We left our hotel before sunrise in order to reach Thiksey for this observance. Once there, we took a seat on the cold stone floor of a dimly lit room. Dozens of saffron-robed monks sat on low benches and chanted, some of them rocking meditatively to the murmur of morning prayers. The chants were occasionally coupled with musical notes when one of the monks would crash a cymbal or blow on a horn. At periodic intervals, the younger men of the monastery dutifully rose and fetched containers of butter tea, which they poured into ceramic cups for the other monks. Outside, daylight crept over the snow-capped peaks and illuminated the village below. The chanted prayers seemed to float away through the open door on a light breeze, drifting over the valley and river to the distant mountains, where they joined the sun in greeting another day.

After the puja, Lisa and I strolled quietly through the rest of the gompa. Inside, a temple contained a colorful two-story Buddha sculpture, crowned by a golden head. The exterior walls were painted a dark shade of red, with splashes of blue, orange and yellow, presenting a vivid contrast to the grey-green backdrop of the countryside. Staircases were lined gracefully with potted plants.

We stopped along a pathway at one point to gaze at a row of prayer wheels. These are metal cylinders that contain rolls of thin paper coiled around an axle. The paper is printed with copies of a sacred prayer and the wheel is meant to be spun whenever someone walks by. As it spins, the prayer is released to the universe, which is supposed to have the same effect as if it were recited. It's also meant to symbolize the turning of the wheel of the dharma, or the setting of the Buddha's teachings in motion.

An elderly monk walked up to the spot where we stood, slowly spinning the wheels and chanting words under his breath. He stopped in front of us and smiled. The man appeared to be in his 70s, with a thin head of gray hair and a circle of wrinkles on his weathered but radiant face.

"Om mani padme hum," he said, in a soft, slow cadence.

We looked back at him, not quite sure what he had just uttered. He then repeated the words, carefully enunciating each syllable.

"Ohm mah-nee pahd-may hoom."

He nodded to us to repeat after him.

"Ohm mah-nee pahd-may hoom."

He corrected my pronunciation of the last consonant, which seemed to be an impossible combination of an 'm' and an 'ng.' I don't think I ever said it exactly right, but he smiled, spun one of the wheels and then gestured for us to do the same.

"Om mani padme hum," he whispered. "Om mani padme hum."

It was our own private lesson in Buddhism, although we didn't grasp it all until later. This chant is perhaps the most important Buddhist mantra and is meant to invoke the blessing of the bodhisattva of compassion. The meaning is not easily conveyed in other languages, but some have translated it into English as, "Praise to the jewel in the lotus." It is said to refer to the awakening of the spark of divinity within each person, resulting in compassion for the welfare of all beings.

The Dalai Lama, who himself is believed to be an incarnation of the bodhisattva of compassion, has written that the meaning of the mantra "is great and vast." At least in part, it signifies that with the correct intention, practice and wisdom "you can transform your impure body, speech and mind into the pure body, speech and mind of a Buddha."

That's a lot of meaning for six syllables. Although part of me wished I had the words and the opportunity to discuss the prayer with this monk, I also realized that any conversation would have distorted the beauty and simplicity of the moment. So I focused on the mantra.

"Om mani padme hum," the monk said, one more time.

Then, apparently satisfied that we had memorized it, he smiled serenely and ambled away, gently spinning the prayer wheels and chanting as he disappeared into the distance.

"When You Go This Country, You Must Take Patience"

Just when everything seemed almost normal again, our trip took a brief turn toward the absurd.

When it was time to depart Ladakh, we arrived at the airport at 6:00 a.m. for a 7:30 flight. We checked in, went to the boarding area and waited. And waited. More than five hours later, we were told the flight was canceled due to high winds. There was no chance of another flight that day, since planes were only allowed to take off from Leh in the mornings.

This problem was fairly unique to Ladakh, since the Leh airport is one of the highest in the world. The only other airports at nearly the same elevation are those in Lhasa, Tibet; La Paz, Bolivia, and Cuzco, Peru. At high altitudes, low air density reduces the amount of lift that an aircraft generates. This can prevent a plane from climbing fast enough to clear the nearby mountains. Since warm air exacerbates the problem, high altitude airports schedule flights for the cooler temperatures of early morning. Therefore, once the afternoon arrived and the wind hadn't died down there was nothing to do but pick up our luggage, find a taxi and return to the hotel. We weren't worried about a room shortage, since no planes landed in Leh that day, either.

The next morning, then, we awoke early once more and went back to the airport to try again. As we stood waiting to check in for our flight, two Indian men walked up and casually put their bags down near the front of the line we were in.

"Excuse me, you are now standing in front of me," said a German man ahead of us.

The Indians ignored him.

"There is a line here," said Lisa.

"Don't worry, we just put our bags down," said one of the men, although he still didn't move from his new position.

Two minutes later, a couple of other men also walked over and set down their luggage in front of us. The first Indian man, who was still standing at the front of the line, said something sharply to one of the later arrivals. What, was he offended all of a sudden? As they bickered we were surprised to see the first man push the second one. Then their arms became entangled and somebody received a punch to the head. They began wailing on each other and a half-dozen men quickly joined in the fight on both sides.

Were we on a movie set, I wondered? Had a gang fight broken out? Just five feet in front of us, punches were flying. One man actually soared through the air and dropkicked another person. A third man was forcefully pushed headfirst into the check-in counter. Bodies and fists were being thrown chaotically. Lisa and I hastily joined dozens of other travelers in scrambling away from the violence.

Then, six armed soldiers rushed onto the scene to stop the fight. Well, sort of. The physical battle stopped, but all of the combatants and all of the soldiers began shouting at each other. A dozen men now, half of them armed, all screaming, gesturing and pushing. The rest of us looked around, wondering where to dive for cover if gunshots rang out. The argument between the Indian men and the soldiers continued for another six or eight minutes, though, and then faded away.

It was all too bizarre. Crazier still was that the airline agents kept checking people in for the flight through all of this. Even when a man collided headfirst with the ticket counter! Was this an everyday occurrence, I wondered? Actually, maybe it was, because when the fight was over the soldiers let all of the combatants go about their business as if nothing had happened.

Interestingly, there were multiple levels of security at this airport because Ladakh is part of the Indian state of Jammu and Kashmir, a region at the heart of a border dispute with Pakistan. Although Ladakh was considered quite safe, the security forces still maintained extraordinary measures, ranging from multiple x-ray checks to pat downs of passengers to a prohibition on such carry-on items as food and batteries. The presence of the armed soldiers was another piece of this stepped-up security, so we naturally assumed that a violent fistfight would lead to people being expelled from the plane. We were half expecting to see the instigators hauled off in handcuffs.

But, no. Instead, the Indian man who first put his bags down at the front of the line, and who had started this entire incident, came back and nonchalantly walked up to the counter—and was checked in before us!

Yes, just when everything seemed almost normal again, India made a return appearance.

When we finally returned to the check-in line, Lisa was so disturbed by what had happened that she went to speak with one of the airline staff and asked if it was safe to allow someone on a plane who had just started a brawl.

"Oh, it's not a problem," said the ticket agent. "He's not violent. Perfectly safe."

Which he turned out to be, in the end. But we still had difficulty imagining many other airlines letting someone board a plane after such an incident.

In any case, we were checked in for the flight and went to wait for the boarding call. And then we waited some more. An hour later, we were told the flight had just left Delhi but there might be another problem with high winds today. Two hours later, as we sat wondering if a second consecutive flight would be canceled, several Indian soldiers walked through the middle of the crowded lobby carrying a flag-draped coffin. More weirdness.

I pulled out my notebook and felt compelled to jot down memories of India and of the peculiar paradoxes that symbolized this country. Obviously, there is the large and talented middle class that lives alongside overwhelming poverty, but there are so many other contradictions. I wrote:

- India has nuclear weapons, and yet every hotel we were in suffered power shortages and much of the country's infrastructure seems to be in a state of disrepair.
- There are world class software engineers, and yet the phones don't always work.
- The country is the wellspring for some of the world's great religions and for Gandhi's philosophy of nonviolence, but there is also a good deal of in-your-face aggressiveness.
- India is an emerging international power, yet the country often seems gripped by chaos. There are no lines, no traffic rules, no consequences for people who start a fistfight in front of an airline check-in counter.

India is every side of every coin. It is the meditators, the yoga devotees, the chanting monks and the wandering holy men. It is the sublime sunrise on the Ganges, the snow-capped Himalayas, and the astonishing explosion of color, smell and sound that is often around every corner. It is also bedlam and madness. It is people bathing on the sidewalk and men urinating against a wall. It is cows, donkeys and goats in the street, blaring horns, dancing bears and legless beggars.

It's just India.

Just then, some mysterious confluence of events led us to meet Dominique. A sixty-something Frenchwoman, she sat down beside Lisa and me and began chatting. She told us she'd been coming to India for 18 years now and that she'd started a foundation to assist Himalayan nomads in Ladakh and Tibet.

"What led a woman from France to set up a foundation in the Himalayas?" I asked.

"About two decades ago, I had a disease that caused paralysis in my legs," she said. "I had many operations. Though I was cured, I still now walk with a limp. After, I decide I want to devote my time to help people. I come here to the Himalayas and I know this is what I should do. These people, they are poor, but they are rich in their culture and their hearts."

"That's very admirable for you to take on this work."

"It is nothing," she said. "I think now it is my calling."

Then she described to us some of her meetings with the Dalai Lama.

"I am not Buddhist. I don't have the belief. But when you meet him, it is like a big light. Then you wonder, maybe I should have the belief," she smiled.

The Dalai Lama told her, she said, that the world was going through a difficult period and would continue to do so for another few years. "After that, he believes there will be more peace. More people will take spirituality into their hearts."

"I hope he's right."

"This period, it coincides with the Bush presidency, I think. Perhaps the world needs to experience this difficult period, then after it will improve."

She sat in silence for a few minutes. Then she looked us in the eyes.

"India has been difficult, yes?"

"There have been many good moments and also many challenging times," I said. "That's what makes it interesting, right?"

"India is difficult place. But good," she said. "This is good knowledge to have when you go back to your home. When you have trouble in India, it's good in a way. Well, trouble is never good, of course. But still, trouble like this is good to remember."

"That's a nice way to describe it."

"When you go this country, you must take patience," she said.

Then she wished Lisa and me a good journey.

Two hours later, four hours after we had checked in, our flight finally departed.

Singapore

"Asia for Beginners"

Singapore does not try to induce culture shock. In fact, it may be the most pristine and orderly city you will ever see. But when we landed there early in the morning after an overnight flight from Delhi, it took a few moments to get over our astonishment at having arrived in such a different world.

In this city-state at the tip of the Malaysian peninsula, we discovered a contemporary metropolis of sleek architecture and perfectly manicured boulevards. Businesspeople in tailored suits talked on cell phones as they sipped a Starbucks coffee and walked past stylish retail stores and international restaurants. It had been less than ten hours since we'd left India and flung ourselves partway across Asia in a plane but it felt more as if we'd jumped several decades into the future.

"It's pretty surreal," I said. "Yesterday there were cows and goats walking along crumbling sidewalks and men urinating against walls. Today it feels as if we're in a futuristic version of Boston or London."

It's actually remarkable how far Singapore has come, given its short history. Prior to gaining independence in 1965, the city was governed by the British for several centuries and then spent two years as part of a Malaysian federation. When the Malays and the Singaporean Chinese had difficulty co-existing, they went their separate ways and became two countries.

In addition to its modernity, Singapore is also distinctive for the way in which it blends East and West. Most everyone speaks English, along with Mandarin Chinese or another Asian language. Also, not only has McDonald's made inroads into the culture, but so have Borders, HMV and Taco Bell. You can grab a quick lunch of pizza or a hamburger as easily as you can find Chinese dumplings and noodle soup.

Our friend Rick, whom we had come to Singapore to visit, described the city as "Asia for beginners." It does provide an easy introduction to Asian culture for anyone who is visiting this part of the world for the first time. Or, for two people arriving here after traipsing through Vietnam, Cambodia and India back-to-back-to-back, it was a nice break from some of the challenges of travel.

Despite Singapore's allure, however, it's doubtful we would've added it to our itinerary had it not been for the chance to visit Rick. Singapore has few compelling tourist attractions and it would have been geographically easier for us to either continue on to the Middle East or find a less distant destination at which to unwind. But Rick is a good friend whom I'd seen only two or three times since he moved away from Boston seven years earlier and I was looking forward to spending time with him and seeing the city through his eyes.

Although he was now based in Asia and working as a Human Resources executive for an American corporation, Rick had gone through a number of previous career incarnations, with stints in the tourist and theater businesses, as an English teacher in Japan and even as an aide to a U.S. Senator. He told me once that he didn't ever mind ending a particular phase in his life, because he knew something interesting would always be waiting for him.

"When you quit a job, it's like stepping off a cliff in some ways," he said. "But if you have confidence in yourself, you begin to know that you're always going to land on your feet. You have to trust in life and in yourself."

In that spirit, Rick had moved to Boston in the mid-1990s without a job. To make money he became a temp worker and began recording meeting notes for a Boston corporation. When he began making his own business suggestions during the meetings, the company was impressed enough to offer him a job. His duties grew rapidly and he eventually moved to Singapore with responsibility for the training of thousands of employees in the Asia-Pacific region.

With most other people, this would be a mind-boggling ascent. With Rick, it was the culmination of another experience. As if to prove it, a few years later he moved on again. He left this job and spent six months traveling and visiting family. Then, when casting about for his next career move, he was lured back to Singapore for a similar position with a different U.S. corporation. That is where he was when we came to visit.

As I thought about it, I realized that some of Rick's earlier life choices had similarities to what Lisa and I were doing, or what Kelly was doing when we met her in Turkey, or what Nancy, Dave, Sarah and Steve were doing in Vietnam, or what Shanti was doing in Ladakh. It was intriguing to think the concept of a life sabbatical might be a growing trend. We all have the ability, it seems, to constantly forge new paths, so long as we have faith in ourselves.

Rick gave Lisa and me the run of his apartment while we were in town and his home soon became a retreat center in the middle of our journey. We relaxed by his pool, did laundry and caught up on errands, emails and trip planning. Then we spent numerous evenings with Rick discovering Singapore.

We went to Indonesian, Mexican and Chinese restaurants, the latter one in the ethnic enclave of Chinatown. While there, we strolled into an herbal medicine store, which sold everything from ginseng and gingko to shark's fin and bird's nest (literally, a nest made from bird saliva). These latter two items are quite expensive as they're considered delicacies in the Chinese culture and are often served at banquets. The store also sold a selection of herbal teas and so we had a cup of chrysanthemum tea, which tasted very much like what I would imagine a flower steeped in hot water to taste like.

As we drank the beverage, a woman explained to us the concept behind the hot and cold qualities of herbs, food and drinks. She said that in Chinese beliefs sickness could be caused by an excess or a deficiency of either hot or cold qualities in the body.

"Whole body must be in balance," she said. "Yin and yang. Too much cold or hot, people get sick."

By chance, a local mother then stopped by the shop with her young daughter who had a cold. The shop owner explained that an excess of heat can cause a cough or sore throat and so she prescribed some herbs and teas that were meant to bring the girl's health back in balance.

Perhaps the most interesting of our food experiences, however, took place at the many hawker centers scattered through the city. These were giant Asian food courts that had evolved from the street vendors who used to populate the Singaporean sidewalks. The government some years ago decided to clear its streets of unregulated food carts but didn't want to do away with hawkers entirely, since they're an institution of Asian life. For this reason, hawker centers were created.

At all hours of the day now, even late at night, one can find crowds of people at these gathering places. The menus reflect the cultural fusion of Singapore, with Chinese, Malaysian and Indian food stalls. A variety of dishes are available, from the commonplace to the peculiar. Some vendors did a brisk business in pig organs or brain stew, for instance, while others stuck to dumplings, noodles and tofu.

Although we stayed away from the most exotic offerings, we were still able to experience a variety of new foods. For instance, there was fish floss bread, a roll covered in dried, shredded fish (the floss) and packed with a sweet mayonnaise-like filling. Or kaching, a pile of shaved ice drizzled with coconut milk and then mixed with, say, berries, corn or beans.

Then, of course, there was durian, a Southeast Asian fruit with a rough skin, almost like a pineapple. Inside, it contains pods of pulpy fruit. The smell is so pungent the fruit has been banned by some airlines and hotels. Some people call durian the "fruit of heaven and hell," maybe because some people love it and others despise it, or perhaps because it has a sweet taste initially but a bitter kick later. When Lisa later told a Thai friend at home that she had tried durian, her friend's response left no doubt as to her feelings about the fruit.

"I hate durian!" she replied. "My parents eat it, but I can't stand it."

Nevertheless, durian is extremely popular. In stores, it is priced according to which region or orchard it was harvested from. Durian connoisseurs are similar to wine lovers in knowing what areas yield the best fruit. We made our purchase from a local vendor who pulled out a machete and chopped the fruit for us. It was sweet and nutty, although with an odd garlic-onion undertone. I didn't quite understand the "heaven and hell" connotation at first, but when a tart aftertaste lingered into the following day it made more sense.

Our time in Singapore also caused me to reflect more on culture, perhaps because this city-state is so economically successful and well-functioning despite being a rather controlled society.

Singapore's economic progress can largely be attributed to the vision of one man, Lee Kuan Yew, who maintained authoritarian control over the country from the 1960s into the 1990s and implemented his vision of a nation governed by Confucian ideals and Asian values. The product was a culture in which social behavior was regulated and individuals were expected to sacrifice for the collective good, but which also resulted in an economically dynamic country that now has one of the highest standards of living in Asia. It has often been said that Singapore is a model for what China would like to someday become.

Along with this modernity, though, is a sterile veneer. Singaporeans have essentially traded some political and personal freedoms for a secure and affluent society and the city can at times feel almost too perfect, as if it's being managed by Disneyworld. Much of this is by design, as the media and entertainment are censored and political opposition is limited. Singaporeans even joke about their home being a "fine city"—that is, if you break one of a myriad number of rules, you are likely to be fined. Littering, spitting, smoking in a public place, or even failing to flush a public toilet can be cause for a fine. An act of vandalism is even worse and will likely result in a caning.

Laws such as these have fed Singapore's reputation in the West for being a police state. But most of the news stories that reach the average Westerner are high profile tales of people executed for drug smuggling, or the case several years ago of the American teenager who was caned for spray painting graffiti. These are extreme cases and, at least from a tourist's perspective, most people have no difficulty staying within the law. Traveling in Singapore did not feel all that different from visiting any other modern metropolis, save for the fact that it was almost unnaturally clean and well-organized.

What I found especially interesting, though, is that Singapore achieved a great deal of success in a short period of time despite shunning some of the values that we in the West have always attributed to our economic success, such as unfettered individualism or limited government. Instead, two of the most obvious characteristics of Singapore are its group-oriented culture and its strong, mostly authoritarian leadership.

Consider the topic of collectivism, for Singapore is nothing if not a group-oriented society. One example of this is that people are accustomed to sharing space. It's common for up to ten people from one family, spanning several generations, to live together in one home. Rick, on the other hand, lived alone in a three-bedroom apartment, which afforded him a guest room and an office.

"This obviously isn't so unusual for an American," he said, "but Singaporeans are usually shocked when they come to my apartment and see how much space I have for myself."

In a similar vein, Rick noted that his co-workers almost always went to lunch as a group. He sometimes joined them, but admitted that locals viewed him as somewhat odd on those days when he pleaded a need to be by himself, either to do personal errands or to catch up with his thoughts.

The group orientation is also apparent in the way the government helps to manage everyday life. For instance, residents have to get government permission to own an automobile and must purchase a license prior to buying a car. In this way, the government can control the number of vehicles in the city and thus try to manage congestion and pollution. Even still, how many Americans, do you suppose, would consent to letting the government decide when they can buy a car?

Since there is this strong sense of group orientation in Singapore, though, I was intrigued one day to read an article in a local newspaper that quoted the Prime Minister as chiding young adults for caring more about their individual lives and careers and being less willing to sacrifice for the greater good of Singapore. This is a growing issue elsewhere in Asia, as well, where there is a tradition of older generations having submerged their personal desires for the benefit of the group, only to be baffled as they watch their offspring develop more individualistic traits.

This got me to wondering whether these were signs of Western values seeping into an Asian society or the inevitable result of a modern, market-oriented economy. The West has no doubt impacted other cultures in terms of economic values and entertainment culture, but if Western values were seeping into the East wasn't it also true that Eastern influences were percolating into the West, especially in the areas of spirituality and health care? Perhaps, I reflected, this was merely another example of the intermingling of global cultures. Trade and travel have always facilitated the cross-cultural exchange of ideas, but technology has now increased the pace dramatically.

LISTENING TO THE SIGNS

On our last night in Singapore we stayed up talking until 3 a.m. We discussed a variety of topics, but at some point the conversation drifted to work and life goals. Soon, Lisa and I would be off to the Middle East and Europe before returning home to begin a new stage of our lives. Although Rick was fairly well entrenched in his job at the moment, he still didn't know how much longer he would stay in Singapore or in his current position. Change was inevitable.

Rick asked me what I'd be doing once our journey was finished.

"Well, I started this process to a degree after our last trip, but I want to work harder to fashion a full-time income out of different writing jobs," I told him. "The consulting firm that I've worked for will continue to hire me on a project basis. My hope is that I can use this as a foundation, and then build on my old journalism experience to do more freelance work. I have so many years of cross-cultural experience now that I want to try carving a niche for myself in writing about culture and travel, and I think my experiences on these trips will help in that regard."

"What about writing a book?" Rick asked.

"That could be an option, too," I said. "It just takes a huge commitment of time and I would need to find a way to work it into my schedule. I also have one or two people who have asked me about the possibility of ghostwriting a book with them."

At this point, Lisa jumped into the conversation, prodded either by several glasses of wine or by experiencing several days of Rick's honesty and bluntness, or both.

"I think he should just put most of that other stuff aside and write his own book," she said. "He doesn't need to make that much money right now. He's got great ideas and I personally think he should use his time to work on his own writing."

"Yeah, why not?" said Rick. "Why mess around with all these other projects?"

"Well, I do have some ideas, but I also have to make a living," I said. "I can't just hole up for a year and write."

"Can't you? Why shouldn't you do bigger, more personal writing projects if you have the opportunity?" goaded Rick, now warming to the topic. "You should be passionate about what you do. Why not take a risk and just do it? Or do you always want to work for other people who took bigger risks? Maybe it's time to try something big on your own."

When a seed is planted, it generally needs time to take root before it can bloom. So as our trip continued, the idea of writing a book continued to germinate. Although I'd previously had thoughts about such a project and had dabbled in writing travel articles after our last journey, a new idea took shape. What about a book centered on the concept of taking a life sabbatical in order to travel?

I had been keeping notes through both journeys and some of the personal insights I'd gleaned during our experiences suddenly took on a new meaning. I saw that a book could be an ideal fusion of my desire to write, my interest in travel and cultural topics and my curiosity about the world. It seems like an utterly obvious idea now, of course, but it was a new thought to me at the time.

A few months later, after we'd returned home, I was in the process of examining my options and trying to summon the nerve to put everything else on hold to write this book. I happened to dust off and read a 12-year-old journal, from when I had spent some time with Rick in Boulder, Colorado.

This is some of what I had written:

Rick and I talked about where we each are in our respective lives. We talked about goals, about the choices we've made in our lives, and why we've made these choices. It is difficult to be less than honest with Rick. I told him that I was excited about getting a master's degree in political science because it would enable me to pursue a number of career options, including writing, teaching, or working in government.

When I said that, he replied, "That's not what you're looking for. I don't sense enough passion in your voice when you say it. What are your real goals?"

I finally had to admit that, deep down, I had more passion for writing and sensed this was my ultimate mission in life. Getting a master's degree was a step on the road to something else, but I wasn't sure what. I had given Rick the standard, safe answer that I have taken to using with people so as to avoid questions. Because, yes, teaching did interest me, but much deeper in my being was a need to write. And not to write grant proposals or marketing materials. I wanted to write things that had more personal meaning to me.

I was astonished to re-read these words of my younger self. Two sets of questions came to mind.

First, what the heck is it with Rick? Was he some sort of human truth serum? How did he draw these things out of me when I'd suppressed them with everyone else? Then, where had I been channeling my passion for the past number of years? True, I had been helping businesspeople learn about other cultures, which was certainly helpful to the world. I was doing it because I was good at it, the cause was worthy and I needed to make money. These are all good and valid reasons for taking a job and I still believe in that work, but I now had to wonder if somewhere inside I was also afraid to risk failure on a bigger, more personal project. Was it now time for me to step off a cliff of my own and finally start being a writer on my own terms?

I continued reading the journal. I read about an evening that Rick and I had spent in a café with three other friends, discussing a variety of topics. At the end of writing about that evening, I had jotted down this note in the pages of my journal:

Rick made an interesting comment tonight. He said he believes that I am going to write a book someday and he is going to be a significant influence on it.

Well.

I put the journal down and went for a walk. I thought, how can I not write a book? There were signs raining down on me from the heavens, tumbling off the dusty pages of old journals that had been hiding in my closet. The message seemed to be that I should start doing work that I was more personally involved in and passionate about.

I found added inspiration in the words of the late teacher and author Joseph Campbell. In his book *The Power of Myth*, a collection of interviews with Bill Moyers, Campbell talked about the perils of not following one's bliss:

CAMPBELL: You may have a success in life, but then just think of it—what kind of life was it? What good was it—you've never done the thing you wanted to do in all your life. I always tell my students, go where your body and soul want you to go. When you have the feeling, then stay with it, and don't let anyone throw you off.

MOYERS: What happens when you follow your bliss?

CAMPBELL: You come to bliss.

Interestingly, some friends of ours invited us out one night to hear a performance by a musician whom they had previously seen in concert. During the show, this performer talked about his journey to becoming a songwriter and his doubts about whether that was the right path for his life.

"It's not like the world needed another song," he said. "But it's your compass—whatever it is, you've gotta figure it out and just do it."

Sometimes we just have to listen to the signs.

Life Lesson #7. *If you want to lead a life of wonder and not regret, then you first have to unearth your passion.* Everyone has a passion. Do you want to sing, paint, teach, travel, dance, run, act, write, grow spiritually, tend to the sick, engage in public service? We all have multiple goals and interests, certainly, but we do tend to have one or two things that we are passionate about above all else. And it's not always what we're currently doing. So if we want our life to be well-lived, we need to unearth that passion and chase it.

Middle East: Egypt and Jordan

BIKINIS AND ABAYAS

On the day Lisa and I arrived in Egypt, Cairo was cloaked in a haze of heat and dust. The North African sun blistered everything it touched and travelers sought relief by clustering around the hotel pool, where there was an appealing swim-up bar.

After checking into our room, we joined the crowd outside for an afternoon of relaxation. Attendants came by to adjust umbrellas, hand out ice-soaked face towels and write down orders for drinks and sandwiches. Nearby, a small band played an unusual mixture of 1960s and 1970s era pop songs.

"I'm hooked on a feeling, I'm high on believing, that you're in love with me ..."

"Hey, Jude, don't make it bad. Take a sad song and make it better ..."

Lisa and I relaxed in blue and green striped lounge chairs and took in the view. A flock of children splashed in the water. Western women strolled by in bikinis, sipping on pina coladas, while Arab females were covered from head to toe in black *abayas*, dangling their feet in the pool and drinking coca-cola. No one seemed the least bit affected by the contrast between the bikinis and the abayas.

"It's interesting," said Lisa, after watching the activity for half an hour. "Some of these kids think it's perfectly normal to see most of their mother's body exposed in public, and the others think it's natural for their mother's body to always be fully covered outside the home."

It was, indeed, a startling difference, one that was more accepted in the relative privacy of a hotel pool than it would be on the Egyptian streets. As we took our own dip in the revitalizingly cool water, the band continued to perform.

"Plenty of room at the Hotel California. Any time of year. You can find it here ..."

Meanwhile, looming curiously over the entire setting was the 4,500-year-old Great Pyramid of Giza. The only survivor of the original seven wonders of the world was just a few minutes from our hotel and provided a dreamlike backdrop to this diverse panorama.

Bikinis and abayas, the Great Pyramid and the Hotel California. It was certainly an unusual mingling of cultures and centuries.

We were at this pool in the first place because Lisa and I decided to treat ourselves in Cairo to the only luxurious hotel of our trip. It was low season in Egypt—since 100 degree daily temperatures don't exactly attract a lot of tourists—and we were able to find an internet deal at a Western hotel chain that was more than 60 percent off the rack rate.

"Let's book it," said Lisa, when I told her about it. "We've been good about keeping costs down, so we can indulge ourselves to make up for all the budget hotels we've stayed in."

So, after a long overnight flight from Singapore, we landed in Cairo in the early morning and by that afternoon were enjoying a dip in the pool. It wasn't exactly a challenging travel experience, but it was certainly a nice way to begin our visit to Egypt.

Honestly, we had no idea what to expect when we arrived in Cairo. Although we'd had a wonderful time in Turkey during our previous journey, Egypt was much more in the heart of the Middle East, both geographically and culturally. Moreover, the U.S. had invaded Iraq in the intervening years, so America was not exactly popular in this part of the world. We'd heard the Egyptians were a welcoming people, but we weren't sure if that hospitality would hold up once they heard what country we were from. As our plane grazed the runway at Cairo International Airport my mind filled with visions of angry locals hissing "Down with America!" as we walked past. Nonetheless, we had long dreamed of visiting this ancient land and so we crossed our fingers and mapped out a three-week journey by train, boat and bus through Egypt and Jordan.

Our first impression after going through immigration did leave something to be desired. We had to run the usual gauntlet of persistent touts at the airport and negotiate over the fare to our hotel. The man who led us to his company's taxi also requested an additional tip just for booking the ride.

"Sir, baksheesh. Baksheesh, please."

When we began driving through the congested, polluted streets of Cairo, past endless blocks of concrete apartment buildings, I mentally prepared myself for a long few weeks.

But then the taxi driver, Karim, began conversing with us.

"Welcome to Egypt," he said. "You will love my country. Very wonderful."

"We are looking forward to our visit."

"Where you from?"

Here goes.

"America."

"America?"

"Yes."

I bit my lip and prepared for the onslaught.

"Very nice. I like America. American people good. Well, not George Bush. I think Bush bad. But American people good."

"Thank you."

"We no like Bush, but we no like Mubarak in Egypt, either. Presidents bad, but people good," he laughed.

Well, maybe we wouldn't have to face angry, hissing locals, after all.

Lisa and I had three primary goals for our stay in the Egyptian capital: see the pyramids, see Cairo, and make plans for the next stages of our trip. The last objective was accomplished when we arranged for an upcoming Nile River cruise and then transportation on to the Sinai Peninsula. We did this through a local travel agency, even though we usually avoided all-in-one deals. But this agent specialized in packages for independent travelers and so we were able to do one-stop shopping for train and boat tickets, van transport and a guide for the temples between Aswan and Luxor, all while avoiding a group tour.

The broker even included an escort for one day in Cairo. Thus, we ended up with a guide to some of the city's historic sites, from the Egyptian Museum, with its astounding array of artifacts, to the large and dazzling Mosque of Mohammed Ali, with its chandeliered prayer space and white marble courtyard. Each site was interesting in its own way but, as was often the case, the chance to converse with our guide was as enticing as any tourist attraction.

Late in the afternoon, when the tours were over, we all went to a café at Khan El-Khalili, a famed shopping bazaar that was built in 1382. There, we ordered drinks at an outdoor table in the shade as hundreds of people meandered through the market's colorful and tangled web of endless alleys and shops. Sabah, who was 32, was dressed in a blue and white checked shirt and a white head scarf. She told us that she lived at home with her mother, two sisters and two brothers. A third sister was married and had her own family, while all of her siblings at home were single adults.

"I still hope to be married," she said. "I have had the opportunity, but I turned down some grooms because they wanted me to stay at home. I want to work after I am married."

This sounded all too familiar, since it was an echo of what we'd heard from Linh in Vietnam and Jorani in Cambodia. It was also unusual, since the majority of guides in these three countries were male. Somehow, we had stumbled into a whole series of female guides and then discovered that they all struggled with the same internal conflict about their lives.

There was, however, a subtle difference in their situations. Linh and Jorani were both in the early to mid-20s and feared never being able to find a husband if they wished to continue working. Sabah was in her early 30s and had already turned down suitors because she seemed confident she'd eventually meet someone who was open to her having a career.

This faint shift in attitude seemed symbolic of these cultures in general. Although it was less obvious in the countryside, Lisa noted that numerous urban Egyptian women appeared more liberated than their counterparts in Southeast Asia. Which was unexpected in its own way, because a majority of Muslim women in Egypt wear a head scarf, called a *hijab*. In the West, our impression of this style of dress is that it's a tool to keep women suppressed. And that may in fact be true in some instances. But we could only judge by what we ourselves experienced and, in this respect, Sabah provided a different take on the topic.

"The head covering is a good thing," she said, "because it shows that women are precious. At home, I don't put on the scarf and I also wear shorts. But in public, my head and legs are not seen by men outside my family. It is also fashionable, I think. I have many scarves, with different colors and designs, to use with different outfits. It is not required to wear the covering, but I prefer it."

"We see the scarf on women," said Lisa, "but not on young girls. Is there an age when females typically begin covering their head?"

"I started when I was 17," said Sabah. "But there is no one age. Some girls start at 12 or 13, and there are some women who never wear it. It is an individual choice."

It may ultimately be a choice, but there is undoubtedly some level of family, peer or religious pressure involved, since the great majority of women do cover up in public. Nevertheless, Sabah was correct in asserting that not everyone followed suit and at least ten percent of the local women we saw went about with their heads uncovered. Moreover, there was considerable variety in the way females dressed. The abayas that we saw by the hotel pool were less common on the Cairo streets and were apparently worn by women from the more conservative families or by visitors from outside the country. Among other females, some had plain hijabs over their head and neck and wore loose fitting clothing, while others displayed colorful designer scarves and dressed in tighter-fitting, more stylish outfits.

The head scarf, it seemed, could be either a religious, cultural or fashion statement, depending on the individual. This realization forced us once again to look below the surface of a culture and to not take everything we saw at face value.

Monuments in the Sand

The Giza plateau is located on the west banks of the Nile River, on the periphery of the Sahara Desert. It once had a view over the ancient Egyptian capital of Memphis and became a funerary complex for several pharaohs who built majestic monuments there. The city of Memphis has long since disappeared, its buildings crumbled and its remains covered by the dust of the ages and by silt from the Nile River. The edifices that were built on the Giza plateau remain standing, however, having outlasted every man-made structure on the planet for 4,500 years.

These are, of course, the Pyramids and the Sphinx. Lisa and I dedicated one of our days in Cairo to wander among these sublime monuments in the sand. We didn't arrange a tour for this particular excursion because we didn't want our time to be scheduled or restricted. A guidebook and several hours to roam were all we desired.

The Giza plateau crowds up against the edge of modern day Cairo, so the journey there isn't the profound experience one imagines of trekking across an expanse of desert and then suddenly stumbling upon the Pyramids. But there is still a palpable sense of exhilaration that comes from finally being there. After arriving, we just stood for a moment and stared at the timeless vista, squeezed between undulating desert sand dunes on one side and the hazy, densely populated suburbs of Cairo on the other.

"The Pyramids were built in about 2,500 B.C. The Great Pyramid of Khufu is first, then Pyramid of Khafre, then Menkaure. They are tombs for three pharaohs."

The voice was that of Bashir, who had driven us here from our hotel. Although we didn't hire a guide, Bashir left his vehicle and walked with us for 15 minutes or so, taking pictures and proudly relating to us some of the history of the monuments.

"They are very large, yes? The Pyramid of Khufu—or you say Cheops, I think?—this alone has 2.4 million blocks of stone."

Apparently, even Egyptian taxi drivers were experts on the pyramids.

"Do you know how long it took to build one pyramid?" asked Lisa.

"Nobody is sure, but we think about 20 years. That is with tens of thousands of workers."

We tried to imagine the scene more than four millennia ago, when this desert landscape would have been a beehive of activity. The slabs of limestone used to build the structures weighed an average of more than two tons each and much of this had to be quarried from a few miles away. The granite used to support the inner chambers came from as far as 500 miles away, in blocks weighing up to 80 tons. Astonishingly, the Egyptians accomplished all of this without the use of wheels.

"It doesn't seem possible," I remarked, "that this was built so long ago. It was 2,000 years before the Greeks built the Acropolis. It was twenty-five *centuries* before Christ."

I tried to visualize just how distant that was in relation to our own era. To project that same amount of time into the future would take us to the year 6500. Which of today's buildings or temples will still be standing then, I wondered?

We thanked Bashir for his time and insights and then set off on our own. Although we initially feared having our experience disturbed by an onslaught of souvenir vendors and camel drivers, the next few hours were surprisingly serene. The Egyptians are apparently striving to keep the Pyramids free of hassles, and so other than a few camels and one postcard salesman we were largely left alone. The site wasn't even very crowded with tourists, another benefit of visiting in low season, and there were never more than a few dozen other people around.

Up close, the Pyramids are even more astonishing than from a distance. The Great Pyramid is 455 feet tall, or the height of a 35 to 40 story building. It is more than twice as high as the Taj Mahal and was the tallest structure in the world for nearly 4,000 years, until the Europeans began constructing their massive cathedrals during the Middle Ages.

For the first few thousand years of their existence, these monuments staggered visitors even more than they do today. That is because earlier travelers didn't encounter the aged, weather-beaten stones that we now see, but rather structures that were surfaced in a white limestone casing which reflected the rays of the sun. They looked like enormous crystals shining in the desert and were visible from miles away. Today, only the Pyramid of Khafre retains any of this casing and then only near its peak. The rest of the limestone was stripped away starting in the 14th century and used in constructing mosques and forts around Cairo.

The Pyramids were also built with remarkable precision. The inner passages are almost perfectly straight and not even the tip of a knife can be inserted into the joints of the outer casing stones. Additionally, they were apparently laid out according to a particular astronomical orientation. One prominent theory is that they're aligned in the direction of the celestial North Pole, according to where stars of the Ursa Major and Ursa Minor constellations were located in the sky in about 2,500 B.C. Because these stars are always visible, the Egyptians associated them with eternity.

Put this all together and it's obvious that the design and construction of the Pyramids was a stupendous achievement for its time. Nothing like these structures was built for millennia afterward, a fact which has always given rise to theories that they were erected by an advanced prehistoric civilization.

Lisa and I roamed the sands for a long while. We sat on enormous stones scattered around the base of the Pyramids and reflected on the mysteries of human history. Did the pharaohs really build these structures in about 2500 B.C.? If so, why was nothing of the sort constructed again? What happened to the designers? Where did this architectural knowledge arise from and where did it disappear to? The Egyptians left few clues as to the answers.

Equally mystifying is the legendary Sphinx, which we visited next. The Sphinx is located some distance in front of the Pyramid of Khafre, where it faces east toward the rising sun. It was carved from limestone bedrock and is said to be the world's largest single-stone statue. With a half-human, half-lion appearance, the figure has been the source of much speculation through the ages. The most accepted theory is that it is associated with the pyramid behind it and may represent a likeness of the Pharaoh Khafre. Others have proposed that the Sphinx is much older and was merely excavated and restored in the time of Khafre.

The most unconventional hypothesis, promoted by the writer Graham Hancock and others, is that the statue is connected to the constellation Leo (the lion) and that the layout of the Sphinx and the Pyramids along the Nile River mirrors the stars of Orion's Belt along the Milky Way. According to this theory, construction had to either take place 8,000 years earlier or at least be based on knowledge of a map of the stars in 10,500 B.C.

Once again, though, history provides little evidence. In this respect, the mysterious Sphinx may be a fitting symbol for the entire Giza plateau. With no definitive answers to these historic mysteries, we are left merely to gaze in awe and to wonder.

When it was time, finally, to leave, Lisa and I lingered for as long as possible, staring into the sun-baked sands and into the impassive face of the Sphinx. Then, in a monument-induced trance, we hailed a taxi.

"You have good time?" asked the driver.

"Yes."

"Good. Pyramids very impressive."

"Amazing."

"So, I take you to papyrus shop now?"

I sighed.

Back to the realities of travel.

Egypt Along the Nile

Two days later, we found ourselves bobbing in the middle of the Nile River in southern Egypt, awash in warm sunshine and a soft breeze. Ali, an old man with a gnarled bronze face, smiled at us as he guided the sails of our felucca, following the wind upstream.

We seemed at that moment to be floating through blue space, with the sky and river differing merely in shades and textures. Beyond the light-filled surface of the water I could see a thin band of green along the river bank, with grass and trees rolling down to the shore. Past that was a dry desert landscape, just hills of windswept sand climbing toward the sky. It struck me that the colors of Aswan were much more vivid than they were in Cairo. The Nile was a more intense blue here and the desert was a deeper shade of amber.

I shut my eyes and felt the motion of the boat as we slowly drifted. Maybe we were too hasty, I mused, in booking four days aboard a river cruiser. Perhaps we should have held out for a felucca trip and journeyed upriver in a traditional sailboat, relaxing on the open deck beneath large masts and triangular sails. Then again, I told myself, several days of constant exposure to the weather during the heat of a desert summer was not really our idea of a good time. So I sat back, turned off my mind and just savored the rest of our afternoon sailing excursion on the Nile.

Later that day, we boarded the boat that would be our home for the next few nights, as we embarked on a trip from Aswan to Luxor. This stretch of the river is sprinkled with the remains of some of Egypt's most spectacular temples and a river cruise is a popular way to explore a lost civilization while experiencing the life of the Nile.

It's been said that without the Nile River there would be no Egypt. Or at least no ancient culture to gaze upon in astonishment. Much of the country is a vast desert, dotted by the occasional oasis, but the river is the artery that gives life to the land. Take it away and the agriculture would dry up, the trade routes would disappear and no great civilization would have ever developed. Even today, more than 90 percent of the population lives within 12 miles of the river.

The Nile also figures prominently into Egypt's own sense of itself, since the country has always been divided into an Upper and a Lower Egypt. Upper Egypt is closer to the Nile's source in Africa, while Lower Egypt is the delta region that empties into the Mediterranean. Not coincidentally, the first capital at Memphis and the current capital at Cairo both lay near the boundary between these territories and the greatest periods of the nation's history have been when the two riverine Egypts were united.

Now that Lisa and I had seen Cairo and the Pyramids, it was time to experience this other feature of the country. We arrived in Aswan after an overnight train ride. The journey was pleasant enough, particularly since we had a two-person sleeping compartment and didn't have to worry about strange visitors in the night. While not luxurious, the train was nicer than the ones we'd rode in Vietnam and India and so we curled up in our bunk beds and fell asleep to the hum of the rails. Then we awoke at dawn to an entirely different world more than 500 miles from Cairo.

Aswan is the nation's southernmost city and is endowed with characteristics of both Africa and Egypt. The Nubian people of the region are darker-skinned than are the northern Egyptians. The majority of the men wore galabayyas, while the women were swathed in long dresses and head scarves. There was more color in the buildings, as palettes of red, blue and yellow shone in the African sun. The city was also smaller than Cairo and life seemed to pass by at a slower pace.

At the train station, we met our guide, Mohammed, and then went to see a few local sights. But this newest stage of the journey really seemed to begin with our felucca ride on the Nile.

"This is best way to feel the river," Mohammed said, as he helped us barter for a ride with one of the many boat owners who hung out by the docks. "It is peaceful."

He was right. We spent two hours on the Nile, then emerged in a tranquil state and boarded the river cruiser, where we were assigned a comfortable cabin with a window view of the passing landscape. The ship was filled with a large tour group of French travelers, but there were a few others like ourselves who had merely booked a cabin and had their own guide. This included two Australian couples and a Moroccan woman who was traveling with her precocious 11-year-old daughter. The schedule was arranged so we could visit ruins in the mornings and early afternoons, then spend the rest of the time relaxing on an upper level sundeck or in our room while the boat steamed northward.

It was a pleasant way to experience the Nile and to view the Egyptian countryside, where the sights have not changed for centuries. Women in purple robes and white head scarves stood knee deep in the river and collected water in jugs. Men and boys dressed in galabayyas and sandals fished with wooden poles. A man in a gray robe herded goats. Boys played soccer in a patchy field of grass, between chipped walls and crooked fences. Donkeys ambled along a craggy roadway, past the white minarets of a rural mosque.

The loveliest picture, though, took place late in the day when the sun went down. As twilight crept in, we sat on the deck and watched a golden disk sink into the desert. In the foreground, date palm trees were silhouetted along the shore. Then the sun split the horizon and the Nile River turned into a shimmering ribbon of dandelion and lilac.

During the first two days, we glided along the river and went ashore a few times to explore the crumbling remnants of centuries-old temples. Most of these were built during the Greco-Egyptian Ptolemaic Era, which was founded by Alexander the Great in 332 B.C. and lasted until a conquest by the Roman Empire in 31 B.C., after which Cleopatra, the last of the pharaohs, committed suicide. During three centuries of rule, the Ptolemies built numerous monuments along the southern Nile, including the Temples of Philae, Kom-Ombo and Edfu.

It was Edfu, dedicated to the god Horus, that most amazed me. But it wasn't the vastness of the temple that seemed most impressive, nor the falcon statues that guarded the entrance, nor even the walls and columns of hieroglyphics inside. Rather, it was when Mohammed casually mentioned to us that, over time, the structure had become almost completely buried in the sand and that part of the local village was built on top of it.

"But ... but," I stammered. "That wall is enormous. How high is it?"

"36 meters," he said. Nearly 120 feet.

"And you're saying that, year by year, the soil accumulated and slowly buried this temple, yet nobody cared or did anything about it?"

"It was a different time. You must remember, the Romans made Christianity the religion of their empire in the early 4th century. After this they tried to stop worship at what they saw as pagan temples. Then in the 7th century the Arabs came with Islam. None of these rulers cared about the ancient civilization or the old religion. At some monuments, stones were even removed and used for building new palaces or mosques. So why would these poor villagers, trying to live and to feed their families, care about this temple if the rulers did not? To them, the pillars and walls sticking out of the sand were just broken old buildings."

"When it was dug out again?"

"In the middle 1800s, a French archaeologist discovered it and was responsible for the excavation."

"That's just amazing to me, how history can be buried like that over time."

"It is not only here. The great Luxor Temple, which you will see tomorrow, was also partly buried in sand and silt from the Nile. And so were many others."

I was unusually startled by this revelation, though I really shouldn't have been. After all, what do archaeologists do? They excavate the remains of history, which lie hidden in layers beneath the soil. The Sphinx had been partially buried at one time, and many of the ruins from the old capital of Memphis were similarly lost. Nevertheless, there was a certain shock value that resulted from actually standing in front of a towering 120-foot high wall that had nearly been obscured by the sands of the centuries. It does make one wonder what else may be buried in the Egyptian earth.

While the first half of our cruise was spent leisurely traipsing through the occasional temple, the second two days were more packed with activity amidst the treasures of Luxor. During Egypt's New Kingdom period, from the 16th to 11th centuries B.C., the city of Thebes was the religious and political heart of Egypt. This is considered the golden age of the pharaohs and today the monuments of Thebes (present day Luxor) are the most stunning relics of ancient Egypt aside from the Pyramids.

On our first morning in Luxor, we had an early breakfast and then headed to the West Bank of the Nile, where the pharaohs built royal tombs in the Valley of the Kings. These were situated west of the river because the Egyptians associated the setting sun with the afterlife. We rode away from the green shores of the Nile into a scorching vista of rocky cliffs and a sandy ravine. The landscape turned brown and barren, with not a trace of vegetation. During the next few hours we explored several tombs in the area, which had been hidden beneath the desert terrain.

Most of the original tomb treasures have been carted away, but numerous vaults still have impressive and colorful artwork on the inner walls and are well worth exploring. I felt a sense of drama about the setting, maybe because of the stark environment or perhaps because we were encountering the final resting place of a who's who of Egyptian pharaohs. As Lisa and I hiked across the sizzling sands and baked in the 112 degree heat, it seemed that Ramses, Amenhotep, Tutankhamun and others were whispering to us across the centuries.

The second highlight of our day was in the center of town when we took a sunset stroll through the Temple of Luxor. Built primarily in the 14th and 13th centuries B.C. by Amenhotep III and Ramses II, this edifice sits astride the banks of the Nile and is a striking example of the grandeur of ancient Egypt. It is particularly eye-catching in the early evening, when the sun goes down over the nearby river and the sky moves from blue to lavender to black. Then, as the sunlight slowly gives way to well-placed lamps within the temple, the changing light casts a supernatural glow over the 3,000-year-old statues and pillars.

The northern entrance is flanked by two massive sculptures of Ramses and a 75-foot-high pink granite obelisk. These are what remain of the six statues and two obelisks that originally guarded the gate. The second obelisk survived, but was given to France in the 1830s and now graces the center of Paris' Place de la Concorde. At the height of Thebes' glory days, this impressive entryway to Luxor Temple sat at one end of a two-mile boulevard that connected it with Karnak Temple. The entire route was lined with sphinxes. Unfortunately, only part of this avenue is now visible and the rest is buried beneath the contemporary city of Luxor.

As we walked into the temple's courtyard, Mohammed pointed in the air to our left.

"Do you see that door frame up there?"

"Yes."

"Why do you suppose Ramses put a door there? It is 25 feet above the ground."

I stared blankly.

"Hah! It is a trick. You remember yesterday when we spoke of these ruins being buried in the sand after many centuries?

"Yes."

"That is the door to a mosque. When Luxor Temple was excavated, that is where the ground was. Many of these columns and walls and statues that you see were buried beneath the city of Luxor."

Once more, I was speechless.

We then walked from the courtyard past a 14-column colonnade, through another courtyard and into the inner chambers of the structure. Egyptian temples were constructed along an axis and were designed so that the further one proceeded, the more intimate and sacred the space became. The innermost sanctuary could only be entered by the pharaoh and the temple's high priest.

As we wandered through the small chapels and shrines of the inner chambers, Mohammed led us into what was known as the Birth Room, where he explained the stories and hieroglyphics carved onto the wall. They depict the myth of Amenhotep III's birth, including scenes where his virgin mother is impregnated by the god Amun and is told that she is going to bear his son. The divine spirit is imparted to her when she is touched by an Egyptian cross (*ankh*).

"Amenhotep used this story to demonstrate his divine nature as a pharaoh," said Mohammed, "but this is a common tale in Egyptian mythology. The pharaohs were sometimes said to be an incarnation of the god Horus, who himself had supernatural origins. After the god Osiris was killed, his wife Isis used magical powers to resurrect him so she could conceive a new child, who was Horus."

Hmmm. Virgin births. Divine conceptions. Even an Egyptian cross. This was interesting.

"What is the meaning of the cross?" I asked. It looked like the Christian cross, but with a loop on the top.

"The cross is similar to the Egyptian hieroglyphic for the word 'life,'" said Mohammed. "There are different theories about what the symbolism is. One idea is that the intersecting pieces of the cross represent earth and sky, and together they give birth to the egg of life."

Then he laughed. "There are many other suggestions, but I like this one, so it is the one I tell you."

As he repeated these tales, I was struck by some of the similarities to Christian beliefs. I was even more intrigued later when I learned that statues of Isis holding Horus in her arms bore a striking likeness to depictions of Mary cradling the baby Jesus. Or that the Egyptians used to celebrate the birth of Horus at the winter solstice, which is December 21. Needless to say, all of these stories and symbols preceded Christianity by centuries.

Is it all a remarkable coincidence, or did Christianity borrow from Egyptian mythology? Perhaps a little of both. They both sprang from the same cultural region of the world, after all, which may explain some of the resemblances. But there are enough differences between them so that a straight line can't necessarily be drawn from one to the other. Furthermore, other societies around the planet also have tales about virgin or divinely conceived births, so this isn't exclusive to Egyptian religion or to Christianity.

What is more fascinating to me, actually, is the very fact that there *are* parallel legends across cultures, especially when these stories form part of a civilization's core beliefs. I don't know what it adds up to exactly (the collective unconscious of humanity? evidence of shared experiences during the mists of prehistory?), but I do know that it has to mean *something*.

From Luxor Temple, Lisa and I said good night to Mohammed and walked back towards our boat, which was nearby. We took a seat at an outdoor table at a café along the river. I ordered a beer and looked out at the Nile as it lapped against the shore under a nighttime sky. As I sat there, I couldn't help but wonder about ancient civilizations and their secrets.

"This is Not Islam"

The next morning, we awoke with a sense of excitement. Although it was our last day in Luxor and our final day touring the sites of ancient Egypt, we were scheduled to visit Karnak Temple. This was the most important shrine in the country for well over 1,000 years and was vastly larger than anything we'd seen so far on our tour of the Nile, so we were prepared to be impressed.

With a bounce in our step, we went out to meet our guide. There was nary a cloud in the pastel blue sky. Sunlight skipped across the rippled surface of the river. As we walked across the bridge that connected our boat to the shore, we saw Mohammed walking down the road to greet us but noticed that he had an anguished look.

"Did you see the news?" he asked. "Three bombs exploded during the night in Sharm el Sheikh. More than 80 people killed."

That single statement changed the arc of our Egyptian journey. Even though we went ahead with the rest of our planned itinerary for that day and, after much discussion, for another week in Egypt, everything that happened from then on was in some way filtered through the prism of that moment.

I explained in the introduction to this book that Lisa and I were scheduled two days later to be in Dahab, a town on Egypt's Sinai coast just one-and-a-half hours from Sharm el Sheikh. Not only was that now a cause for concern, but we rightly wondered if we should even go on with the present day's activities. We didn't have details about the bombing and didn't know if there was any risk of a follow-up attack, but regardless, it somehow seemed wrong to do anything remotely enjoyable in the aftermath of such an incident.

As we stood there and looked at the strangely normal street scene around us, though, Mohammed convinced us to go ahead with our plans. There would be more security, he said, and we should focus on the moment. We finally agreed, and when we arrived at Karnak soldiers peered in the back of our van and swept underneath the vehicle with mirrors, looking for bombs.

In retrospect, visiting the temple was the right call. There was little else we could have done, other than to sit around for 12 hours and wait for that evening's train. One way or another, we were going to be in Luxor for the rest of the day and Karnak was certainly worth visiting. Although the complex was in more of a state of ruin than Luxor Temple, it was remarkable to see the scale of the site. It's one of the largest religious structures ever built and, during a period of about 1,500 years, 30 pharaohs contributed their own edifices and designs. No single feature is unique, but as a whole it's a lesson in the history and architecture of ancient Egypt.

As much as the chance to explore Karnak Temple, however, even more valuable for us that day was the opportunity to converse with Mohammed in a way that we hadn't previously. He stepped out of his official persona as a guide and opened up more, sharing his dismay with the terrorist bombers and his opinion that a tolerant Islam didn't support such violence.

That afternoon, when our Karnak tour was over, we had several hours free before needing to be at the train station and so we decided to roam through Luxor's shopping bazaar. We stepped into stores that sold artwork, jewelry, pottery and rugs, walked through market stalls that displayed boxes of produce and barrels of spices, and meandered past teahouses where old men in galabayyas inhaled the aroma of apple tobacco from hookah pipes. At one point, the call to prayer from a nearby mosque drifted melodiously over the entire setting and people knelt on carpets and prayed. Through it all, televisions were on wherever we went, all broadcasting news of the previous night's bombings. The locals were all saddened by it and they were all insistent that it didn't represent the beliefs of most Egyptians.

"Ah, this is foolishness! This is not Islam," said one shopkeeper, in a comment that was repeated to us in some form by a dozen other people.

In part, it was experiences such as these that convinced us not to join the rush of travelers who sped their departure from Egypt in the next two days. It wasn't the only reason, since the logistics of changing our next flight were challenging given that we weren't supposed to fly again until we reached Amman, Jordan. We were also saddened by the prospect of missing some of the destinations ahead of us, which included Mt. Sinai, the Red Sea and the ruins of Petra. In the end, though, the warmth of the people did go a long way toward persuading us to remain in the country.

We eventually learned that the attacks were the work of indigenous Sinai residents and were likely directed at the Egyptian state. The people of the Sinai have a tribal society and resent the government's control over their way of life. Among some, these grievances have merged with a desire to forge a purer Islamic society. So, by attacking tourist areas, they're able to damage the Egyptian economy and thereby weaken the government. It's believed now that radical groups from the Sinai were behind a 2004 bombing in Taba, the 2005 strike in Sharm el Sheikh and a later 2006 attack in Dahab.

Of course, even if the ultimate target was the Egyptian government, the attack still happened in a tourist area and dozens of people died. So Lisa and I weren't completely successful in putting this incident out of our minds. In the end, though, we were glad that we stayed in Egypt. We had some great experiences during the following days and had conversations with locals that might not have been possible under normal circumstances. It was a small gift, but a cherished one.

Which led me to Global Rule #6. *We have to resist the urge to label entire societies based on the actions of extremists.* It's easy for fear to take hold of us when our impressions of a country are based mostly on televised images of rage and carnage. That doesn't excuse the senselessness of those individuals who resort to violent tactics, but we should know this usually represents only a small percentage of the population. Most individuals around the world are peaceful, caring human beings with a heartfelt sense of a shared humanity.

"Boston Red Sox are World Champions"

"Hello, is Miss Lisa there?"

"Uhhhh, yes. One minute."

"Hello?"

"Hello. Miss Lisa?"

"Yes?"

"This Salim, from front desk. I just check you in. I notice now on your passport that today your birthday, yes?"

"Oh. Well, yes, today is my birthday."

"Good, so I call to wish you happy birthday!"

"Wow, thank you, Salim. That's so nice of you!"

"Hope you have nice birthday in our hotel!"

We were in Dahab. About 30 hours earlier we had awoken before dawn in St. Catherine for our middle of the night hike. After the marvel of watching the sun rise from atop Mt. Sinai we lingered on the summit for as long as possible, looking out at a panorama of rocky peaks that stretched out like a mountainous sea. Then we began the downhill trek along a winding path scattered with boulders, through a honey-colored landscape that shimmered under an impossibly blue sky. Along the way we walked with Bedouin tribespeople clad in white robes and keffiyehs, and were trailed by snorting camels with red, blue and green blankets thrown over their saddles.

Back in St. Catherine, we had a hot shower to wash away the dust and sweat of the hike, then grabbed some lunch and set off for Dahab, which we reached in mid-afternoon. Our first night in town was spent at a hotel that we'd booked on the internet, but the next day we decided to switch lodging places. We weren't thrilled with the cleanliness of the first inn, nor its location along the busiest section of the main street, where it was impossible to leave our room without being assaulted by a swarm of salesmen.

"Hello, sir. You eat at my restaurant?"

"OK, maybe drink then. Very hot, you need cool drink."

"Ma'am, you want buy carpet?"

"Nice jewelry here. Come see!"

"You come back later, then?"

It didn't take us long to find a better deal at a hotel that wasn't even listed in a guidebook. Just a ten minute walk down the same road, we booked a $28 room with a balcony that overlooked the sea. Our new lodging was outside of the main shopping area, so we were able to come and go in peace. It was at this hotel, immediately after we checked in, that Lisa received a call from the front desk clerk wishing her a happy birthday.

Perhaps it was a good omen because Dahab didn't seem at first like the most obvious place to relax after the events of the previous few days. As noted, the town was just down the coast from the site of the bombing in Sharm El Sheikh. We were also just a few hours' drive from Israel, and from the center of town we could look across the Red Sea's Gulf of Aqaba and see the mountainous coast of Saudi Arabia, which looked almost close enough to swim to.

Nevertheless, Dahab seemed a world away from, well, the world. Parts of it still felt like the Bedouin village it once was, while the Saudi mountains turned a beautiful shade of pink in the sunset and lent an aura of serenity to the landscape. Despite the obvious business of tourism, which was overwhelming for about a two-block stretch in the center of town, there was otherwise a quaint sense of peacefulness about the place.

In the mornings, we could get out of bed and go across the road to an outdoor restaurant for eggs, toast and coffee. All along the shore was a string of open air cafés, furnished with low tables and cushions. There, we often relaxed with a drink for hours, just watching the waves drift by. One day, we took a camel ride along the beach, guided by a local Bedouin. We also took advantage of the fact that the Red Sea has some of the best diving and snorkeling in the world, with a stunning variety of dazzlingly colorful sea life. Additionally, many locals seemed unusually happy to see us. Although there were many other tourists in town, the hotel clerk noted that about 50 percent of guests had canceled their reservations after the incident in Sharm el Sheikh.

We stayed in Dahab for five nights and could easily have spent twice as long there. There were no reasons to set an alarm clock, no temples or museums to visit, no must see attractions aside from the marine world that existed beneath the waves. It was a perfect little break for us just before our round-the-world journey hit the homestretch.

One night, while nosing through a news stand in search of a current copy of *Time* or *Newsweek*, we struck up a conversation with a university student who worked there. Khalil told us he was from Upper Egypt, near Luxor, and came to Dahab in the summer to work. He lived with the store owner, he said, and so received free room and board in addition to 300 Egyptian pounds a month ($50–55).

"I am working on my English," he told us. "Would you mind coming back here in the evenings for the next few days while you are in town and speaking to me, so I can practice?"

"I think your English is already very good," said Lisa, "but we'll come back and help you with English if you will talk to us about Egypt and your culture."

"Agreed," he replied.

Khalil said that just speaking English was helpful to him, but he was especially interested in learning idiomatic expressions that were particular to our country.

"Like what?"

"For instance, you like to say 'bats in the belfry,' yes?"

"Bats in the belfry?!"

"Yes, an English man last month, he tell me this popular saying."

"Maybe in England," I laughed. "Actually, I have heard that saying before, but it's not used so much in America. I think it refers to someone who has a few screws loose."

"A what? A few screws loose?"

"Sorry! That's another saying. They both mean someone who is a little bit crazy, or eccentric."

"So to English person I say, "He has bats in the belfry," and to American I say, "He has a few screws loose?"

"Uhh, sure. I suppose."

This conversation wasn't exactly going as I had expected.

After talking for a while, we said goodnight and Lisa promised to come up with a list of sayings for him. And she did. The next evening, we went back to the news stand.

"Ah, welcome, my friends," said Khalil when he saw us. "OK, I take break and we talk."

We walked about 20 yards away and sat on a wall overlooking the sea. Initially, we discussed some of the differences between different regions of Egypt. Khalil was dressed in jeans and a t-shirt, but he said at home he would wear more traditional clothing.

"If I wore a galabayya here in Dahab, people would see me as a simple person from the country," he said.

This was similar to what we'd experienced. The only people in Dahab who wore traditional dress were the local Bedouins, but in Luxor galabayyas were common and in Aswan they were almost the rule. Similarly, these local customs affected how tourists were expected to dress. In Dahab, some foreign women walked around in shorts and bikini tops, but that would be shockingly unacceptable in southern Egypt.

As we conversed that evening, Khalil told us he was studying to become a teacher, though he didn't know how realistic of a goal that was in the short term.

"I want to be married, but it will take me 100 years on that salary to earn enough money for a wedding. So perhaps I work abroad for some years, like in Saudi Arabia, to make money. In future, then, maybe I teach."

"Could you ever work in a Western country?" asked Lisa.

"Ah, I love to travel to West. But it is unrealistic, I think. Very expensive for Egyptian to go to West, especially America. Almost impossible financially. And even then, it is very difficult to get visa."

"That's sad," said Lisa. "We enjoy traveling so much. I wish everyone had the opportunity."

Then Lisa broke the sadness by pulling out her list of American sayings.

"Ah, wait one moment, I almost forget," said Khalil, rushing back to the store.

He returned a minute later with a small bag, which he gave to Lisa.

"You tell me yesterday you are going to have dinner to celebrate your birthday. So now I give you birthday gift."

It was a small jar, filled with colored sand that formed a picture of a camel walking in the desert and the words "Happy Birthday Lisa." An artisan who worked next to the news stand had made it especially for the occasion.

"Wow. That is so sweet, Khalil!"

"Ah, it is a small gift. But you should have nice birthday in Dahab, yes?"

"Thank you so much!"

"OK, now we can see your sayings."

Lisa had actually done an impressive job of preparing a list. It included some more traditional sayings ("piece of cake"), some contemporary phrases ("totally cool, dude"), and even one expression that couldn't really be considered an idiom at all.

"Boston Red Sox are world champions."

I laughed when I saw it on her list.

"That's a great saying, but it's really not in the same category as the others."

"Oh, it will be a great conversation starter when he talks to Americans," said Lisa.

"What does this mean?" asked Khalil.

Lisa briefly explained to him the story of how, in American baseball, the Red Sox had not won a championship from 1918 until 2004. She told him how exciting it was for the city of Boston in October of 2004 and how tens of thousands of people, including me and Lisa, had lined the streets and the river for a victory parade afterward. I had to give her credit—she wasn't even a baseball fan when I met her, and she still didn't exactly love the sport, but nine years of living in Boston had apparently gotten to her. Now she was promoting the Red Sox to an Egyptian university student.

"All Americans will know about baseball," she told him. "But if you happen to say this to Red Sox fans they will love you for it."

"OK," smiled Khalil. "I will remember this saying."

"Maybe the next American he meets will be a Yankees fan," I said hopefully.

The next day, and the day after that, whenever we saw Khalil, he greeted us the same way.

"Boston Red Sox are world champions."

EASY, RIGHT?

Sometimes travel is a collage of sights and wonders. Sometimes it's a string of delightful personal encounters. And sometimes it's just another eye-rolling, sigh-inducing day of trying to get from one place to another.

From Egypt, our plan was to travel to Jordan by bus and boat. We were going to visit the ruins of Petra, then make our way to Amman for a flight to Europe. The travel connections out of Dahab seemed relatively straightforward. We would take a morning bus to the port city of Nuweiba, catch an early afternoon catamaran across the Gulf of Aqaba, be in Jordan by mid-afternoon and then find transport for the final two-hour trip to Wadi Musa, the town nearest to Petra's ruins.

Easy, right?

Lisa and I arrived at the Dahab bus station at 10 a.m., where we were met by several individuals who insisted the bus to Nuweiba wasn't running that day. In light of this unfortunate event, however, they were willing to sell us a seat on a van or taxi that was going in the same direction.

"Thanks, but we'll wait to see if the bus shows up."

"OK, but we leave now. When bus doesn't come, you will be still in Dahab."

We had seen enough scams in enough countries by now to take our chances with the bus. Which did finally arrive, albeit half an hour late. Still, it delivered us without incident to Nuweiba in plenty of time to make the ferry's scheduled 1 p.m. departure.

The first real mystery of the day arose when nobody at the port seemed able to sell us a ferry ticket. We went to the boat terminal and were told the ticket office was down the street on the next block. So we trudged down there, found the ticket office that was described to us, and were informed by a different person that we were still in the wrong place. Tickets had to be purchased at the ferry terminal.

"But we just came from there. They sent us to you."

"Sorry, no ticket here."

Everyone seemed to agree that a ferry was leaving that afternoon, but tickets for the boat apparently couldn't be purchased anywhere. As we shuffled from one place to the next, we met two young men, from Germany and Switzerland, who were having similar difficulties. Then an American couple stumbled by. Then two girls from Korea. Soon we were a motley crew of international travelers, carting our luggage back and forth along the same dusty street in the mid-day heat, going from building to building in search of tickets for a boat whose departure time was growing imminent.

Finally, a tourist policeman walked by and decided to help. He herded us into a departure hall, where we had our passports stamped and were loaded onto a standing-room only bus. Still no tickets or explanation, but at least we were moving somewhere. The bus drove us a few hundred yards through a seaside parking lot and deposited us at the foot of a fairly large boat, where hundreds of Arabs were massed in a shapeless line, trying to get on board.

Unfortunately, this ship didn't look like anything like the catamaran that we were told left every day at 1 p.m. for a one-hour crossing of the gulf, so we thought perhaps they'd brought us to the wrong boat. For all we knew it was a ferry to Saudi Arabia. Eventually, we tracked down an official looking person who spoke some English.

"Where is the ferry to Aqaba, Jordan?"

"This the ferry."

"No, we're looking for the fast ferry. For the catamaran that leaves at 1 o'clock."

"No fast ferry today. Day off. Only slow ferry."

Day off? Since when does a catamaran have a day off?

Ugh. We had confirmed the ferry schedule the previous night with *two* travel agencies in Dahab, and the German and Swiss travelers had been given identical information. But unless we wanted to spend the night in Nuweiba we now had no choice but to take the slow ferry, which meant a three-hour ride instead of a one-hour trip. So we joined the scrum of people and began pushing our way through a throng of shoulders, elbows and luggage.

As we edged slowly forward, we watched the boarding process unfold. Dozens of local travelers ahead of us made their way to the front of the line, were asked multiple questions by security officials and then had their tickets and passports scrutinized closely. Well, that all made sense, I figured, since this ferry was about to cross part of the Red Sea from Egypt to Jordan, a mere one week after a terrorist bombing took place a few hours down the road.

There was, of course, a slight unresolved problem. Namely, that we still didn't have tickets for the ferry. This was a great mystery to us, since nobody had wanted to sell us a ticket, nobody asked for evidence of a ticket when our passport was stamped, and yet every non-Western traveler in line with us seemed to have a ticket receipt.

"We may yet be spending another night in Egypt," said Lisa.

When we finally reached the front of the line, I took a deep breath and prepared myself for the inevitable. Surely we were about to be tossed out of there and told to return the next day once we'd paid for a ride. But instead, when Lisa and I pulled out our passports the guard immediately waved us past with a flick of his wrist, never bothering to look inside the documents or ask for our tickets. After a moment of shocked disbelief, we realized what had happened. Everyone whose travel documents were being scrutinized was from an Arab country. Lisa and I, on the other hand, owned U.S. passports and looked Western. We were evidently freer to move back and forth between these countries than the locals were.

I felt elated and guilty at the same time. Elated that we were finally on the boat, but guilty that we were allowed to board with a wave of the hand when all these other individuals had to endure extensive questioning. But that, apparently, is the value of an American passport, a value that I now appreciated more than ever before.

And the tickets? We were finally able to purchase them on the boat, at a second checkpoint.

"It really would have saved us a lot of anguish," I said, "if someone had just told us an hour ago that we could pay after we boarded."

With a deep exhale, then, we walked onto the ferry, ready to relax in our seat for the three-hour trip to Jordan.

Easy, right?

Except there were no seats. The few inside rooms with seating had long since filled up, so we wandered the outside decks for at least 20 minutes, stepping over entire families who were sleeping on blankets or crouched in the corners. Almost every foot of deck space was spoken for. In talking to a crew member later, we learned there were 900 passengers on board. This included the six Europeans, Americans and Koreans we'd met while searching for the ticket office. There was also an older Danish couple whom we met on the ferry. That made eight Westerners, two Asians and apparently 890 or so Egyptians, Jordanians and Saudis. Needless to say, we stood out.

In the midst of our wandering, we stopped to use the bathroom. When I walked in, men were lined up at the sinks, washing their face, head, mouth, hands and feet for the ritual cleansing that takes place before prayers. That in itself was fine. Even sort of captivating in the abstract. But the reality of dozens of people spraying water on themselves from a row of continuously running faucets was not a pretty site. All the sinks were overflowing and the floors were flooded, while men stuck their bare feet under running water or slurped it into their mouths. After staring slack-jawed for a moment, I decided to splash my way through the deluge to a toilet. There, I discovered the facilities were already so overused that every basin was clogged and filled with urine and feces. Oh, my. I held my breath and escaped as quickly as possible.

After that unpleasantness, we found a self-service restaurant, where we ordered a soda and sat at a table, hoping we could wait out the journey there. We were later joined by the two other Americans and the Danish couple.

Then we waited.

The ferry didn't leave at 1 p.m., as allegedly scheduled, but at 3:30. And it wasn't a three hour ride, but a four-and-a-half hour trip.

"It's just Egypt," said the Danish couple, who had done this trek before. "Don't worry, everything runs more smoothly in Jordan."

OK, so instead of getting to Aqaba, Jordan, in mid-afternoon, as we'd originally anticipated, we actually arrived at 8 p.m. By the time we disembarked and made it through immigration, it was 8:45. The currency exchange window at the terminal was closed and all the buses to Wadi Musa were long since departed. So now our only choice was to negotiate a taxi ride. A *two-hour* taxi ride, and without any local currency in our pockets. Sigh. We walked outside and geared up for a marathon negotiating session.

We were pleasantly shocked, however, when it took a mere 30 seconds to book a ride at exactly the lowest price recommended by Lonely Planet. Not only that, but the taxi driver cheerfully offered to take us to an ATM at a nearby bank. Then, as we set off for the long drive, he began joking with us.

"Look, our streets our clean and orderly. Not like in Egypt. Hahaha. Look, I'm stopping at a red light. Not like in Egypt. Hahaha."

It took a moment to sink in, but then I realized he was right. The streets *were* clean. The vehicles *did* drive in separate lanes and stop at traffic lights. Hmmm. Other than in Singapore, this was the first time in months that we'd seen anything resembling orderly traffic.

Half an hour later, as we began our journey through the vast emptiness of the Desert Highway north of Aqaba, the driver stopped at a roadside drink stand.

"I get tea. You want tea?"

"Sure," I said.

I got out with him to buy some tea, but he beat me to the punch and bought it for us. A taxi driver was buying me a cup of tea? Either the tea was drugged, I thought, or I had entered a parallel universe.

"Jordan hospitality," he said.

So there we stood by the side of a lonely road at 9:30 p.m., breathing in the warm evening air, looking up at stars in the Middle Eastern sky and drinking a cup of tea with our taxi driver.

Well, if another eye-rolling, sigh-inducing travel day could end with a moment like this, then perhaps it was all worth it. Two problem-free hours later, we were at our hotel in Wadi Musa.

ENCHANTING PETRA

Two centuries ago, a Swiss explorer named Johann Ludwig Burckhardt stood at the edge of the 2,000-year-old city of Petra, which no non-Bedouin had laid eyes on for centuries. It was unusual for Westerners of the time to travel through the empty deserts of the Middle East so Burckhardt had spent several years preparing for his trip. He moved to Syria in 1810, where he became fluent in Arabic and studied Islamic law. Then, posing as a Muslim, he set out in 1812 for a journey to what is now southern Jordan.

Burckhardt had heard tales of amazing hidden ruins near the present day town of Wadi Musa. When he reached the village there, he was able to convince local Bedouins to serve as guides so he could sacrifice a goat at the tomb of Aaron, the brother of Moses, in the nearby Edomite Mountains. His deception worked and Burckhardt was able to trek through a veiled valley and behold the so-called lost city of Petra, whose existence to that point had been just a legend in the West.

Thankfully, it's no longer necessary to go to such lengths to view the extraordinary remains of Petra, even if it's still not the easiest place to reach. Anyone not traveling with a tour group has to either hire a driver or deal with an irregular bus schedule to Wadi Musa. And even then the ruins can only be seen after some hiking. But that, really, is what makes Petra so special. In order to get there, one has to walk into a mountainous valley the same way people have done for centuries. Not only do we appreciate the ruins more, but the setting itself is part of the spectacle.

The morning after our ferry experience, Lisa and I woke up in Wadi Musa and set out to explore the famed remains of Petra. This began with a half-mile walk down a parched trail to reach the Siq, a narrow gorge that serves as an entryway to the hidden city. The Siq itself then entails another half-mile hike, but it's one of the most fantastic walks you will ever take.

It is essentially a path through a mountain, a fissure in the rock that was opened thousands of years ago by an earthquake. Or, if you believe ancient legends, this may be where Moses struck a rock with his shaft and brought water gushing forth for the Israelites who were wandering the desert. The name Wadi Musa means "Valley of Moses." Whichever way the rock fractured, though, the fact is that it provides the only access to Petra aside from a trip over the mountains, which is why the area was able to remain hidden for centuries.

The trail winds between towering 600-foot rock faces. In some places, it opens wide to the sun and at other times narrows to a slit of just a few feet. The cliffs have been sculpted by nature into a whimsical whirl of shapes and the colors of the rock seem to dissolve into each other, turning from tan to burgundy to cream. It's a spectacular sight, but it's only a warm-up for what is to come. After twisting marvelously through the Siq for ten minutes, the path suddenly empties into a slender valley and brings visitors face to face with the stunning image of Al Khazneh.

Al Khazneh, or "The Treasury," is the most famous building at Petra. It's an elaborate collection of columns and statues that—unbelievably—was carved directly out of a red sandstone cliff. Although the interior is plain and unimpressive, the 130-foot tall facade is as extraordinary as any other ancient ruin in the world. It's all the more remarkable because it wasn't constructed piece by piece but was rather chiseled whole from a mountain of stone. In the morning sun, it shines with a pinkish radiance, which gave rise to the most famous line about Petra, from a poem that describes it as "a rose-red city half as old as time."

The structure was apparently built as a tomb. It's called the Treasury, though, because of an old Bedouin myth that it was created magically by the Egyptian Pharaoh as a place to store his treasures and lighten his load while he pursued Moses and the Hebrews through the desert. A ten-foot high urn near the top was said to be the repository of these riches. This urn is now ridden with bullet holes, presumably from people who believed it truly held ancient treasure rather than merely being an ornament carved from solid rock.

Although the Treasury is the most famous edifice in Petra, it's just one of more than 800 such monuments in the area. These were built by the Nabataean people who lived here from the 3rd century B.C. to the 4th century A.D. The Nabataeans never forged a great empire, but they built a prosperous society through their control of trade routes, particularly for frankincense, which was the most valued commodity of its day. Interestingly, most of the local structures are tombs and temples, leading to the belief that the inhabitants lived in tents and maintained their nomadic heritage even in the face of these spectacular building projects. The Nabataean civilization was fabulously successful for several centuries but began a slow decline when sea-based trade routes replaced desert caravans and thus eliminated Petra's source of wealth.

Lisa and I spent two days exploring the enchanting hills and valleys of the region. We climbed to a collection of tombs, carved from stone walls that were the color of raspberry-vanilla swirl ice cream. We traipsed through a striking amphitheatre, where rows of seats for several thousand people were sliced out of the rocky foothills. And we hiked up a steep trail of more than 800 stairs cut into the rock in order to reach a Nabataean temple called the Monastery. Once again, we found ourselves gazing at the talents of people who preceded us by more than two thousand years and pondering the centuries-long emptiness of yet another ancient city.

On the afternoon we reached the Monastery, which seemed like a mirage in the desert with soaring golden pillars molded from a mountainside, we saw that a drink stand was incongruously located across from the monument. The locals apparently used donkeys to haul supplies up the trail and then sold drinks to wandering travelers. It was actually a brilliant idea and we took advantage of it to replenish our fast emptying water bottles. Later, as we sat there admiring the view of the Monastery, a local teenager came over and began talking to us.

"Where you from?" he asked

"United States."

"Ahhh, United States. U.S. is cool! Cool in school!" he beamed.

Then, while walking through the desolate landscape above the Monastery, where there is a dramatic view across the surrounding mountains, we came across a solitary Bedouin and his goats.

"Welcome," he said. "Enjoy your visit to my home."

These moments were small but, just as with the taxi driver who bought us tea, they were emblematic of the welcoming nature of all the people we met in the area. One night at a restaurant in town, two local men even insisted on moving to a different table so that Lisa and I could have the better seats with a window view.

"Really, we can't take your seats. You were here first and this other table is perfectly fine."

"No, no, you must. You are guests in our town. We see this view all the time, you should sit here."

When they insisted, we reluctantly switched seats with them.

"It's really not necessary, but thank you."

"It is our pleasure. Do you enjoy Wadi Musa and Petra?"

"Very much. Everyone here has been so kind and welcoming."

"Yes, it is our culture. A Bedouin tradition."

"What do you mean by that, 'a Bedouin tradition?'"

"The Bedouin people have lived in the desert of Jordan, of Arabia, for many centuries. They are nomadic people. You know?"

"Yes."

"Well, because life in the desert was harsh, the Bedouin had a tradition of always taking care of passing strangers. It was a matter of honor. They would prepare a great meal for a guest, and would give shelter and meals for at least three days without even asking who you are. So today in Jordan, maybe we live in houses now instead of tents, but we continue this Bedouin tradition of hospitality."

"Well, we're honored. We feel very welcome."

"We hope you enjoy your stay in Jordan."

When it was time to leave Wadi Musa, Lisa and I headed to the local bus station in order to find transport to Amman. We had a flight to Prague the next morning at the ungodly hour of 3:40 a.m., so we planned to find a cheap hotel in the Jordanian capital where we could get a few hours of sleep and a shower before heading to the airport.

The only challenge in traveling to Amman, we learned, was a lack of reliable public transportation. A bus ran a few times a week, but not on the day we needed it. Minibuses ran more frequently, but there was no set schedule. We asked at our hotel, then at several travel agencies, and everyone gave us the same response.

"In the morning, at perhaps 8 a.m., you should go to the Shaheed roundabout in the center of town and ask if a minibus is traveling to Amman."

So we did.

And there was not.

In the end, though, it wasn't a problem, as we quickly found a service taxi (a shared ride in a private taxi). There was already one paying customer in the vehicle, an ophthalmologist from Amman who had a part-time practice in Wadi Musa. The fare, we were told, was 3.50 Jordanian dinars (about $5) and the taxi needed to wait for a fourth passenger. Or, if all three of us agreed to pay 4.50 dinars (just over $6 each) then he would leave immediately.

That was a no brainer for us. For a little more than $2 extra we could leave right away and wouldn't have to share the backseat for a three-hour drive. The ophthalmologist readily agreed, as well, and so we set off for Amman.

It was a fun little road trip. Lisa, me, a middle-aged Jordanian ophthalmologist who was dressed in Western style clothes and spoke fluent English, and an elderly taxi driver who was dressed in a traditional robe and spoke only Arabic. As with pretty much everyone we met in the country, both individuals were incredibly friendly.

That ride, sadly, marked the end of our brief visit to Jordan. Although there were many more ancient and biblical sites to visit in the region, they'd have to wait for a future trip. There is seemingly never enough time to see everything and, in any case, we had allotted most of our recent schedule to Egypt. But we were most sad, I think, to be leaving the people, who had all treated us with kindness and respect.

As if to emphasize that fact, when he dropped us off our taxi driver gave me a high-five. And with that, our journey through the Middle East was over.

Central Europe

BACK IN THE WEST

Following our middle of the night flight from Amman, Lisa and I landed at the Prague Airport, booked a room at a hostel, got on a bus that took us to a train station, rode a subway into the center of the city, and then finally walked several blocks to our lodging place.

There is nothing remotely interesting about any of this, I know. And yet we were fascinated.

We were fascinated because, during the hour or so that it took us to get from the airport to the hostel, not a single person talked to us, asked us where we were from, offered us a ride or a room or a good deal, or even so much as looked at us.

Yes, our first impressions of Prague, oddly enough, were that it was orderly and hassle free. In the next few days, we certainly came to appreciate so much more about this lovely Central European city, but after a few months of traveling in South Asia and the Middle East it was hard not to immediately notice that individuals kept to themselves, taxis had meters, buses and trains ran on schedule and everyone stood in straight lines.

The culture was less exotic and exciting than what we'd recently experienced, to be sure, and we did have some moments of regret about this because it meant that our string of adventures was coming to an end. At the same time, there was some relief at having our space back. Honestly, I was taken aback by how relaxed and unencumbered I suddenly felt. I mean, this was still the Czech Republic, right? We weren't exactly in California. What we were, though, was back in a society that we recognized.

We were back in the West.

This experience reminded me of our conversation with Shanti in Ladakh. She had conveyed to us how she, as an Indian, felt isolated when she lived in London because there was too much privacy and individualism, while we at the time were having the opposite challenge in India. Our arrival in Prague, it seemed, was more proof that we all derive our expectations about life from the world that we know best.

Shanti, Lisa and I had noticeably similar experiences because we were all comparing an Eastern society with a Western one, and the core worldviews of these cultures couldn't be more different. The West, for instance, has an ethos of individualism while the East has a group-oriented culture. In the West, we tend to emphasize the material world, but in the East there is more recognition of a non-physical realm. Westerners also tend to compartmentalize everything, from our schedule to our personal space, while Easterners have an outlook that accentuates holism and relationships.

Neither of these ways of thinking is right or wrong, obviously, it's just the way cultures are. For me, at least, it makes the world an even more fascinating place, because most of the traditions and behaviors that we first notice about other countries—such as whether individuals approached or didn't approach Lisa and me on the street—are nothing more than manifestations of the cultural lens through which we view the world.

Perhaps, I reflected, we could all learn from one another's culture and worldview. This notion led me to Global Rule #7. *Each culture in the world has something unique to contribute to our global civilization.* If each person's life has a unique pattern and purpose, then the same may be true for every culture. Perhaps we need to reorient our thinking and, instead of focusing on what separates us, begin to consider what each culture offers to the world. Imagine if we were all able to understand and learn from, for example, the Indian acceptance of chaos and uncertainty, the Cambodian reverence for the extended family, Turkish sense of hospitality, the French taste for pleasure, the American optimism and belief in the future, the Thai devotion to faith, the Japanese loyalty to the group or the Kenyan appreciation for nature. Imagine.

Café Culture

I love cafés. I think in a previous life I must have lived in Paris or Vienna, where I probably spent my days as a starving artist haunting the cafés that are part of the life of those cities. When I first began traveling to Europe two decades ago, coffeehouses hadn't yet become a staple of the American landscape and so I used to return home with a wistful nostalgia for the languorous afternoons that I had spent relaxing, thinking and writing in European cafés.

Thankfully, the situation has improved somewhat in the U.S. since then. But when Lisa and I arrived in Prague, one of the things I was still most looking forward to was the chance to experience the legendary café culture of Central Europe.

It's popularly believed that the first cafés sprang into existence in Vienna. There is a famous story that Turkish soldiers left behind sacks of coffee beans after being defeated in a 1683 battle. The Viennese were mystified by these beans, but a Polish officer took ownership of them and opened Austria's first coffeehouse. It's an enticing tale but, even if it's true, cafés had already been founded in other parts of Europe by this time, including in Paris and London, and the first coffeehouse anywhere was likely opened in Istanbul in the 1400s.

However, even if the Viennese receive more credit in this respect than they may deserve, what is still indisputable is that they fell in love with the culture of the coffeehouse and turned it into an art form. From Vienna, cafés spread through the Austro-Hungarian Habsburg Empire and became part of the cultural fabric of such cities as Prague and Budapest. Some have even suggested that Central Europe itself is best understood as those Habsburg territories where coffeehouses are most deeply rooted. The French and Italians may be equally famous today for their cafés, but these gathering places are undeniably a vital part of Central European life and are nearly impossible for visitors to avoid. Which was fine with me.

In Prague, one can find a café most anywhere, but the cobblestone streets of the Old Town are the best place to encounter the city's history. So on our first day in town we merged the two goals and scoped out a place to relax with a drink near Old Town Square. This medieval plaza has been a hub of activity since at least the 1100s, when it served as a marketplace. Today it's one of the most atmospheric squares in Europe, in part because Prague is one of the few cities that wasn't shattered by bombs during World War II.

Even though the streets are jammed with tourists, it's still hard not to be charmed by the architecture and ambiance of the place. The entire Old Town is a work of art, with blue, pink and yellow facades glinting in the sun, delicate carvings around door frames, elaborate paintings on outside walls, statues of lions, cherubs and mythological figures jutting from rooftops and balconies, and pots of colorful flowers draped from almost every window. I felt as if I'd been dropped into a bakery and the buildings around me were fluffy pastries and brightly decorated cakes.

It seemed remarkable that just a few decades earlier this city made only a faint appearance on the travel map. During the middle to late 20th century, the Cold War was simmering and this part of Europe was under the control of the then Soviet Union. Although the Czechs, Poles and others had little in common with the Russians, they were still relegated to that mysterious territory behind the Iron Curtain. Today, of course, it's a different story, as history has turned a page and swarms of travelers have returned to these lands.

When Lisa and I mapped out our round-the-world journey, we decided to end in Europe and wanted to visit a part of the continent that we hadn't seen before. Central Europe was a natural choice and Prague was an obvious starting point. So that first afternoon, we indulged in a cappuccino in a Czech café and contemplated the final stages of our trip.

"Just a few more weeks, then we'll be back home," I said. "New city, new home, new job."

"It doesn't seem possible," said Lisa. "But I guess at the end of our last trip it was also hard to believe it was about to end. I think we're going to be glad we decided to finish in Europe, though. Maybe it's less exotic than Cambodia or Egypt, but there's also a lot we haven't seen in this part of the world. And Europe may be somewhat less tiring, which will be a good thing when we do get home and have to dive into work and unpacking and everything else."

"Yeah, I know we have to think about all those things soon. But you know what's funny? Here we both are, talking as if the trip is about to end, when we still have three weeks of traveling left. That's more than an average vacation, normally. We're in Prague! We're sitting in a café in front of a church and a town hall that were built in the 1300s. And we have a lot of Europe still ahead of us."

"Yeah, it is funny. Three weeks seems short compared to everything we've just done, but if we were at home thinking about taking a three-week vacation, we'd be thrilled."

She finished her cappuccino and set down her cup.

"So let's go explore Prague."

And so we did. For the next few days we wandered the city streets, from the narrow lanes of Old Town to historic Wenceslas Square. We toured Prague Castle, which looms magically over the skyline. We took in the view from the 14th century Charles Bridge, a captivating walkway over the Vltava River that is garlanded by 30 sculptures. We spent an evening listening to a classical music concert in a centuries-old church and we had dinner in a Czech beer garden.

Each day, of course, we also relaxed over coffee in the cafés of Prague.

"Please, I Beg You"

Nothing really prepares you for Auschwitz. This World War II concentration camp is about 35 miles west of Krakow, Poland. It opened in 1940 on the grounds of a deserted Army barracks and was initially designed to hold Polish political prisoners. Later, when the Nazi regime tried to exterminate the Jewish race, Auschwitz and nearby Birkenau became gruesome death camps. More than one million people died here, the vast majority of them Jews who were killed in gas chambers. Countless others succumbed to starvation, disease, hard labor, torture or medical experiments.

Today, it is a somber and heartrending place to visit. The red brick dormitories sit silently, mocking the sunshine that rains down on them. Inside, there are rows of wooden planks that once served as beds, covered with straw and threadbare blankets. In another section of camp, the gas chamber and crematorium are unspeakably distressing sights.

Perhaps most shocking of all, though, are the enormous piles of shoes, suitcases, hairbrushes and human hair. Upon arrival at the camp, all new prisoners were stripped of their possessions and had their hair cut. They were stripped, really, of their identity. But little pieces of each individual lived on in the belongings that were left behind. Many of the suitcases, in fact, still bear the names and addresses of their owners.

Otto. Eva. Herman. Sara. Peter. Marie. Hanna. The names are printed in white lettering on black or brown bags and fill entire rooms with their sadness, reminding visitors that each one belonged to a human being who was murdered by the Nazis for no other reason than his or her ethnicity.

I began writing some of these thoughts down when Lisa and I left Auschwitz and were on a bus back to Krakow, which is the city we traveled to after Prague. But I stopped after a few minutes, because there isn't always much to say after such an experience. It's disturbing to confront the cruelty that human beings are capable of inflicting on one another and writing down the details of what I saw didn't seem to do justice to the reality of the situation. So I closed my notebook and sat in silence, watching scenes from the Polish countryside cascade past the window of our bus.

As we drifted past farms and villages, my mind wandered back to a visit I'd made years earlier to a different concentration camp. Fort Breendonk, in Belgium, didn't have a gas chamber and was considerably smaller than Auschwitz or

Birkenau. But it was no less cruel of a place and the impact of seeing it was magnified by the presence of a man named Frank, who had been a prisoner at that camp. I recalled the stories Frank told us and, as I thought about them, they began to illuminate and bring to life some of the scenes I had just witnessed at Auschwitz.

That day in Belgium, Frank greeted my group at the entrance to Breendonk but then let us walk through the camp on our own before saying very much. So my initial encounter with the Belgian concentration camp was not unlike what Lisa and I had just experienced in Poland.

I walked through dark, chilly cement corridors, hidden from the sun. Saw the austere barracks rooms in which prisoners slept for a few hours each night. Felt a sense of fear inside the torture chamber when I glanced at the long crack in the cement floor that was used to collect the skin and blood of tortured prisoners. Contemplated the sharpened triangular cement blocks in the middle of the room and could almost hear the screams of prisoners who, stripped naked, were hoisted to the ceiling and dropped onto these slabs.

Outside, I stood by the gallows area where prisoners were executed by hanging and the row of wooden poles where they stood to face a firing squad. In the dungeon, I closed the door behind me and stood in utter blackness. I wondered what drove men to such atrocities against other human beings. Or, I might add, what drives people even today to such dreadful acts, in places like Sudan or Iraq.

It was an emotional experience, as Auschwitz had just been. But, still, it was intangible. I knew all these events had occurred, but the actions were so far removed from my conception of normal human behavior that, as horrified as I was, I had difficulty putting it into sort of any contextual framework.

And then we spoke with Frank.

This thin man with an easy smile was aged and ailing when I met him, but when he was healthy enough to work he still tried to spend time with visitors to Breendonk. He said he wanted to do his part to keep alive the memory of the horrors that occurred there.

"When my generation is dead," he said, "no one will be around who actually remembers the terror. The world should not be allowed to forget."

Frank was a political prisoner at Breendonk. After being arrested, he told us, he endured a cramped, six-day train ride in a locked wagon. People were squeezed together like livestock. It was the dead of winter, there was no heat on the train and the prisoners were not fed at all during the journey. Of the 4,000 people who started the trip, only 800 were alive at the end.

Once they arrived at the camp, the situation was equally bleak.

"We were made to work all day, often without a break. And very little to eat. Some watery coffee or thin soup, then a piece of bread and maybe a tiny piece of meat. Our beds were just wooden planks and in the winter we had nothing to keep us warm but very thin blankets. The guards would beat or torture a prisoner for very small things, like for being tired and not staying in line on the way to work. Sometimes, to set an example, a guard would decide to execute a prisoner in front of everyone. Maybe for almost no reason."

He stopped and paused before he spoke again, with a catch in his voice.

"Then, you know, there were some women here who gave birth after they were imprisoned. One time, a guard took a new baby from the mother's arms and threw it into a fire. The mother cried and begged at the guard's feet, but he showed no emotion. Another time, some guards threw a baby high into the air and used it as target practice in front of the mother."

Frank told us the only way he endured the suffering was by keeping alive a flickering hope that the war would end and he might once again taste freedom. But he also came perilously close to not surviving his imprisonment.

He explained that prisoners usually had no toilets available during the day and were often not allowed any breaks, so people had to urinate in their own clothes as they worked. But, since they also had bug bites and sores on their bodies from unsanitary living conditions, the urine would leak down their leg, seep into the sores and begin to burn. If they wet themselves during the winter, meanwhile, their pants would freeze and cut raw the skin of their legs.

"One day, I just couldn't take it anymore, so I urinated outside in the field. The guards saw that and they beat me. They beat me unconscious. Later, I awoke and saw stars in the sky. I thought, 'maybe I'm in heaven.' But then when I was really awake I started feeling pain, real pain, everywhere in my body. So then I thought, 'I'm alive,' and I start to feel around me for the ground. But I got a big surprise. You know what I felt? Arms and legs."

Frank had discovered, to his horror, that he'd been left for dead and was lying atop a pile of lifeless bodies. Somehow, he mustered the strength to crawl off the pile and back to the barracks. There, other prisoners heard his taps on the window and brought him inside. They hid him in trash cans to avoid detection by the guards as they nursed him back to a semblance of health.

"And all the stories I tell you are just the tip of the iceberg," said Frank. "There is so much more that is left unsaid."

When the fighting finally ended and the prisoners were released, Frank weighed 80 pounds. But he was free. Small and weak, he made his way back to his home village. When he got off the train that took him home, the first person he saw waiting for him on the platform was the young woman whom he had courted before the war. Through all the dark days of his confinement, he had given up hope of ever seeing her again.

"When I saw her standing there, smiling and waiting for me, what could I do but marry her?" he said, in a voice filled with affection.

Despite this happy ending to a dreadful experience, though, Frank was otherwise filled with bitterness.

"When the war was over, I ... hated ... every ... German," he said, slowly emphasizing every word.

It took him years of effort to purge himself of hate. But the most remarkable part of this story, perhaps, is that he succeeded. Frank said his wife helped him slowly learn to appreciate life again. When we met him, more than four decades after his imprisonment at Breendonk, he kept emphasizing to us the importance of love.

"Give love," he said. "That is all that is important. A little every day. I have my wife and my family and I am as happy as I can possibly be."

The other thing Frank spoke about with passion was the need for forgiveness. It made such an impression on me, that this man who was jailed for his political views, who was starved, tortured, beaten and left for dead, saw it in his heart to forgive.

"I don't say this lightly," he told us. "Because we can never, ever, *ever* forget the horrors of the war. That is why I cannot remain silent about what happened in this prison. But there is a time when we must forgive."

Then he made a plea to us.

"My friends, you should always strive to understand each other and the world. That is the hope for the future. Remember the horrors of war so they are not repeated and learn to understand each other. And, you must always love."

He looked at us intently one more time. I don't think there was a person in the room with a dry eye.

"Please, I beg you. I beg you on my knees. Learn to love each other."

On the bus, my eyes welled up again remembering Frank. The love he exuded after the cruelty that he'd experienced still stunned me. But before I had a chance to think much more about it, we were suddenly back in Krakow.

As we walked from the bus station to our lodging place, the contrast with the solemnity of the concentration camp was staggering. I marveled at the sun-dappled market square, cobblestone lanes and streetside cafés. At that moment, it seemed inconceivable to me that sixty years earlier this part of the world had been at the center of such terror.

For the next few days, we wandered contentedly through Krakow. But amidst the medieval Old Town, the exquisite cathedrals and the sidewalk artisans, my mind kept coming back to one thing, which is that an extraordinary spiritual dichotomy seemed to exist in the city.

It is the nearest city to Auschwitz and has therefore experienced some of the worst atrocities that man has ever carried out against other human beings. But at the same time, there is a strong sense of spirituality in the area. For one, it is the home of Karol Wojtyla. He was born in nearby Wadowice and served 15 years as Archbishop of Krakow before passing into history as Pope John Paul II. Everywhere in town there are photos and memories of the late Pope, who had one of the most esteemed papal reigns ever and is apparently on his way to sainthood. For these reasons alone, one could say that Krakow has experienced some of the most hideous evil and some of the most vital spirituality of the past century.

But the spirituality, or the mysticism, goes one step further. That's because Krakow has the unusual distinction of being the supposed site of one of the world's seven chakras. According to some Hindus, the planet has seven chakra points or energy centers. These are said to include Jerusalem, Mecca, Rome, Delphi, Delhi and Velehrad, along with Krakow. The specific site is alleged to be in a corner of Wawel Hill, where the royal castle is located. Hence, this spot tends to attract the occasional seeker who comes to meditate or to see if he or she can feel the power of the universe emanating from the earth.

Concentration camps, energy chakras and popes. If that isn't another example of two aspects of the same reality existing in one location then I don't know what is.

As we roamed through Krakow, these thoughts and notions kept mingling in my mind. The pairing of energies in Krakow and the ideas that Frank had articulated at Breendonk. And then another insight came to me. The last one, it turns out, of our journey.

Life Lesson #8. *Life is a choice. What we choose is up to us.* Every day, we are faced with choices. Do we base our decisions on love or on fear? Do we approach each day with passion or indifference? Do we take chances for happiness or do we play it safe and risk regret? Do we look ahead with optimism or back with bitterness? The choices we make on these questions shape everything else in our life. Our families and our careers, our successes and our failures.

These choices play out on both a universal and a personal level. Karol Wojtyla certainly made different choices in Poland in the 1940s than did the Nazi regime of the time. Frank managed to overcome his bitterness and choose happiness. Most of us, thankfully, are never faced with experiences or decisions that are quite that profound, but the choices we make still have real consequences for our lives. For instance, are we spending all of our time at the office and neglecting our personal life because we want to or because we think we have to? Do we blame our unhappiness on a difficult childhood even though we've been an adult for two decades? Are we miserable at work even though we won't consider finding a new job?

If we don't like the thoughts that are controlling our life, we always have the freedom to choose other thoughts.

A Rainbow in Slovakia

Lisa and I were on a train in Slovakia when our sabbatical came to an end. Not literally, for we were on the road for another two weeks, but there was a moment when I realized that our journey had reached a turning point and seemed to be transitioning from a sabbatical to a holiday.

That day, we were traveling from Krakow to Vienna and much of our route cut through Slovakia. There was a gentle mist floating in a still blue sky and, as we curved through the Slovak countryside, I gazed at farmhouses scattered amidst cocoa and mint colored fields. I thought about the people who lived in these homes and wondered how different my life might be had I grown up on a European farm. Would I have the same interests that I do now? Would I still care about travel? Or, even further removed from my own reality, what if I'd been a Turkish carpet salesman, Masai warrior, Vietnamese fisherman, Indian shopkeeper or Egyptian taxi driver? There were so many different lives that I could have been born into.

"But, you know," I said to myself. "It doesn't matter. As difficult as it is for me to imagine being someone else, it's no doubt equally difficult for them to imagine being me. That's part of what makes this world so interesting."

Rather than contemplate other potential lives, I mused, what was most important was simply to make myself into the best version of me that I could be. This life sabbatical, it seemed, had been a step in that direction and I was pleased that we had taken a chance and embarked on this journey.

Then, I saw a rainbow.

It wasn't unusually large or spectacularly brilliant, but as our train clattered along the rails, I looked out at an arc of color stretched across the fields of Central Europe. And, for some reason, that was it. I knew our journey was ending. Maybe it was because we were nearing the finish line and looking toward home, or perhaps it was simply that we'd learned what we needed to learn from the world for the time being and now it was time for the next chapter of our lives to unfold.

In any case, for the next two weeks my notebook pages didn't fill quite as quickly and the reflections slowed to a trickle. But that was OK. Maybe our trip was less insightful the rest of the way, but we still enjoyed ourselves as much as we had previously. We made the usual tourist stops, sure, but even more than that we tried to simply absorb the places we visited and to collect cultural experiences when we could.

In Vienna, we hung out in the famed coffeehouses, spent an evening at a wine tavern in a building that Beethoven used to live in, and whiled away an afternoon at a thermal bath and sauna. During a stopover in Salzburg, we ate bread and cheese on the banks of the Salzach River and enjoyed a view of the Alps. In Munich, we drank beer and ate monstrous pretzels in a Bavarian beer garden. Then, when the rain wouldn't let up in southern Germany, we escaped to sunnier Heidelberg and strolled along the dreamy Neckar River in the shadow of Heidelberg Castle.

We ended our odyssey in Paris, because we wanted to finish someplace fun and romantic and because Lisa and I had great memories of the city from our previous visit. So we spent several summer days walking the boulevards, reading in cafés, eating crepes and chocolate, relaxing in the sunshine among the flowers and sculptures of the Luxembourg Gardens, drinking wine while sitting in the grass near the Eiffel Tower, and taking time to simply contemplate the amazing experiences we'd had around the world.

Then we boarded a plane for home.

Home

When the trip was over, Lisa and I settled into our new home in Arizona. We unpacked our life, she started a new job, and I began writing more intently about travel and culture. I created a website devoted to cross-cultural topics and then, after several months, finally collected all of my materials and dove into this book.

As I went through the writing process, I reflected often on the places we saw, the people we met and the insights we gained into ourselves and the world. But there always seemed to be a few final sentiments striving to get out that I hadn't yet been able to express. One day, then, while sitting in a café east of Tucson, I was inspired by something or other—a shaft of sunlight streaming through the window, perhaps, or the aroma of a cup of coffee, or a vibrant Southwestern sunset that made the sky look as if it had been finger-painted by angels—and a torrent of memories from our trips came tumbling back to me.

I remembered the stark beauty of central Turkey, where a carpet dealer took time out of his day to drive us to a local bath. The Masai tribespeople who showed us their traditions. The Balinese dancer who stomped out fire with his bare feet. The Himalayan monk in India who taught us a Buddhist chant. The Beijing grandmother who served us moon cakes. The Indian pilgrims who bathed at sunrise on the Ganges River in Varanasi. The ancient wonders of Egypt. The cafés of Prague and Vienna. The young Vietnamese woman who gave us a ride on her motorbike. The Japanese mother who thought that perhaps we were friends in another lifetime.

All at once, then, words jumped from my pen and formed sentences on the page in front of me.

Our time on the road can often seem like nothing more than a jumble of people and experiences, I wrote, and yet, just like in our lives, it all somehow fits together into its own perfect whole when all is said and done. We're all on intersecting journeys. Lisa, me, everyone we met on our trip, everyone who will be motivated to pick up this book and read it. Maybe it's a journey through one lifetime, or maybe through several lifetimes.

What I now know is that the enchantment of travel is intertwined with the experience of life itself, with the opportunity to dive into the splendor of our planet and explore worlds previously unknown to us. There is a sublime pleasure inherent to travel and all travelers have known the same feeling—the sense that we are tapping into the transcendent, that we are watching the universe unfold its stunning diversity before our eyes. We are somehow more alive when we travel. Our senses break open and we're more alert to the energy of the life around us. Even at travel's most difficult moments, we are conscious of having experiences that are subtly altering our existence.

The only unfortunate aspect of travel, of course, is that every trip must come to an end. But we can at least take solace in knowing that the rest of our journey continues.

Life Lessons and Global Rules

Following is a compilation of all the "Life Lessons" and "Global Rules" that appeared in this book:

Life Lessons

1. *Our life as a whole can best be understood as a progression of smaller lives.* Just as the earth has its seasons, our lives consist of a series of cycles, each with its own strand of interests and opportunities. Perhaps, in the end, what we all really need is some type of sabbatical experience every seven or so years in order to reflect on our lives and refocus our energies.

2. *Each person's life has a distinctive pattern and purpose.* Our lives often make more sense than we realize, but we rarely take the time to put all of our experiences into context. All too often, our gaze remains fixed on the current moment. We can see where we are, but we don't always perceive where we've come from or where we're going. The rhythm and meaning of our existence, however, becomes more comprehensible when we can look at our lives with some detachment from our daily to-do lists.

3. *If you want to grow, do something that makes you uncomfortable.* If public speaking alarms you, go do it. Or train for a marathon. Go skydiving. Disagree with someone who intimidates you. Go back to school. Drive cross-country by yourself. Get naked on a clothing-optional beach. Start your own business. Leave your job and travel around the world. Don't do anything stupid or unsafe, obviously, but the point is, once you stare down something that scares you, you become filled with a sense of confidence and freedom. The world feels lighter and less daunting.

4. *Life is all about taking that first step, even if it seems risky, and then the next step and the step after that, until we finally reach our desired objective.* Every person who crosses the street in Vietnam has to overcome a fear of walking into traffic, every traveler has to conquer a fear of the unknown, and most everyone in life has to deal with a fear of failure or rejection. In each case, all we can do is trust our inner self and have the nerve to take that first step. Sort of like walking into traffic in Hanoi, if you take it one move at a time, go with the flow and allow space for adjustments, it often turns out fine.

5. *We are all engaged in a never-ending process of becoming, but the way in which we grow depends on the life experiences we select for ourselves.* No one's life is static and we are all perpetually evolving, whether we are trying to or not. So if we want to be better, more confident, more interesting people in the future, then we need to choose worthwhile experiences in the present.

6. *A successful person isn't one who never fails, but one who knows how to persevere in spite of setbacks.* You certainly learn from successes, but you often learn more from failures. So whether you're trying to do well in business, athletics or just life, it helps to know that you can pick yourself up again whenever you get knocked down.

7. *If you want to lead a life of wonder and not regret, then you first have to unearth your passion.* Everyone has a passion. Do you want to sing, paint, teach, travel, dance, run, act, write, grow spiritually, tend to the sick, engage in public service? We all have multiple goals and interests, certainly, but we do tend to have one or two things that we are passionate about above all else. And it's not always what we're currently doing. So if we want to know our life has been well-lived, we need to unearth that passion and chase it.

8. *Life is a choice. What we choose is up to us.* Every day, we are faced with choices. Do we base our decisions on love or on fear? Do we approach each day with passion or indifference? Do we take chances for happiness or do we play it safe and risk regret? Do we look ahead with optimism or back with bitterness? The choices we make on these questions shape everything else in our life. Our families and our careers, our successes and our failures. If we don't like the thoughts that are controlling our life, we always have the freedom to choose other thoughts.

Global Rules

1. *It is only by interacting with others, and even debating them, that we can ever begin to know each other.* We are stuck in a world in which too many people believe they are absolutely right. Which, of course, means that anyone who holds a different opinion has to be wrong. But absolutism leads nowhere, except to conflict. It's not that everyone should always agree, but rather that we should be able to reach some sort of common understanding of our differences. We should at least be able to appreciate what it is that we disagree about. Most travelers, I believe, understand this. Many politicians, unfortunately, do not.

2. *We are all silently and permanently molded by the assumptions of the culture in which we are raised.* We cannot change this about ourselves, nor can we change anyone else's cultural perceptions. This means, of course, that if we want other people to understand and appreciate our way of life, then we are obligated to understand and appreciate theirs.

3. *Religions are different because cultures are different, but at heart they are all seeking the same thing, which is an understanding of the transcendent.* Each faith seems to undertake the same search, ask the same questions, and perhaps even arrive at the same answers in different forms and different words. All of humanity is longing to touch the divine and we find inspiration wherever we believe we will, in whatever place or faith we already believe is blessed.

4. *Our perception of the world depends on our perspective of the world.* If you live in India, you embrace uncertainty; if you live in Germany, you embrace order. If you live in New York, you're in the center of the world and anything is possible for those who take initiative. If you live on Easter Island, you're isolated from the world and have to rely on your community. If you live in Ushuaia, Argentina, you're looking up at the planet; if you live in Hammerfest, Norway, you're looking down. We may believe the world is an objective place, but our experience of it is still subjective and our perceptions are influenced by where we live.

5. *The world would be a saner place if more travelers went into politics.* Consider the different perspective government leaders would have if they'd spent months of their lives taking buses and trains through other countries, staying in local hotels and conversing with foreigners in bars and cafés. Envision a world where presidents and prime ministers had experience as private citizens wandering through

Asia, Africa, Latin America or the Middle East simply because they found it interesting. Think of how their own personal experiences with different cultures, faiths and worldviews would influence policy discussions.

6. *We have to resist the urge to label entire societies based on the actions of extremists.* It's easy for fear to take hold of us when our impressions of a country are based mostly on televised images of rage and carnage. That doesn't excuse the senselessness of those individuals who resort to violent tactics, but we should know this usually represents only a small percentage of the population. Most individuals around the world are peaceful, caring human beings with a heartfelt sense of a shared humanity.

7. *Each culture in the world has something unique to contribute to our global civilization.* If each person's life has a unique pattern and purpose, then the same may be true for every culture. Perhaps we need to reorient our thinking and, instead of focusing on what separates us, begin to consider what each culture offers to the world. Imagine if we were all able to understand and learn from, for example, the Indian acceptance of chaos and uncertainty, the Cambodian reverence for the extended family, Turkish sense of hospitality, the French taste for pleasure, the American optimism and belief in the future, the Thai devotion to faith, the Japanese loyalty to the group or the Kenyan appreciation for nature. Imagine.

978-0-595-44391-8
0-595-44391-5